Studies in Social Ecology and Pathology
General Editor: NIGEL WALKER

Death on the Road

Studies in Social Ecology and Pathology

1 · Freedom and Justice within Walls:
The Bristol Prison Experiment
F. E. EMERY

2 · Death on the Road:
A Study in Social Violence
F. A. WHITLOCK

Death on the Road
A STUDY IN SOCIAL VIOLENCE

F. A. Whitlock

Foreword by R. J. Smeed

Professor of Traffic Studies,
University College London

TAVISTOCK PUBLICATIONS

in association with

HICKS SMITH AND SONS

First published in 1971
By Tavistock Publications Limited
11 New Fetter Lane, London EC4
Printed in Great Britain
in 10 point Times New Roman
By Butler & Tanner Ltd
Frome and London

© *F. A. Whitlock 1971*

SBN 422 73230 3

Distributed in the USA
by Barnes & Noble, Inc.

And the watchman told saying, He came even unto them and cometh not again; for the driving is like the driving of Jehu the son of Nimshi: for he driveth furiously.

2 Kings 9: 20

Contents

Acknowledgements

Anyone who sets out to explore a subject well outside the range of his normal activities will sooner or later run into formidable difficulties created by his own ignorance. In general, psychiatrists are not over-familiar with the complexities of road-accident research, and it was not long before the present author encountered problems of selection and procedure which would probably have been child's play to those more experienced in this field. Fortunately, help, advice, and encouragement were most generously provided by a host of individuals and organizations, and it is regrettable that not all of this assistance can be acknowledged by name.

The major part of the work was carried out during six months' sabbatical leave from the University of Queensland, and it is a pleasure to thank Dr D. J. West of the Department of Criminology of the University of Cambridge for hospitality shown; also the Library staff of that Department who helped by providing documents of criminal statistics required for one part of this study. Further assistance was provided by the Library staff of the Official and Government Publication Room in the University of Cambridge Library.

My thanks are also due to Mr R. F. Newby, Statistician of the Road Research Laboratory of the Ministry of Transport, Crowthorne, who gave up time to advise on statistical procedure, unearthed a mass of useful information, and permitted me to use the Library, whose staff provided further guidance to relevant literature.

Similar assistance was generously given by the Librarians of the Ministry of Transport Library in London and the London School of Economics, which was able to provide a wealth of statistical data from the countries surveyed in this investigation. Special thanks are also due to Mr J. A. Lain, Statistical Officer of the Royal Society for Prevention of Accidents in London, who provided me with figures for accidents and other data in the towns and counties of Great Britain.

When official texts failed to reveal the information required, numerous inquiries to individual embassies and offices almost invariably led to additional help. The assistance provided by the x · *Death on the Road*

Agents-General for the Australian States in London, and the Librarians of Australia House, New Zealand House, and Canada House are here gratefully acknowledged. It is a pleasure also to thank Mr C. H. G. Witt of the Royal Netherlands Embassy and officers of the Embassy of the Duchy of Luxemburg for providing access to a quantity of data unobtainable elsewhere.

I am particularly indebted to my colleague Mr M. Weston, Lecturer in Clinical Psychology, for advice on statistical methods, and to Dr. H. Silverstone, Reader in Medical Statistics, and Miss J. Caine in the Department of Social and Preventive Medicine of the University of Queensland for help with some of the statistical analysis. Once again, it is a pleasure to acknowledge the help given by the Library Service of the University of Queensland, and special mention must be made of the Librarians in the University Medical Libraries. Additional thanks are due to the Queensland Parliamentary Library staff, who were able to provide British Government Command Papers which seemed to be otherwise unobtainable in Brisbane.

Mr S. E. Solomon, Deputy Commonwealth Statistician of the Commonwealth Bureau of Census and Statistics in Brisbane, was a most valuable supplier of data relating to Australia, and further information on road traffic was obtained through the good offices of the Librarian of the Main Roads Department of Queensland. Information on Australian criminal statistics was most generously provided by the Chief Police Commissioners of the six Australian states, and I am grateful to Mr Paul Wilson of the Department of Government in the University of Queensland for further assistance in this matter.

The patient typing and retyping and drawing of charts and figures rested in the capable hands of my secretaries, Mrs M. Beckford, Mrs Valerie Monoghan, and, later, Miss B. Little. Finally, a special word of thanks is due to all those relatives, friends, and colleagues who patiently through many months have tolerated and discussed my preoccupations. Helpful comments and criticisms have led to modifications and amplification of the original study. But, needless to say, I alone am responsible for its final shape and the conclusions, however speculative, which have been drawn from the mass of data given by so many informants.

Foreword

Many people are concerned about their likelihood of being killed or injured in road accidents, and many more about the similar risk to their families and friends and about the possibility that they may cause death or injury to others. There is, therefore, concern about road safety among a high proportion of the world's population and it is of major importance that the subject be investigated in the most revealing possible way.

Professor Whitlock's book is a major contribution to thought in this field. He has reviewed a high proportion of the scientific papers dealing with the subject in general – as opposed to dealing with particular aspects of it – and he has made some major analyses of his own. I do not agree with all of his views, but his book should be studied by everybody seriously interested in the subject.

There can be no doubt that some general trends in road-accident fatalities and casualties can be discovered even apart from the obvious one that their numbers are increasing. For example,

(i) There is a general tendency for road fatalities per registered motor vehicle to decrease as motorization (motor vehicles per person) increases.

(ii) There is a general tendency for road fatalities per head of population to increase as motorization increases.

(iii) Despite the very large differences in traffic conditions in different countries, the number of road fatalities in a given country can, to a large extent, be predicted from a knowledge of the population and the number of motor vehicles only.

(iv) The number of pedestrian fatalities in a country is largely determined by its population and is not very dependent on its degree of motorization.

(v) As motorization increases, there is a tendency for injuries to occupants of motor vehicles to increase in number relative to injuries to pedestrians.

(vi) There is a general tendency for road-user behaviour to improve as motorization increases.

It can be confidently expected that more such tendencies will be discovered, and that they will greatly assist in formulating rational policies for dealing with the road-accident problem. Professor Whitlock's book is a major step forward in this direction.

R. J. SMEED
Professor of Traffic Studies,
University College London

1 · Introduction

The gods are just, and of our pleasant vices
Make instruments to plague us.

King Lear

It is uncertain where death may await thee,
therefore expect it everywhere.

SENECA, *Epistles*

Towards the end of 1966 I was invited to give a talk on some aspect of Australian society. The nature of the audience necessarily imposed some limitations on the choice of subject, even though some facet of social pathology was clearly appropriate for the occasion. However, for a newcomer to discuss some less favourable aspect of a society to which he had been welcomed would be a somewhat hazardous proceeding unless, of course, the topic chosen was one capable of arousing the concern of most members of the audience. My limited knowledge of Australia, and my understandable bias towards a psychological rather than a purely sociological type of approach to social problems, created additional restrictions on the scope of the lecture. However, one public health problem of a universal and increasingly important nature seemed in the circumstances suitable – road traffic accidents.

No one can live for long in Australia without becoming acutely aware of the appallingly high rates of death and injury on the roads. In the twelve months 1931–2, 818 persons were killed on the roads of Australia, giving a death rate of 12·5 per 100,000 of the population. By 1966–7, the total deaths had nearly quadrupled (3,201) resulting in a death rate of 27·1 per 100,000 (Appendix II, *Figure 3A*). In 1965, 4·2 per cent of male deaths in Australia occurred in road accidents, whereas only 1·8 per cent of females died in this fashion; an indication at least that death on the road is an affliction predominantly of the male sex. In 1966, 1,122 male drivers and 535 male passengers were killed. In contrast, 107 female drivers died, although the number of female passengers killed (447) was only a little lower than the male incidence. Compared with the 564 male pedestrians who were killed on the road, only half that number of women (279) met their end in this way. Such a finding has three possible explanations; that there are fewer female than male pedestrians; that women are more careful than men on the roads; or, more probably, that more male than female pedestrians are rendered careless or incompetent by excess of alcohol.

Facts of this nature indicate a problem of considerable magnitude which has been causing concern throughout the world. Nevertheless, despite growing awareness, very little has been done successfully to bring this epidemic under control. In Australia its impact is more forceful than the similar problem in Great Britain where road-death rates, despite the greater road congestion, are about half those found in Australia. Such differences invite investigation which becomes all the more compelling when one considers the common ethnic, social, and cultural background of the two communities. What, one might reasonably ask, are those differences in temperament, personality, and attitude to driving which distinguish the Englishman from the Australian on the road? For although there are notable disparities between road construction and traffic densities in the two countries, it seemed improbable that these two factors alone could account for the contrasting accident and death rates.

A few years ago Gorer (1955) stated that in his opinion the central problem for understanding the English character was the problem of aggression. 'The English gentleness', he wrote, 'would seem to be a comparatively new phenomenon. A psychologist . . . would suspect the aggression has changed direction, instead of being manifest in public life it was being discharged elsewhere.' The author went on to suggest that other possible outlets for aggression are the family and phantasy. He concluded that aggression had not disappeared or diminished in potentiality. 'It is seriously controlled,' he wrote, 'so that it rarely appears in overt or public behaviour.' He observed that outlets were provided by humour and motiveless destruction of property, i.e. vandalism. One hundred and fifty years ago or more, the quality of aggressiveness in English public life was, according to Gorer, something of a byword in Europe. Today it could hardly be said that the Englishman compares too badly in this respect with his European neighbours. I would like to propose that some, at least, of this hidden aggression becomes more manifest when the owner of the car gets behind its wheel and drives on to the public highway.

In Australia, the quality of aggression seems to be nearer to the surface. For the most part it is kept under rigid control and certain strong conventions of address and behaviour in public and social life suggest that these conventions have not arisen by chance but were devised largely in response to the need to curb aggressive behaviour. Not infrequently, this aggression bursts its bonds, and the national newspapers – like newspapers in most parts of the world – report a startling increase in the average number of assaults, drunken violence, homicide, and mass rape. The use of alcohol in Australia, which differs from prevailing customs in Great Britain, may have something to do with this state of affairs. In England and Wales in 1964, convictions for public drunkenness amounted to 15·4 per 10,000 of the population. In Australia during the same year, the figure was 117 per 10,000, falling only slightly in 1965. It is possible, of course, that Australian police attitudes towards public drunkenness differ markedly from those prevailing in Great Britain, leading to higher arrest rates in Australia. However, I submit that this is inconsistent with common observation, a fact suggesting that aggressiveness, excessive drinking, and road accidents may be causally interrelated.

Needless to say, outbursts of aggression are not confined to road transport. Violent death by suicide, homicide, other forms of accidental death, and violent crime can all be looked upon as manifestations of the quality and quantity of aggression in a given society. Examination of statistics showed that, compared with England and Wales, Australian rates for suicide, homicide, and violent crimes known to the police were all decidedly higher. Evidence of this nature suggested a tentative hypothesis: that road-death and injury rates are recognizable indices of the total sum of aggression in a given society; and that the higher these death and injury rates rise, the higher in general will be other manifestations of social aggression as measured by violent death and violent crime. The measures of misuse of alcohol, a drug known to lead to the release of aggressive behaviour in susceptible persons, could also be regarded as indicators of the extent of violent behaviour in society. Some support for this theory was obtained from its application in limited fashion to the annual statistics of the six main Australian states. How well the theory would be upheld if it were applied more widely was not known. The testing of this hypothesis by examination of the vital, criminal, and other statistics of 27 world states, 48 states of the United States of America, and the 10 Canadian provinces is the main subject-matter of this book. At the same time, additional support for the theory that road violence as measured by death and injury rates is but one aspect of the total aggression of a society was forthcoming from a number of relevant publications. Crime, alcoholism, suicide, and road-death rates seemed to be discussed together sufficiently often to permit some feeling of confidence that the association was not a chance one. The literature on each of these aspects of social pathology is extensive, and I would not pretend that it has been covered *in toto*. Nevertheless, as reference to subsequent chapters will show, aggression and violence as traits of personality run like leitmotives throughout much of the writing about the psychological aspects of road accidents. It is, of course, possible that this aggression is itself but one manifestation of some wider aspect of social disorganization and pathology. Divorce rates, illegitimacy rates, delinquency rates, prison and mental-hospital admission rates, could all be examined in relation to the central question – why do some societies have higher road-death rates than others? Death rates from certain diseases might also provide a further index of aberrant behaviour, and for this reason deaths from cirrhosis of the liver – significant because of the relationship of cirrhosis to alcoholism – were included as one of the variables of social pathology. The extent of dependence upon narcotic and other drugs, had figures for this disorder been available, would also have been of considerable interest. Finally one might have to consider how far such social disturbances as strikes, lockouts, and unemployment could be classed as symptoms of social pathology. No doubt the list could be extended considerably, but unfortunately the limitations imposed by official statistics have inevitably curtailed further explorations along these lines. Hence, although there is some evidence that other aspects of social pathology might well be relevant to road deaths and injuries, the more limited hypothesis concerning the relationship of these misfortunes to other manifestations of aggression in society is the one which has been most closely tested and examined in the following pages.

Needless to say, it should always be remembered that a correlation does not necessarily imply a causal relationship; and that although, in my opinion, aggressive behaviour is one of the major causes of traffic accidents, other factors such as road surface and congestion, vehicle reliability, and climatic conditions all contribute to the end-result. Many of these aspects of road accidents have been examined in detail by engineers and others better qualified than I to express opinions on complex technical problems. Consequently, the emphasis in this book on the personality of the driver who becomes repeatedly involved in road accidents may appear excessive. However, daily observation of human behaviour in the clinic and on the roads seemed sufficient justification for this approach to traffic accidents, which, in the last analysis, almost invariably require a human driver behind the steering-wheel before they can occur. The epidemiological data are sufficiently clear to warrant the conclusion that, however safe we make roads and vehicles, our efforts will be vitiated unless vehicle usage can be modified and controlled at the same time.

REFERENCE

GORER, G. 1955. *Exploring English character*. London: Cresset Press.

2 · The extent and nature of the problem

'There's been an accident!' they said,
'Your servant's cut in half; he's dead!'
'Indeed!' said Mr Jones, 'and please
Send me the half that's got my keys.'
HARRY GRAHAM

In 1964, in those countries of Europe making returns of road accidents to the United Nations, 68,629 persons were killed and 1,841,036 injured more or less seriously by motor vehicles. In the same year in the United States of America, 47,700 persons were killed and 1,700,000 injured. As one writer commented (editorial in *New England Journal of Medicine*, 1965), 'This is an appalling statistic . . . [yet] it is a remote fact that apparently impresses only those in safety work, law enforcement, medicine, religion and burial services.' By 1967 the annual figures for road deaths in the United States of America had risen to over 52,000.

Norman (1962) noted that

two deaths were registered in 1896 in Great Britain as due to motor vehicles; one was registered in the United States in 1899. From these small beginnings a terrible stream of death and injuries has followed. In 1951 the United States recorded its millionth death in road traffic accidents and other countries which have become highly motorised have suffered similarly . . . in highly motorised countries road traffic accidents are now the commonest cause of death in adolescents and young people, particularly males. A large proportion of the beds in male surgical wards of hospitals are occupied by young men injured in road accidents, many of them maimed or permanently disabled.

Austin (1966) has observed, 'Since the beginning of the century more than a quarter of a million people have been killed on the roads of Britain and during the last ten years – 1954–63 – the total casualties have numbered 3,076,434 of whom 61,452 were killed,

735,376 seriously injured and 2,279,606 slightly injured.' In most Western countries motor accidents constitute the commonest single cause of violent death, exceeding by far any other accidental cause of death. In Great Britain in 1963, after road deaths, death by suicide was the next highest cause. The figures for Australia have already been discussed, and similar findings could be quoted for many other countries in Western Europe and the Americas. The Canadian road-death rates show equally formidable increases over the twenty-two-year period 1944-66 (Appendix II, *Figure 4A*).

These are impressive figures, which could be reinforced by additional statistics relating to human and economic loss. Young men between the ages of 16 and 25 show the highest age-specific death rate from road accidents, and Norman observed that such incidents are by far the commonest cause of death for men aged 20–24. The man-years lost are consequently high, and in the United States of America in 1955 well over one-quarter of the 1,470,496 man-years lost due to premature death were on account of road accidents. The economic loss is equally severe. In 1964, the United States National Safety Council estimated that the cost of road accidents amounted to $8,100 million from wage losses, property damage, medical expenses, and insurance costs.

Despite the enormity of these figures, road-death and injury rates have astonishingly little impact on the general population. For the most part a new 'record' receives brief notice in the press; the majority of readers, after expressing perfunctory concern, remain indifferent or apathetic. Not until a friend or relative is killed on the road do we begin to be dismayed by this daily carnage. This public apathy over what amounts to an international disaster of considerable magnitude has been commented on by a number of writers, and Doherty (1965) is possibly correct in suggesting that horror fascinates rather than acts as a deterrent to rising road-accident rates. For those having to cope with the mutilated bodies of young people killed in car smashes, this is a disturbing conclusion which may well be germane to the general thesis that violence and aggression on the roads have deep roots in the psychological characteristics of the individuals concerned. However, a more likely explanation of the general apathy of the public is the comparative rarity of such incidents in the lives of most drivers. In the USA in 1959, the average driver would have had to drive 400,000 miles before becoming involved in an accident resulting in an injury to any party concerned in the collision severe enough to cause death or disablement beyond the day of the accident. At an average speed of 30 miles an hour, this represents a driving-time of 13,000 hours; or, for an annual driving-distance of 10,000 miles, 40 years of driving before becoming embroiled in an accident of greater or lesser severity. The belief, firmly embedded in the minds of most drivers, that accidents happen to other people is obviously supported and reinforced by figures of this kind. Consequently, we continue to take risks or drive dangerously simply because such behaviour for the most part goes 'unpunished' by accidents. We all make driving errors; and most of us are prepared to take a chance on occasion. In the majority of instances we 'get away with it'. The risk taken is rewarded rather than punished and, inevitably, new learning in the shape of better driving behaviour does not take place. If this is the common experience of most drivers, perhaps it is hardly surprising that lack of interest in road-accident statistics is the prevailing attitude.

It is instructive to contrast our indifference to road deaths with our reactions to other forms of accidental and violent death. Natural catastrophes such as earthquakes, floods, and fires horrify us sufficiently to cause us to subscribe to charitable organizations bringing relief to persons in the stricken areas. Yet the number of persons dying each year from major disasters of this kind is small when compared with the annual world road-death toll. In Australia the rare occurrence of a swimmer being killed by a shark is widely reported and often followed by demands for greater safety in terms of nets and beach patrols. Half a dozen young people killed on the roads at the weekend barely get a paragraph in daily newspapers other than those devoted to the reporting of local affairs. The comparative rarity of natural cataclysms may have something to do with our immediate and appropriate response to such occurrences. We empathize more easily with the victims because we can enter into the horror of the situation. Road accidents leave us indifferent owing to our built-in belief that such disasters will not happen to us.

Most major air-travel organizations have a very good accident record, largely because of the stringent regulations governing inspection, maintenance, hours of flying and so forth. Yet a good many persons – including the present author – experience some apprehension towards a coming air journey, even though they know as an intellectual proposition that their chances of being killed during a flight are considerably lower than the hazards of death encountered daily when driving on the public highway. In 1958 in the United States of America, the road-death rate per 100 million vehicle-miles travelled was 2·3. The comparable air-travel statistic gave a death rate of 0·43. It would appear to be five times more dangerous to journey on the roads than by air, but we continue to show confidence in our ability to handle the more hazardous form of road travel. A partial explanation may lie in our conviction that, whereas in automobiles we have control over our own fate, in aircraft we have to accept that we are in the hands of others. We believe that, faced by an emergency on the road, somehow we would manage to escape. We are far less optimistic about our chances of emerging unscathed from an air crash, which, admittedly, when it occurs has an irrevocable impetus that cannot be controlled. On the roads we assume that all will be well, even though anxieties about our children are aroused, largely because of their inexperience and vulnerability. We advise and exhort them to take all reasonable care – and promptly fail to apply such advice to ourselves.

Compared with road-traffic accidents, war and war casualties affect us far more intensely. During the First World War the United States of America lost 126,000 dead and 234,300 wounded. In the Second World War casualties amounted to 291,557 killed and 670,846 wounded. On the basis of the 1964 figures for road casualties in the United States of America, the number of deaths in World War I would be exceeded in less than three years and the number of injured in just over one and a half calendar months of normal peacetime driving. In the Vietnam war, by 30 December 1967, United States military forces had suffered 9,353 deaths and 32,355 seriously wounded. These figures, incurred over a period of five years, understandably arouse national concern because of their tragic and irrevocable nature. Yet an almost equal number of persons – men, women, and children – were killed on the roads of the United States in just over two months in 1966. The current toll of Australian casualties in Vietnam at the time of writing (May 1968) amounts to 194 killed and 836 wounded. The same number of persons were killed on the roads of Australia in 22 days during the twelve-month period ending June 1967. These battle casualties rightly receive the maximum publicity in the national and local newspapers of Australia, yet we remain comparatively indifferent to the far more disastrous and avoidable road-death and injury rates occurring each year.

Earthquake is often held to be the most fearsome and cataclysmic of natural disasters. In the course of, and subsequent to, the Great Lisbon Earthquake of 1755, some 10,000–15,000 persons are said to have died (Kendrick, 1956). This event so shocked the civilized world that it produced major changes in political, philosophical, and religious thought and practice. More recent disasters in Alaska, Yugoslavia, and Turkey were widely reported in newspapers throughout the world, yet the 117 deaths in the Alaskan earthquake in 1964 were exceeded during 22 hours of driving on the roads of the United States. No doubt many deaths in a short space of time in a limited geographical area are far more impressive than the same number of deaths extended in time and space caused by a large number of smaller accidents. Yet one suspects that it is not so much the spatial and temporal qualities of the disaster which impress us, as our readiness to empathize with the victims of major catastrophes while obstinately failing to react appropriately to casualties occurring every hour on our roads. Fires, floods, and shipwrecks take their annual toll far more dramatically than the numerically greater road deaths and injuries. Major air disasters seem always to receive front-page treatment in the world's newspapers when they occur. The destruction of the airship R101 in 1930, when 47 lives were lost, and of the Hindenburg zeppelin in 1937, with 36 dead, led to the abandonment of this form of air transport. No doubt other technical factors contributed to the greater use made of other forms of aircraft, but catastrophes of this kind must have played a part in bringing about the abandonment of airships in favour of aeroplanes as the major form of air transport. So far the vastly greater number of deaths and injuries occurring each day on the world's roads has failed to lead to the necessary modifications in road and vehicle design calculated to minimize the risk incurred whenever a car is driven on to the highway. A major indictment of the motor industry such as that provided by Nader (1965) has not wholly converted manufacturers to the provision of fully tested safety devices in their products. Seat belts, for example, are still 'optional extras' in the majority of motor vehicles sold. The evidence is overwhelming that seat belts minimize injury risks when accidents occur and it is astonishing that they are not yet obligatory items in the structure of the motor vehicle, as essential as brakes and the steering-wheel. Only in recent times has legislation in a number of countries – including the United Kingdom and Australia – made mandatory the fitting of seat belts in all new vehicles.

Even so the *wearing* of seat belts by driver or passengers is not enforced by law.[1]

Our attitude to motor-vehicle accidents appears even stranger when one considers the entertainment value of such mishaps. I have yet to see a film dealing with motor racing which did not make spectacular crashes one of the principal features of the production. Evidently a good many spectators derive positive pleasure from such scenes, and it is probably true to say that those who attend motor race meetings vaguely or explicitly hope for similar disasters 'in the flesh'. From another point of view, road accidents are high comedy. No one who has watched the Keystone Cops can deny his whole-hearted appreciation of the crashes, explosions, and other disasters that appear to be built-in features of the vehicles depicted in this series of films. Of course, we know that the accidents are not real – and laugh accordingly. The motor race films, however, attempt to give verisimilitude to spectacles that may not cause us to laugh but certainly hold us enthralled.

In summary, therefore, we seem to have reached a stage when road accidents and death rates fail to impress us, an attitude which contrasts strongly with our reactions to other forms of disaster. Apathy and indifference seem to be fairly universal attitudes towards these rising figures, and we appear to accept death on the road as a commonplace, an ordinary hazard in our daily lives. We are also more fatalistic about this hazard than we are about minor variations in our bodily health. Yet road deaths and injuries constitute a major public health problem requiring every conceivable measure to bring it under control. We already know some of the contributory causes. Others we can guess at. Some are probably unknown, including the exact contribution of driver psychology to this disturbing state of affairs.

The epidemiology of road accidents has been reviewed by Norman, Austin, and others and it would be superfluous to reiterate all their findings. However, certain points require emphasis because of the clues they provide to aetiological factors that are not dependent solely on vehicle construction or road design. Quite obviously, road-death rates will depend very much on the population at risk, the number of motor vehicles on the roads, and the density of traffic. It is difficult to take all these variables into account, but if one calculates road-death rates on a population basis, one obtains a picture

[1] Except in Victoria, Australia, by a new law coming into force in 1971.

very different from that provided by death rates calculated per million vehicle-miles driven each year. According to the Royal Society for the Prevention of Accidents, road deaths per 100,000 of the population in Great Britain rose from 11 in 1957 to 15 in 1966. During the same period the rate per 100 million vehicle-miles fell from 10·8 to 7·8. Figures from the United States of America show rather similar trends. These findings, of course, do not minimize the shocking extent of death and injury on the roads, but at least they suggest that greater use of the motor vehicle may be leading to better control of its lethal potentialities.

Such figures say little about the persons involved in accidents. The 1966 figures in Great Britain showed that fatality and serious injury rates rose steeply between the ages of 17 and 20 and then slowly declined. For motor-cycle riders the casualty rate was even more dramatic, rising very sharply between the ages of 17 and 19 and then falling equally suddenly. Lee (1963) has estimated that in Great Britain a youth aged 16–19 owning a motor-cycle has an 8 per cent chance of being killed or seriously injured on the road. Passenger casualties from road accidents most commonly are found in these younger age-groups, but pedestrian death rates are highest in early childhood, falling in adolescence and adulthood, only to rise again in old age. If all forms of road accidents are considered together, the mortality rate for males is 3–5 times higher than for females. Whereas male deaths are particularly heavy between the ages of 15 and 25, falling to their lowest level in middle age, women show less dramatic changes, although their death rates, as with men, tend to rise in later life. The steep rise in casualty rates in Great Britain on Saturday nights between the hours of 10 p.m. and midnight have often been commented on, and few would doubt that heavy drinking on Saturday evenings has something to do with the phenomenon. The fall in casualties by 49 per cent between the hours of 10 p.m. and midnight in Great Britain during the month of November 1967, following the introduction of the breathalyser test, despite a 1 per cent increase in road traffic compared with the previous year, is further evidence in support of the role of alcohol as a major cause of road accidents (*British Medical Journal*, 1968). Figures of the kind quoted indicate clearly the particular groups at risk on the road. Young men lacking in driving experience, whether in cars or on motor-bicycles, show the highest rates just as they show the highest rates of delinquency. Whether or not there is some causative association between these two well-known facts is one of the topics to be examined later.

These epidemiological data, of course, tell us little about the underlying causes of the verified facts. Male and female differences in personality, driving skills, and attitudes to motor vehicles, the effects of experience, and the effect of alcohol, all seem to be aspects of the problem. The psychological make-up and emotional state of drivers involved in repeated road accidents are also important features of varying relevance. It remains to be seen whether closer examination of these phenomena will demonstrate understandable and preventable disturbances which, if rigorously controlled, could lead to reduction of current road-casualty rates.

Concentration on the behaviour of aggressive youth on the road should not obscure the contribution made to road accidents by older members of the community. A substantial number of young men survive the initial exposure only to become dangerous in middle life for other reasons. There appears to be general agreement that alcoholism is more likely to lead to drunken driving than is normal social drinking. Alcoholism is essentially a disorder of the middle-aged male who runs into trouble at a time when his capacity to maintain his heavy alcohol consumption is deteriorating. The frequency with which the alcoholic is involved in accidents following excessive drinking has been noted in a number of studies throughout the world. Generally speaking, the offender is a middle-aged man, but recently Birrell (1968) has claimed that in Victoria in Australia young men are the worst drinking drivers, a finding somewhat at variance with observations made elsewhere.

The relationship of road accidents to criminal behaviour is an aspect of this topic considered only in comparatively recent times. That a proportion at least of accident-repeaters and violators of traffic regulations is recruited from the more delinquent section of society appears to be a well-established fact. Antisocial traits falling short of overt criminal behaviour seem also to be well-documented features of a number of persons involved in traffic accidents. Clearly, such observations are of importance when one considers the youth and sex of the majority of delinquents and the similar age and masculinity of those injured on the roads.

Finally, the relationship of the mental and physical health of drivers to the causation of accidents is an issue which at present remains undecided. The proportion of accidents due to the sudden or chronic illness of driver or pedestrian is unknown, but once again it is as well to bear in mind that the heaviest incidence of death and injury on the road occurs in the age-group that, in the nature of things, is composed of the healthiest members of the community.

Without anticipating the conclusions to be drawn from the statistical data to be presented in later chapters, one is compelled to ask how the rising road-death and injury rates can be controlled. A good deal of attention has rightly been focused on the restriction of the use of alcohol by drivers, but less attempt has been made to delineate and control those psychological attributes which add measurably to the vulnerability of certain types of road-users. Why some persons behave dangerously or recklessly on the roads is a question to which many answers have been given. An answer purely in terms of human psychology may be inadequate, even when all other aspects of the environment have been taken into account. If aggressive behaviour is a variable basic to the whole problem, then a proper assessment of this variable as a major contributory factor to road accidents is more than overdue. Undoubtedly psychiatric and psychological methods are relevant to this examination, but it may well be that the contributions of the ethologist and the sociologist will in the long run prove more illuminating.

REFERENCES

AUSTIN, M. 1966. *Accident black spot*. Harmondsworth: Penguin Books.

BIRRELL, J. H. W. 1968. *Australian*, 17 August.

BRITISH MEDICAL JOURNAL 1968. 2 March, p. 588.

DOHERTY, T. T. 1965. Facts versus emotion in traffic safety. *Med. Sci. Law* 5, 147–50.

JEFFCOATE, G. O. 1962. The chance of being killed in a road accident for people born during different years. *J. roy. stat. Soc.* (A) **125**, 583–7.

KENDRICK, T. D. 1956. *The Lisbon earthquake*. London: Methuen.

LEE, J. A. H. 1963. Motor-cycle accidents of teenagers. *Proc. roy. Soc. Med.*, **56**, 365–7.

NADER, R. 1965. *Unsafe at any speed*. New York: Grossman Publications.

NEW ENG. J. MED. 1965. The unsafe driver. Editorial in Vol. 272, pp. 47–8.

NORMAN, L. G. 1962. *Road traffic accidents.* Public Health Paper No. 12. Geneva: WHO.

ROSE, G. N. G. 1968. The artificial delinquent generation. *J. crim. Law, Criminol., Police Sci.* **59,** 370.

UNITED STATES NATIONAL SAFETY COUNCIL. 1964. *Accident facts.* Chicago.

3 · The nature of accidents and accident proneness

All nature is but art, unknown to thee;
All chance, direction which thou canst not see.
ALEXANDER POPE

Two concepts much abused by expert and layman alike are 'accident' and 'accident proneness'. Most of us believe that we understand what is implied when we read that a person has been killed or seriously injured in a road accident. Yet the more we learn about such contingencies the less certain do we become about their inherent nature. A similar conclusion applies to the notion of accident proneness, a term used by most persons as inaccurately as words like 'inferiority complex' and 'repression'. The domestic servant with a propensity for destroying one's best glass and china may be labelled accident prone. As a result she may be advised to seek employment in an ironmonger's store, where the more enduring qualities of carpenter's tools and garden implements provide less scope for her maladjustment. That such advice might be based on an inexact appreciation of the nature of the problem is one possible consequence of applying poorly defined concepts to practical affairs.

To many people accidents are fortuitous events occurring in a random fashion entirely by chance, to be classed with acts of God and other misfortunes. However, as more has become known about accidents and their causation, the elements of chance and randomness have diminished under the impact of more precise statistical assessments of what actually occurs. Indeed, the pendulum has swung far from the belief that accidents are chance misfortunes to the equally extreme belief that all accidents are caused by conscious and unconscious factors potentially under the control of the individual. Convictions of this nature have led to the development of the notion of accident proneness which, under the influence of Dunbar (1943, 1959) and others (Dunbar *et al.*, 1939), became an enduring personality trait correlated with other recognizable psychological characteristics. This trait was initially held to be of a stable and lasting nature, a tendency that would dog the life of its unfortunate possessor for the rest of time. Concepts of accident proneness of this kind implied that prediction of this particular propensity was possible, with consequent elimination of the affected persons from dangerous employment. This policy was in fact tried in a number of instances, with results that were, to say the least, somewhat disconcerting. In one study, following the elimination of the so-called accident-prone workers, the accident rate for all other workers in the subsequent decade increased rather than diminished (Adelstein, 1952). However, findings of this unexpected nature have not yet wholly eliminated accident proneness from the categories of personality. Hence it might be advantageous to examine critically the origins and development of this concept to discover how far it is acceptable and useful today.

It is not easy to provide an adequate definition of an accident for, as Froggatt and Smiley (1964) commented, 'An event is not listed as an accident unless some form of trauma occurs.' In fact, what is normally termed an accident is really the outcome of an accident, because near misses, slips, and errors do not enter into official statistics in any way. Arbous and Kerrich (1953) argue that any concept of accident proneness that regards it as an inherent trait of the individual must include all forms of accidents experienced by that person. As they rightly point out, all episodes of an unforeseen or hazardous nature leading to minor injury or no injury are almost certainly eliminated from memory and official statistics. This leaves us with only those events resulting in major injury, loss of work, or death as a basis for the assessment of an individual's experience of accidents.

One definition of accidents is as follows: 'In a chain of events, each of which is planned or controlled, there occurs an unplanned event which, being the result of some non-adjusted act on the part of the individual (variously caused) may or may not result in injury' (Arbous and Kerrich, 1953). Such a definition is reasonably all-inclusive, but unfortunately, potentially traumatic encounters of this kind not resulting in injury or damage to property are unlikely to be classed as accidents. Suchman (1961) noted that accidents were the product of a number of situational factors, including, for example, a susceptible host, risk-taking, poor appraisal of hazards, the nature of the environment, and the degree of familiarity of the host with that environment. Suchman felt that the greater our understanding of all these factors, the less likely we were to label a set of events as accidental. It is doubtful whether this is correct, since all traumatic events on the road leading to death, injury, or damage to property are classed as road accidents, even though we may have very precise information about the events leading up to them. Consequently, an understanding of the causes of accidents does not necessarily enable us to do away with the term. In the last analysis we have to fall back on some operational definition devised to meet the need of a particular situation, and so we find ourselves limited to those phenomena of an unpleasant, unforeseen, and damaging nature which occur apparently against the wishes of the host and which, if they do not result in injury or damage, fail to be classed as accidents. A definition of this kind would at least include most of those situations analysed in such a publication as *Accident Facts* (US National Safety Council, 1965) whatever the circumstances of the collision or trauma might be. Nevertheless, one cannot but agree with those authors who have argued that if we are to continue with the concept of accident proneness we have to consider all those near misses, slips, and minor aberrations from what is expected occurring in the life of any particular individual classed as accident prone.

The concept of accident proneness dates back to the original paper by Greenwood and Woods in 1919. The term 'accident proneness' was not, of course, used by these original investigators, since it was not introduced until 1939 by Farmer and Chambers in their paper, 'A Study of Accident Proneness among Motor Drivers'. However, Marbe (1926), working in Germany, talked of the accident habit, and later workers have discussed accident-repeaters and accident liability. Generally speaking, most people have come to assume that accident proneness is an enduring personality trait liable to manifest itself at any time of life, whereas accident-repeaters or persons showing the accident habit more commonly are those known to have had a number of accidents over a limited period of time, without any necessary imputation of specific personality qualities. Accident liability refers to all the circumstances surrounding an accident and goes far beyond the individual who is actually involved.

Greenwood and Woods carried out a study on female munition workers in Great Britain at the end of the First World War. They noted that a minority of the workers were responsible for a majority of the accidents, a finding which has been confirmed repeatedly by other investigators since that time. They made a statistical examination of their findings, and noted that the actual apportionment of accidents differed from what was expected, assuming that accident experience was a random event in the population conforming to a Poisson distribution. Putting it more simply, some persons appeared to have more accidents than they should have, even though it was to be expected that by pure chance a number of persons would have more accidents than the majority of the workers.

To explain this observation, it was necessary to discover the basis for the accident experience of the population under study. Initially it was assumed that accidents occurred randomly but, as already mentioned, the distribution among the population was not of a wholly chance nature. An alternative hypothesis suggested that an individual who had experienced one accident would in consequence go on to have more accidents. In short, whereas the first accident was a random event, the second and further accidents were in some way determined by this first experience. However, the statistical analysis failed to support this particular possibility. Finally, it was concluded that for reasons unknown certain persons had more than their fair share of accidents, assuming that environmental and exposure risk remained constant for the entire period and group. This, of course, is the most important aspect of the study, but one that has been largely disregarded by later workers.

The work was carried further by Newbold in a series of papers around 1926. She surveyed accident-room attendances based on 22 factories, 8,962 workers, and 16,188 accidents. The periods of exposure varied from three months to two years. Every attempt was made to provide comparable groups, but this was not always wholly successful. However, it was noted as usual that a small number of workers influenced markedly the distribution of accidents in the population under study. Like Greenwood and Woods she did not find that one accident influenced future accident rates, but she noted that accidents decreased with age and experience. Fortunately the accidents suffered by the group under investigation were not severe, but it was observed that the more serious accidents tended to involve older workers. The individuals who had the most accidents also had the greatest number of minor ailments, and men and women seemed to be equally affected by these. Newbold maintained a cautious attitude to her findings, but felt that they were in keeping with those of the earlier investigators. Certainly she did not go beyond the statistical facts in order to ascribe psychological and other attributes to persons affected by repeated accidents.

As mentioned earlier, the term 'accident proneness' was coined by Farmer and Chambers, who found that motor accidents were not statistically random events. They carried out an investigation into the incidence of accidents among five groups of omnibus drivers, using psychological and psychomotor tests in support of the statistical findings. The five groups were not homogeneous in terms of age, driving experience, or even route of driving. Nevertheless, these authors concluded that accident proneness was manifest in all kinds of accidents throughout all conditions of exposure. Furthermore, it was shown that experience, although it lessened accident rates, did not affect differences between those who were specially prone and those who were not. Unfortunately, the inability to control the quality and quantity of exposure of the groups throws doubt upon the results of the investigation. Farmer and Chambers were not able to demonstrate an enduring psychological trait, but on the basis of psychometric test findings concluded that such a trait existed. 'Accident proneness', they wrote, 'is no longer a theory but an established fact.' But, as a number of authors have since pointed out, this statement went far beyond the data.

The concept of accident proneness was taken further by workers in the psychosomatic field in America, notably Flanders Dunbar, who wrote a number of papers on this particular topic. Her views are summarized in her book *Mind and Body* (1955), in which she claimed that a personality trait of accident proneness is a proven fact. Persons showing this trait, she said, were impulsive, looked for short-term gratifications rather than aimed at long-term goals, were casual in their attitudes to sex and family, were concerned about their health, were resentful of authority, and had shown childhood neurotic traits. The circular nature of the reasoning used to support the hypothesis seems at times to have escaped the critical sense of the author. 'Accidents happen quickly,' she wrote, 'and the damage is usually obvious to those whom the victim wishes to impress.' Psychodynamic interpretations of an equally tautological nature were offered as proofs that persons involved in accidents had some unconscious need for trauma of this kind.

Dunbar compared a group of fracture patients with cardiac patients, and on some basis not entirely explicit divided accidents into true accidents and personality-factor accidents. She claimed that 90 per cent of the fracture patients had personality-factor accidents, compared with 12 per cent of the cardiac patients, whereas 10 per cent of each group had had true accidents. Presumably the personality-factor accident is based upon the alleged personality profile, which to say the least is a tautological argument hardly convincing to those who do not accept the underlying psychodynamic hypothesis. The fracture patients were described as

> jerky, tense, restless people who were popular, made up their minds quickly and aimed at immediate rather than long-range goals. They responded to actions rather than thoughts. From early childhood their responses were impulsive. In childhood they were likely to have run away from home, played truant, told lies and been guilty of stealing. Early neurotic traits were common. As adults they were always in a hurry, were tense and often were heavy smokers. Many were interested in sport, body culture and heavy machines. They were boastful, took chances, left school early and found it difficult to hold a regular job. The outstanding feature in their development was a continual conflict with authority, at first within their families, then at school, later towards social and religious bodies, employers and finally in their marriages. There was a high incidence of childless marriages, small families and divorce. Accidents tended to occur when strong aggressive feelings were aroused in the patient and pressure from outside authorities had become too great. Aggression showed in a wish to punish themselves in order to punish those whom they regarded as responsible for their frustration. The majority of the patients had at least one over-strict parent.

Later Dunbar had to modify her original views because it was pointed out that some of these so-called accident-prone personalities ceased to have accidents as they grew older. She postulated that in a good many instances accidents were precipitated by specific worries or situations. In short, she assumed that the personality structure remained unchanged, but that the propensity to become involved in accidents only occurred when certain strains were imposed upon the subject.

Understandably, a number of investigators have turned their attention to the problem of accidents in childhood, and the matter has recently been reviewed by Vaughan (1965). Langford *et al.* (1953) found that children involved in road accidents more frequently came from families where the mother was working or pregnant, where there was illness in the mother or in a near member of the family,

C

and where the families were overcrowded with poor play facilities. This author concluded that accident proneness in children exists, but that it is only one aspect of a more general problem of emotional disturbance. There may also be special instances when the accident satisfies some unconscious need. Krall (1953) claimed that accident-repeater children showed more aggressive behaviour than others. Some of these earlier studies on children have come under criticism in recent years. The fact that accident-repeaters come from large families and broken homes, have more frequent changes of school, and are known more often to school and home social agencies, implies that the home background might be responsible for accident proneness and aggression, both of which coexist independently. Once again, there is a failure to control exposure risk and a host of other factors that certainly could contribute to differences between groups.

The best-known paper on accident proneness in motor-vehicle drivers is that by Tillman and Hobbs (1949), who demonstrated that, in two groups of taxi-drivers in Canada, one group had a higher number of accidents and traffic violations than the other. They went on to examine the life-style of the accident-repeaters, who showed marked aggressive antisocial tendencies, more frequent appearances in Court in both youth and adult life for non-traffic offences, a higher incidence of venereal disease, and a greater rate of attendance at social and welfare agencies. The authors concluded that a man drives as he lives, and that the belief that sitting behind the wheel of a car releases certain latent tendencies that are well under control in other circumstances is in fact incorrect. Unfortunately, they also concluded that these accident-repeaters had some specific trait denominated by the term 'accident proneness', and, of course, they were not able to control the exposure risks of the two groups they were studying.

A very much more ambitious attempt to control environmental factors was provided by Häkkinen (1958) working in Helsinki, Finland, where he carried out an investigation of accidents among public transport drivers in that city. As far as possible, he compared drivers who had the same amount of exposure and who drove on the same routes within the city, but, even so, he was not able to make absolutely exact comparisons. Nevertheless, he concluded that some drivers consistently had more accidents than others when driving under similar conditions. This study has been criticized by Smeed (1960), who pointed out that, although this was on the whole the most satisfactory attempt to demonstrate accident proneness in vehicle drivers, the author had not been wholly successful in controlling age-groups and a number of other factors.

It is necessary at this stage to summarize the position as it stood some 10 to 15 years ago. The careful statistical studies of the earlier workers and the cautious interpretation of their results had been supplanted by the enthusiastic personality-profile studies of psychosomatic theorists. These workers incautiously argued that they could demonstrate specific personality qualities in individuals involved in repeated accidents. Underlying the outward manifestations, they claimed, was a traumatophilic drive which they seem to have inferred largely from the observation that certain individuals had experienced a fair amount of damage to themselves in the course of their lives. Undoubtedly, some of these subjects manifested aggressive behaviour in a number of situations, but it was going beyond the facts to assume that the accidents in which they were involved were brought about by unconscious wishes for punishment for their antisocial behaviour. Furthermore, all these studies repeatedly failed to control the risk of exposure to accidents for the accident-repeaters and the control groups. This, of course, is very difficult to achieve, but unless it is carried out successfully it makes nonsense of any theory of accident proneness. Furthermore, as already pointed out, slips and near misses are not included in the statistics of accidents, even though one might well presume that persons who do have repeated accidents in the conventional sense might also have very much higher near-accident rates than control groups. This has never been conclusively demonstrated, because it is quite impossible to obtain data on such trivial events. Indeed, one of the major criticisms of so many of these studies is that they are based on retrospective evidence. People's memories of accidents, unless these mishaps were of considerable severity, can hardly be regarded as reliable. Consequently, most studies of accident proneness have had to be based mainly on documentary evidence of serious accidents sufficiently severe to require medical treatment. Anything less will not be included in the final statistics.

Dunbar claimed that 80-90 per cent of all accidents were due to personality factors that could be diagnosed before the habit developed. She and others believed that a study of the personality and life situation of these individuals would allow one with some confidence to diagnose the trait of accident proneness. Such persons, it was said, should be eliminated from dangerous occupations, with a consequent fall in accident rates. A number of authorities have attempted to do this, and, as already mentioned, in one particular study, following the elimination of the so-called accident prone, the accident rate increased rather than decreased. It is, of course, difficult to obtain adequate controls for these experiments, but one of the most famous studies in industry, the Hawthorne experiment at the Western Electric Company, was not able to show that attention to accident proneness in a control group and an experimental group led to changes in the expected direction. In fact, in both experimental and control groups the rates went down, largely, it would seem, because of the interest being shown by management and unions in the activities of the employees.

Schulzinger, in his book *The Accident Syndrome* (1956), wrote, 'Numerous studies of the frequency distribution of accidents have indicated with monotonous regularity that most accidents occur in a relatively small group of individuals. This finding furnished the statistical basis upon which the psychological theory of accident proneness was founded.' He went on to say, 'In 25 years of experience the author has been unable to confirm the above observation. The concept of accident proneness as a fixed personality factor which compels or generates accidental injury throughout life or long periods of time is incompatible with my findings.' He noted Franz Alexander's statement that 'in the unconsciously provided accident the accident prone expresses his resentment and revenge, at the same time atoning for his rebellion by his injury'. Schulzinger felt that this sort of interpretation was impossible to demonstrate as a conclusive truth, and, like a good many others, argued that many interpretations can be put upon the facts, depending largely upon the theoretical standpoint of the observer. Unless one controls the factors of age, experience, and exposure in experimental and control groups, one's findings are bound to rest on a shaky basis.

One of the most searching critiques of accident proneness was provided by Arbous and Kerrich (1953), who started their article by noting that many people believed that accidents were not fortuitous events but were largely determined by personality traits and unconscious wishes of the individual sufferer. The alleged enduring nature of these personality traits required that their possessor should be prohibited from engaging in dangerous occupations. However, accident proneness can be based only on statistical and mathematical testing of data and cannot be inferred solely from the number of accidents incurred by the individuals being studied. Undoubtedly, the statistical data are valid, but the existence of a set of lasting personality traits has never been conclusively proved. It would appear more likely that from time to time certain groups of individuals become more liable to repeated accidents. It is going far beyond the facts to assume that this liability is due wholly to underlying personality traits and tendencies. Circumstances, environment, host susceptibility, and a number of other factors all have to be taken into account, for it is rare indeed to discover individuals who have shown a lifetime of repeated accidents. Far more commonly they have bursts of repeated accidents which then cease, possibly for the rest of their lives, assuming, of course, that they survive the initial exposure.

Schulzinger found that the number of accidents was higher in youth and fell after the age of 21. Twice as many males as females were involved in accidents, while most accidents were relatively infrequent solitary events. That the irresponsible and the maladjusted have more accidents and more emotional strain at the time of an accident seems to be generally accepted. Car accidents involved more frequently young men under the age of 21 on hot, humid days, at weekends or on holiday, in the late evening or during a rush hour after dark, at a time when the individual was driving aggressively. Other factors included inexperience, excessive speed, fatigue, ingestion of alcohol, specific psychological conflicts, sociopathic traits, and disturbed childhood.

Undoubtedly, differences are to be found between persons who have repeated road accidents and persons who avoid these disasters. Sociopathic and criminal traits have been demonstrated among the accident-repeaters, but this observation largely confirms the Tillman and Hobbs statement that a man drives as he lives. However, the great majority of serious road accidents are single events in the lives of their victims, and the accident-repeater is a comparatively unusual person. Even so, one cannot argue that a person who has repeated accidents will also have a specific trait labelled accident proneness. All that one can say is that some individuals have repeated accidents and that numerous factors contribute to these events. The causes of repeated accidents do not remain constant throughout the subject's life, but vary according to time and place and other circumstances.

Menninger (1938) described an individual who showed behaviour of a kind which could be interpreted as suicidal or as equivalent to a suicidal act. There appeared to be some relationship between this type of subject and the so-called accident-prone personality, since Menninger's patients had experienced more accidents, had undergone more surgical operations, were more commonly dependent on drugs or alcohol, and even sought martyrdom more frequently than the rest of the population. It is difficult to test the truth of this type of descriptive psychiatry, but a recent study (Whitlock and Broadhurst, 1968) examined the incidence of violent events of this kind in the lives of patients who had made suicidal attempts. They were compared with matched control samples of psychiatric and non-psychiatric patients, and it was found that persons who attempted suicide had more frequently than the others experienced accidents of varying degrees of severity in their lives. Unfortunately it was impossible to control risk of exposure or driving experience for the three groups, and the most that could be said about this study is that it pointed to the possibility that persons who made suicidal attempts were prone to seek violent solutions to their difficulties, without necessarily postulating a specific trait of accident proneness.

Accident proneness seems to be one of the legacies of the personality-profile stage of psychosomatic theory. It has survived longer than most of the other profiles mainly because of the popular acceptance of the notion that some persons are accident prone. No doubt it is more comforting to ascribe one's misfortunes to a malign psychological quirk for which one bears no responsibility than to face the possibility that accidents occur for no reason other than our carelessness or inattention. If this is true it might explain the popular acceptance of the accident-prone concept in contrast to other psychosomatic personality profiles which were less publicized outside medical circles. In fact, this trait of accident proneness has never been conclusively demonstrated, and it might be better if the term was dropped from psychiatric nomenclature. Such a recommendation does not eliminate the problem of the accident-repeater on the road. Certainly, in one respect he will differ from his counterpart in industry or in the home; because of the severity of some road accidents the first collision might well be the last, so eliminating the victim from the ranks of those who have repeated crashes of this nature. Consequently, although the accident-repeater is a significant contributor to road-casualty rates, his problems may differ considerably from those of the man who is killed in the first disaster or who brings his driving career to an end owing to subsequent permanent incapacity. These two groups of road casualties may have similar psychological attributes; they may differ widely in this respect. The methodological problems of assessing premorbid personality traits of those killed or permanently incapacitated in road accidents may effectively prevent anyone from demonstrating psychological differences between accident-repeaters and those who have one fatal or wholly incapacitating disaster. Most investigators, in consequence, have concentrated their attentions on the accident-repeaters but, as will be seen later, at least one class of individual – the alcoholic – is noteworthy for his contribution to fatal single-vehicle accidents. He may not always have experienced accidents of less severity prior to the final débâcle. These theoretical problems are not solved by the use of the term 'accident prone', and, whatever value the concept may have had as an explanatory hypothesis of accidents in industry or in the home, it seems hardly applicable to the field of road accidents, where the complexity of the variables involved makes any single theory of causation untenable.

REFERENCES

ADELSTEIN, A. M. 1952. Accident proneness: a criticism of the concept based upon an analysis of shunters' accidents. *J. roy. stat. Soc.* (A) **115**, 354.

ARBOUS, A. G., and KERRICH, J. E. 1953. The phenomenon of accident proneness. *Indust. Med. Surg.* **22**, 141–8.

DUNBAR, H. F. 1943. *Psychosomatic diagnosis.* New York: Hoeber; London: Cassell.

—— 1955. *Mind and body.* New York: Random House.

—— 1959. *Psychiatry in the medical specialities.* New York: McGraw Hill.

——, WOLFE, T. P., TAUBER, E. S., and BRUSH, A. L. 1939. Psychiatric aspects of medical problems. *Amer. J. Psychiat.* **95**, 1319.

FARMER, E., and CHAMBERS, E. G. 1936. *A study of accident proneness among motor drivers.* Report 84, MRC Industrial Health Research Board. London: HMSO.

FROGGATT, P., and SMILEY, J. A. 1964. The concept of accident proneness: a review. *Brit. J. indust. Med.* **21**, 1–11.

GREENWOOD, M., and WOODS, H. M. 1919. *The incidence of industrial accidents upon individuals with special reference to multiple accidents*. Report 4, Industrial Fatigue Research Board. London: HMSO.

HÄKKINEN, S. 1958. Traffic accidents and driver characteristics. Finland Institute of Technology, Helsinki.

KRALL, V. 1953. Personality of accident repeating children. *J. abnorm. soc. Psychol.* **48**, 99.

LANGFORD, W. S., GILDER, R., WILKING, V. N., GENN, M. M., and SHERRILL, H. H. 1953. Pilot study of childhood accidents. *Pediatrics* **11**, 405–13.

MARBE, K. 1926. *Practical psychology of accidents and industrial injuries*. Munich and Berlin: Oldenbourg.

MENNINGER, K. A. 1938. *Man against himself*. New York: Harcourt; London: Harrap.

NEWBOLD, E. M. 1926. *A contribution to the study of the human factor in the causation of accidents*. Report 34, Industrial Fatigue Research Board. London: HMSO.

SCHULZINGER, M. S. 1956. *The accident syndrome*. Springfield, Ill.: Thomas.

SMEED, R. J. 1960. Proneness of drivers to road accidents. *Nature* **186**, 273–5.

SUCHMAN, E. A. 1961. A conceptual analysis of the accident phenomenon. *Social Forces* **8**, 241–53.

TILLMAN, W. A., and HOBBS, G. E. 1949. The accident prone automobile driver. *Amer. J. Psychiat.* **106**, 321–31.

UNITED STATES NATIONAL SAFETY COUNCIL. 1964. *Accident facts*. Chicago.

VAUGHAN, G. 1965. Accident proneness. In J. E. Howells (ed.), *Modern perspectives in child psychiatry*. Edinburgh: Oliver & Boyd.

WHITLOCK, F. A., and BROADHURST, A. 1968. Attempted suicide and the experience of violence. *Journal of Biosocial Science* **1**, 353–68.

4 · The psychology and psychopathology of drivers

Rage supplies all arms. When an angry man thirsts for blood, anything will serve him as a spear.

CLAUDIUS

There is no passion that so much transports men from their right judgement as anger.

MONTAIGNE

A widespread belief that road accidents are due to personality factors rather than mechanical faults of the vehicle is embodied in the saying that the nut *behind* the wheel is the real problem on the road. Following his investigation into the roadworthiness of a number of makes of vehicle Nader (1965) had good reason to doubt the general applicability of this saying, but many authors have felt that the human contribution to accidents greatly exceeded those of the roads or vehicles. Sanchez-Jiminez (1967), for example, claimed that 90 per cent of road-traffic accidents were due to the personalities of the drivers concerned, while Selzer and his colleagues (1968) estimated that 80–90 per cent of road deaths in the United States of America were due to driver-error. Bearing in mind that the causes of accidents are multiple and complex, it is not always easy to distinguish between a primary, secondary, or tertiary cause of an accident. For example, a car may swerve to avoid running over a dog on the road. As a result of the swerve, the vehicle overturns and the driver is injured. A more ruthless driver might have killed the dog rather than risk an accident, whereas other mortals have an instinctive aversion to killing anything on the road, often at considerable risk to themselves. Perhaps in this case the vehicle was travelling too fast to permit less hazardous avoidance tactics. The speed might have been due in part to the desire of the driver to keep a particular appointment. Was the accident caused by the dog, the camber of the road which resulted in the vehicle overturning, the temperament of the driver, or his speed due to his emotional state at the time? No simple answer can be given to a question of this kind, but most investigators would agree that personality factors contribute to rather than constitute the prime cause of road accidents; and that the more frequently an individual is involved in accidents the more likely will one find a deviance of personality which could be highly relevant to that driver's accident record.

It has also to be remembered that for the average driver serious accidents are rare events. The word 'average' implies a statistical quality of normality which will include, among its many variables, normal personality. The majority of road accidents are fairly trivial events involving individuals with unremarkable personality traits. Consequently, it might well be argued that concentration on the personality structures of drivers involved in accidents is unlikely to reveal anything very startling. However, there is good evidence supporting the opinion that certain drivers have more than the expected sum of accidents and that these persons make significant contributions to the overall frequency of these emergencies. It may well be that human fallibility, congested roads, and a number of environmental factors will always have as their outcome a number of accidents of greater or lesser severity. The problem, therefore, is to discover those individuals peculiarly at risk, and for this reason particular attention has been focused on the personalities of drivers involved in repeated accidents, accidents involving flagrant disregard of the traffic regulations, and accidents to whose cause alcohol consumption has made a significant contribution. If such persons could be detected and restrained prior to their obtaining a driving licence, one might hope to see a decline in road-accident rates.

Needless to say, psychological aspects of road accidents are not solely matters of personality. Such factors as age, sex, and social class, and their differential effects upon behaviour, are all highly relevant to the overall problem. Learning theorists understandably derive their hypotheses from conditioning and deconditioning experiments, many of which may have a very real relevance to driving skills. Some of these factors may also have a bearing on the ease or difficulty with which applicants succeed in passing driving tests required before a driving licence is granted (see Sanchez-Jiminez, 1967). Some persons will manifest disabilities which include defects of intelligence and emotional stability and the presence of mild neurological disorders which could interfere with motor skills.

Road and automobile engineers are properly concerned with the psychology of perception, reaction times, information load, and the ergonomics of design. Intrinsic to car-driving is a constant inflow of all kinds of information; and on the basis of what is perceived actions have to be taken, some of which are of an emergency nature. Anything that distracts attention from, delays reception of, or distorts incoming information can produce inappropriate reactions on the part of the driver. Consequently, attention has been focused on the layout of dashboard instruments, the positioning of controls, the size, colour, and lettering of road signs, and the design of roads. Pedestrian behaviour is partly dependent on a somewhat similar list of design problems, all of which need to be solved in order to avoid confusion, to provide clear information, and to permit the use of roads by pedestrians and motor vehicles with a minimum of danger to either.

Interference with information can be caused by visual or auditory impairment; poor visibility, which obscures the various signals; fatigue, which reduces the perceptual set and lengthens reaction time; and emotional tension of various kinds leading to inappropriate behaviour on the part of the driver. All these aspects of psychology are related to the important functions of vigilance and preparedness. By vigilance is meant that intelligent appreciation of changing situations conducing to immediate and appropriate responses designed to control or allow for the various contingencies presented to the driver. This state of vigilance will vary considerably between persons, and from one time to another in the same person. Familiarity with the vehicle and the route can undoubtedly alter perceptual set, leading to the well-known phenomenon of automatic driving. Depending to some extent on the experience of the driver will be his capacity to drive safely in this 'unconscious' fashion without impairing his ability to respond immediately to sudden changes in the incoming information. A good many aspects of car-driving can be compared to learned behaviour similar to that required for other complex motor skills. Typing, playing a musical instrument, and the operation of a telegraph are good examples of comparable learned techniques which ultimately can be carried out automatically by mechanisms working below the threshold of full consciousness. Indeed, safe and accurate operation of complex pieces of apparatus requires the fullest possible development of this automatic behaviour. Unfortunately, the inexperienced driver may show a lowering of vigilance or perceptual set well before he has acquired perfectly integrated automatic responses. Should an emergency occur during such a phase of driving, a failure to respond immediately or appropriately might be the expected consequence. Furthermore, the sudden anxiety engendered in the inexperienced person on such occasions would also contribute to his or her inappropriate reaction. It would seem, therefore, that vigilance and preparedness are important qualities whose impairment for one reason or another increases the risk of fractional delay between stimulus and reaction – with traumatic possibilities for the driver and others on the road.

The degree of vigilance of a driver can to some extent be estimated by monitoring his use of the rear mirror in his car. Quenault (1967) examined 50 car-drivers who had been convicted of careless driving and compared them with matched, non-convicted controls. The careless drivers carried out more unusual manœuvres, had more near-accidents, were overtaken less frequently, and made less use of their rear mirrors. Quenault used the word 'dissociated' to designate those persons 'who appear to drive with a degree of awareness of the relevant presented information which is below that necessary for safe driving. Their mirror usage is either very low or non-existent . . . to some degree these drivers lack anticipation and show poor judgment of traffic situations.' And, as Quenault remarked, these persons are not easily identifiable: 'It is only when they get behind a steering-wheel that this pattern emerges.'

This particular study, of course, tested out only one class of delinquent driver, but one might also expect such a person to have more than his fair share of accidents or near-accidents. However, it would be going beyond the facts to postulate a particular class of personality showing these qualities of dissociated driving. Certainly behavioural characteristics of this kind may not account for the actions of the driver who, with a ruthless disregard for the rights and safety of others, pulls out from the kerbside into a stream of traffic without warning or a rearward glance to observe whether the road behind him is clear.

The epidemiological data have shown that certain classes of individual are more likely to be killed on the roads or to be involved in repeated accidents. Male exceed female deaths in all age-groups. Young men under the age of 25 are particularly at risk, and Minden (1964) in England found that drivers under the age of 20 had seven times the minimum rate of fatal or severe accidents. Leygue and his colleagues (1966) felt that a driving experience of less than five years was an important finding in accidents involving young persons. Middle-aged men are more likely to have accidents – often fatal – due to excessive alcohol. Older citizens as well as very young children tend to swell the toll of pedestrian deaths. This age and sex differentiation has received much comment for, even allowing for the larger number of male than female drivers, the death rates among young men are quite disproportionate. In one other significant sphere does the social pathology of young men greatly exceed that of young women – criminal behaviour. One would certainly agree with Baroness Wootton's comments (1959) on criminal and motoring behaviour when she says, 'If men behaved like women the Courts would be idle and the prisons empty'; and so, one might add, would be a large number of surgical beds reserved for the acute admission of road casualties.

Age, experience, and ability to learn are probably inseparable from the more general problems of personality and their relationship to safe and unsafe driving. Louer (1952), after noting the high accident rates of male drivers aged less than 30, found that men required some five years before improvement in their accident records occurred, whereas women seemed to improve right from the start of their driving experience. Russell Davis and Corley (1959) found that better-educated drivers had fewer accidents, but that personality qualities – estimated by psychometric tests – did not differentiate accident-repeaters from the single-accident group. In general, of course, men learn to drive earlier in life than women, a fact that may be of some importance when it comes to assessing their capacity to learn to drive safely. The accident-repeaters in Davis and Corley's study more frequently had criminal records, a finding that could be related to personality qualities that presumably had not been detected by more formal testing.

The subject of accident proneness has already received consideration, and in this connection it is also worth noting the remarks of Haddon and his colleagues (1964) who, following a review of papers on this topic, wrote, 'The foregoing studies indicate that accident proneness is a psychological abstraction based upon a statistical enquiry. As often happens when a statistical distribution is given theoretical significance, the concept quickly assumes much more than was originally intended.' They went on to reject accident proneness as a global personality trait, while recognizing that psychological factors were of major significance in the production of accident situations. Hence it becomes all the more necessary to examine closely those persons involved repeatedly in road accidents in order to estimate those psychological characteristics which appear to correlate with these recurrent misadventures.

Running through numerous papers on this topic is the theme of aggression and its expression and control as a dominant personality trait in individuals who have repeated road accidents. Selling (1941) felt that such persons failed to anticipate risks, were unable to stop in time, and were often young and drove aggressively. They also had a past record of delinquency. In a further paper (1941) he compared 50 drivers found guilty of hit-and-run offences with 500 persons found guilty of other traffic violations. Eighty per cent of the hit-and-run drivers had previous motoring convictions, and 38 per cent had two or more criminal convictions. The social and psychological characteristics of persons who have repeated accidents were described in greater detail by Tillman and Hobbs (1949), who, as already mentioned, compared drivers having accident-free records with accident-repeaters. The second category of drivers drove aggressively, showing little concern for the safety and rights of others. The authors concluded, 'it would appear that the driving habits in the high accident records are simply one manifestation of a method of living . . . truly it may be said that a man drives as he lives'. In support of this opinion, Canty (1953) remarked: 'It has often been said that a person behaves in a manner totally different from his usual pattern when he is behind the wheel of his car. This is not so. His personality does not change. There is one significant difference: when the driver is in his own car there is more freedom to demonstrate the presence of unsocial, irresponsible and, even, antisocial traits.'

This conclusion agrees well with clinical observations on the antisocial or psychopathic personality. The qualities characterizing these individuals may not be manifest on all occasions, but this should not mislead us into thinking that there has been a change of personality. Faced with the inevitable frustrations of the road, sociopathic personalities are more likely to demonstrate their poor frustration tolerance by the outward expression of aggression. The consequences in terms of loss of life and property are all too familiar. Conger *et al.* (1957) using psychometric and projective tests, found that accident-repeaters showed poor control of hostility and were more overtly aggressive than the accident-free control group. Mental immaturity is another quality found by an Australian investigator

(Listivan, 1958). In a further paper Conger and his colleagues (1959) showed that persons involved in repeated road accidents were more likely than persons not so involved to demonstrate impulsive hostility, poor reality-testing, emotional lability, impaired intellectual function, a highly personalized, idiosyncratic fantasy life, and withdrawal from interpersonal relationships. These antisocial attitudes figure prominently in the findings of many other observers who comment upon high anxiety, tension, and little control of aggression (see also Alonso-Fernandez, 1966, and Pelaz, 1966). In a number of papers, Selzer and his colleagues (1962-8) have commented on the psychological make-up of persons – mainly alcoholics – involved in road accidents. In one study (1968) of 96 drivers responsible for fatal accidents, there were significant findings of paranoid thinking, suicidal tendencies, depression, and expression of violence. Fifty-two per cent of the accident subjects compared with 18 per cent of controls had experienced social stress within the past year and 20 per cent of accident subjects had been involved in major rows within six hours of the accident. Once again, there is evidence of poor control of aggression coupled, in a proportion of cases, with suicidal impulses.

The employment of psychometric instruments to test the personality qualities of individuals involved in road accidents has produced conflicting findings. Brown and Berdie (1960), using the Minnesota Multiphasic Personality Inventory, showed that drivers with high accident and violation rates scored more highly on the psychopathic and hypomanic scales. Eysenck (1962), applying his well-known tests for extraversion, introversion, and neuroticism, predicted that extraverts would be more liable to accidents arising from the occurrence of involuntary rest pauses during their driving and felt that there was evidence to support this view. Elderly persons and those who had suffered brain damage were more likely than young healthy individuals to suffer from numerous and lengthy involuntary rest pauses, thus constituting a definite hazard on the road. Unfortunately Eysenck's predictions seem not to be supported in his paper by experimental work carried out by himself on drivers and, consequently, the significance of involuntary rest pauses in elderly and brain-damaged drivers can only be regarded as a speculative possibility. The effects of extraversion and drink are cumulative. Consequently, extraverts are doubly at risk owing to their fondness for conviviality and only a clear understanding of the position would discourage them from driving while under the influence of drink. This statement, too optimistic over the possibility that drivers take heed of the results of experimental psychology, overlooks the fact that the large majority of persons involved in serious accidents on the roads are young and healthy rather than elderly and brain-damaged. The relationship of misuse of alcohol to age, to be discussed later, may also modify Eysenck's prediction.

Shaw (1966) in South Africa, using the Thematic Apperception and Social Relations Tests, found that drivers classified as bad accident risks showed emotional and mental immaturity, little control of aggression, high anxiety, insecurity and tension, and a high incidence of antisocial attitudes. This investigator concluded that people drive as they would *like* to live. A World Health Organization conference (WHO, 1966) commented on the psychological problem of too much information, the effect of car radio on alertness, and the usefulness of speed limits in reducing information load. Quenault, in the study already referred to, was not able to distinguish between careless drivers and the unconvicted control group by psychometric tests which included the Maudsley Personality Inventory. From a more descriptive point of view, Goldstein (1964) observed that most drivers believe that accidents happen to others, that minor bumps and knocks should not be counted as accidents, and that most drivers expect reasonable conditions for driving and responsible attitudes on the part of other drivers. Preston and Harris (1965) found that persons involved in accidents had a higher incidence of traffic violations and were more prone to blame others when they occurred.

Although there is some conflict between the various findings, there seems also to be general agreement that the use of the car as a means of expressing aggression is a common factor contributing to violence on the road. Sometimes this aggression overflows and becomes manifest as bouts of fisticuffs between participants in accidents, an aspect of life on the road that has been commented on by Bennett (1965) and by Raphael (1967). I recall witnessing recently in Australia an episode involving two (presumably) adult males in a car park attached to a large supermarket. The area was crowded, and both drivers wished to move out of the car park simultaneously. Neither would give way to the other and eventually a notable slanging match ensued which fortunately concluded when the less aggressive or more mature participant permitted his rival to go ahead of him. Raphael recounts a number of instances of naked aggression on the road, the majority of which could be multiplied by any observant driver who keeps his eyes open during his travels. This quality of aggressive driving is, of course, well known to motor salesmen, who employ a variety of phrases to sell their wares, implying that only the aggressive and virile are fit subjects to sit behind the wheel. Perhaps these outbursts of aggression are partial consequences of our need in civilized society to contain or channel aggression into acceptable modes of behaviour. As Lorenz (1966) has commented, 'I believe . . . that present day civilised man suffers from insufficient discharge of his aggressive drive. It is more than probable that the evil effects of the human aggressive drives . . . simply derive from the fact that in prehistoric times intraspecific selection bred into man a measure of aggressive drives for which in the social order of today he finds no adequate outlet.' Later he continues, 'Anyone who has ever driven a fast car when really angry knows . . . what strong inclination there is to self-destructive behaviour in a situation like this.' As an example of aggressive driving leading to high road-accident rates, Lorenz cites Margolin's work on Ute Indians, a tribe formerly known for its outstanding fighting qualities. Since these were curbed by social and legal reforms, there has been a marked rise in the incidence of neurosis and accidental injury. The rates for motor-vehicle accidents among the Ute Indians far exceed those of any other racial group. In their statistical analysis of accidents in the USA, Iskrant and Joliet (1968) showed that American Indians had abnormally high death rates from motor-vehicle accidents, drowning, and mishaps with firearms. Such findings are compatible with the explanation that inability to employ the former fighting qualities of their race has led to their manifestation as other forms of violence resulting in accidental deaths.

The young adult male with sociopathic traits or other impairment of psychological health and impulse-control figures prominently in many of these reports. Anger as a contributory factor to road accidents has been commented on by psychologists, psychiatrists, police, and clergymen. One author (Skillman, 1965) remarked particularly about this emotion and its relationship to frustration as a factor in road accidents. He wrote, 'The man who has sat a yard behind another's tail fuming over what he thinks as road hogging gets some of the annoyance out of his system by cutting in sharply when he finally does pass. Other people hoot belligerently to let people know that they think they are driving badly. The uprush of anger in their victims is sometimes quite surprising. I have seen a driver go almost black in the face.' The author observed the higher incidence of vulnerability as defined in his book of Australian males compared with English and United States drivers. Anger seems to increase the vulnerability factor, and in Australia a certain kind of embitterment went with this high vulnerability rate. The author suggested that this was an extrapunitive characteristic. The measurement of this trait has received little attention, although Preston (1964) used the Rosenzweig Picture Frustration Test when comparing accident proneness in attempted suicides and in automobile accident victims. Unfortunately, the two groups were not strictly matched, but, as might be expected, the test failed to differentiate individuals exhibiting suicidal behaviour from those whose dangerous driving resulted in serious accidents.

The behavioural and psychological characteristics of aggression have been discussed in a number of recent publications (Carthy and Ebling, 1964; Berkowitz, 1962; Buss, 1961) and it would be beyond the immediate scope of this monograph to examine this topic in detail. How far aggressive behaviour is due to built-in cerebral mechanisms in the human species is not entirely certain. Studies of territoriality in animals have shown that they have an aggressive response to threats to the integrity of the area marked out by the individual and this response seems to be innate in many species. Learning and child-rearing theorists tend to argue that a good deal of aggressive conduct is the result of early experience of violent behaviour at the hands of others – notably parents – during childhood. However, whatever the truth might be, there is undoubtedly a type of personality, the aggressive psychopath, who appears to have very low tolerance of frustration coupled with a ready resort to violence in order to overcome his difficulties. Such persons seem not to respond to normal measures of socialization and rarely learn from past experience. They act impulsively without much thought for consequences to themselves or to others. Nevertheless, it is still far from clear whether these individuals suffer from an excess of aggressive drive or behave as they do mainly because they have never had the opportunity to learn adequate control. As might be expected, when these personality qualities occur in conjunction with excessive drinking, the results can be peculiarly dangerous both to the subjects and to others. According to Berkowitz (1962), frustration is conducive to the manifestation of aggressive behaviour; and, whatever else might be said about driving on our congested roads, frustration is one of the principal experiences of all who get behind the wheel of a car.

It would be tedious to relate the numerous frustrations and irritations to be encountered on the road. We all have our private lists of pet aversions ranging from the trivial to the potentially catastrophic. Their effect upon observers or victims varies from mild expressions of astonishment at human folly to dangerous surges of rage liable to result in counter-aggressive behaviour as reckless as the act which provoked it. If frustration is fundamental to the calling forth of aggression then one might expect that those least able to tolerate such restraints will be the ones most at risk on the road. The antisocial psychopath whose aggressive and criminal propensities have been examined in the greatest detail will almost certainly be encountered amongst repeated violators of traffic regulations and will also be responsible for more than the expected number of serious accidents involving himself and others. In general, the young are less tolerant of restraint – particularly restraint imposed by vehicles driven by cautious older citizens – and once again one finds a high proportion of young men among traffic offenders and accident victims. Nevertheless, an explanation of road aggression solely in terms of frustration will probably be insufficient to account for all the facts. Such an explanation might suffice for the reckless behaviour of certain well-recognized personalities. Other aspects of violence will require examination; for however much a man might 'drive as he lives', there is good reason to presume that a large number of otherwise mild-mannered persons manifest surprisingly aggressive behaviour once they get behind the steering-wheel of their cars. The irrational nature of much of this conduct can be inferred from the quality of the behaviour and its expression by persons who normally show most of the features of civilized, social restraint.

Needless to say, the more unusual or disturbed personalities do not show their qualities solely on the highway. An examination of personality in relation to traffic accidents suggests that those most frequently involved in such incidents will also have other antisocial characteristics, not the least important of which will be criminal tendencies. Such propensities existing in conjunction with car ownership and a misuse of alcohol have obvious implications so far as road-accident rates are concerned. It will be necessary therefore to examine the evidence that a proportion of road offenders and accident-repeaters are noteworthy for their criminal records as well as their list of violations of traffic rules.

REFERENCES

ALONSO-FERNANDEZ, F. 1966. Psychology of road traffic accidents. *Rev. Psic. gen. y apl.* **21,** 947–60.

BENNETT, R. O. 1965. The traffic hot-head: an unsuspected motoring menace. *Police Chief* **32,** 20–30. Washington.

BERKOWITZ, L. 1962. *Aggression.* New York: McGraw-Hill.

BROWN, P. L., and BERDIE, R. F. 1960. Driver behaviour and score on the MMPI. *J. appl. Psychol.* **44,** 18–21.

BUSS, A. H. 1961. *The psychology of aggression.* New York: Wiley.

CANTY, A. 1953. Quoted in T. C. Willett, *Criminal on the road.* London: Tavistock, 1964.

CARTHY, D., and EBLING, F. J. (eds.) 1964. *The natural history oj aggression.* New York and London: Academic Press.

CONGER, J. J. *et al.* 1957. Personal and interpersonal factors in motor vehicle accidents. *Amer. J. Psychiat.* **113,** 1069–74.

—— 1959. Psychological and psycho-physiological factors in motor vehicle accidents. *J. Amer. med. Assoc.* **169,** 1581–7.

EYSENCK, H. J. 1962. The personality of driver and pedestrian. *Med. Sci. Law* 3, 416–23.

GOLDSTEIN, L. G. 1964. Psychological aspects of traffic accidents. *Traffic Dig. Rev.* **12** (7), 10.

HADDON, W., SUCHMAN, E. A., and KLEIN, D. 1964. *Accident research.* New York: Harper.

ISKRANT, A. P., and JOLIET, P. V. 1968. *Accidents and homicide.* Cambridge, Mass.: Harvard University Press.

LEYGUE, F., DUPLOT, P., and HOFFMAN, F. 1966. Investigation into the influence on accidents of the age of the driver, his driving experience, and the age and power of the vehicle. *Internat. Rd Safety and Traffic Rev.* **14,** 13–22.

LISTIVAN, I. A. 1958. Psychological aspects of car accidents. *Med. J. Australia* ii, 282–5.

LORENZ, K. 1966. *On aggression.* London: Methuen.

LOUER, A. R. 1952. Age and sex in relation to accidents. *US Highway Res. Board Bull.* **60,** 23–35.

MINDEN, J. M. 1966. Accident rates of car drivers by age. *Internat. Rd Safety and Traffic Rev.* **14**, 28–9.

NADER, R. 1965. *Unsafe at any speed.* New York: Grossman Publications.

PELAZ, E. 1966. Driver psychopathology. *Rev. Psic. gen. y apl.* **21**, 961–7.

PRESTON, C. E. 1964. Accident proneness in attempted suicides and automobile accidents. *J. consult. Psychol.* **28**, 79–82.

——, and HARRIS, S. 1965. Psychology of drivers in traffic accidents. *J. appl. Psychol.* **49**, 284–8.

QUENAULT, S. W. 1967. *Driver behaviour: safe and unsafe drivers.* Road Research Laboratory, Ministry of Transport Report L.R. 70.

RAPHAEL, A. 1967. Violence on the roads. *Guardian*, 17 November.

RUSSELL DAVIS, D., and CORLEY, P. A. 1959. Accident proneness in motor vehicle drivers. *Ergonomics* **2**, 239–46.

SANCHEZ-JIMENEZ, J. 1967. Personality of the driver and the cause of accidents. *Rev. Psic. gen. y apl.* **22**, 143–59.

SCHUMAN, S. F., PELZ, D. C., EHRLICH, N. J., and SELZER, M. L. 1967. Young male drivers, impulse expression, accidents and violations. *J. Amer. med. Assoc.* **200**, 1026–30.

SELLING, L. S. 1940. Personality traits in automobile drivers. *J. crim. Psychopathol.* **1**, 258–63.

—— 1941. The psychopathology of the hit-and-run driver. *Amer. J. Psychiat.* **98**, 93–8.

SELZER, M. L. 1967. Automobile accidents as an expression of psychopathology in an alcoholic population. *Quart. J. Stud. Alc.* **28**, 505–16.

——, and PAYNE, C. E. 1962. Automobile accidents, suicide and unconscious motivation. *Amer. J. Psychiat.* **119**, 237–40.

——, ——, GIFFORD, J. D., and KELLY, W. L. 1963. Alcoholism, mental illness and the drunk driver. *Amer. J. Psychiat.* **120**, 326–31.

——, ——, QUINN, J., and WESTERVELT, F. H. 1966. A depression–aggression syndrome related to accidents caused by alcoholic drivers. *Proc. 4th Internat. Conf. Alc. and Traffic Safety.* Indiana, 1966.

——, ROGERS, J. E., and KERN, S. 1968. Fatal accidents: the role of psychopathology, social stress and acute disturbance. *Amer. J. Psychiat.* **124**, 1028–36.

——, and WEISS, S. 1966. Alcoholism and traffic fatalities. *Amer. J. Psychiat.* **122**, 762–7.

SHAW, L. 1966. The practical use of projective personality tests as accident predictors. *Internat. Rd Safety and Traffic Rev.* **14**, 30–6.

SKILLMAN, T. S. 1965. *Road safety.* London: Reappraisal Society.

TILLMAN, W. A., and HOBBS, G. E. 1949. The accident-prone automobile driver. *Amer. J. Psychiat.* **106**, 321–31.

WOOTTON, B. 1959. *Social science and social pathology.* London: Allen & Unwin.

WHO. 1966. Epidemiology of road accidents. *WHO Chronicle* **20**, 393–406.

5 · Crime and the accident-repeater

*In some instances of my observations, psychoanalysis has re-
vealed that guilt feelings persisting for many years after a
disastrous car accident and seemingly completely irrational, had
good justification in the unconscious homicidal wishes of the
driver.*

G. BYCHOWSKI, *Evil in Man*

Two well-established facts point to a close association between
criminal behaviour and road-casualty rates: young men have the
highest rates for both these classes of social disturbance; and the
relationships between alcohol and violent crime and vehicle accidents are among the oldest and best-tested aspects of human mis-
behaviour. Rape, assault, and homicide frequently occur when
assailant or victim or both are partially intoxicated. Similarly, the
disastrous effect of excess alcohol on transportation has been
recognized since the earliest times. Noah was mercifully sober when
he piloted the ark to safety, but a good many seafarers subsequently
have had reason to regret the intemperance of their captains. As one
recent commentator pointed out (Editorial, *Medical Journal of
Australia*, 1968), the problem of drink and driving is not a new one,
for the Romans introduced legislation in an attempt to reduce the
number of collisions between drunken charioteers. Since the inven-
tion of the internal combustion engine the effect of alcohol upon
driving skills has been the subject of so much attention that regular
international conferences are now held to consider the problem. One
might therefore infer that violent crime, alcoholic excess, and
dangerous driving will be three closely related problems.

Surprisingly, until recent times little attention has been given to
the criminology of the traffic offender and the driver involved in
repeated accidents. A number of reasons can be offered for this
neglect of a fairly obvious aspect of the problem, not the least
important of which are public and judicial attitudes to motoring
offences. The reluctance of juries to convict for dangerous or drunken

driving is one of the better-known features of prosecutions for these classes of offence. The reasons for the unwillingness to condemn a fellow-driver for offences which a number of jury members may have committed themselves without being detected are said to be due to the strong empathy with the accused and a feeling of 'There but for the grace of God go I', which is not extended to the more conventional and established forms of criminal behaviour. Indeed, as Elliott and Street (1968) have pointed out, the term 'manslaughter' for the offence of killing a person by negligent driving was so abhorrent to juries that the less loaded verdict of causing death by dangerous driving has been substituted in many countries. The empathy between jury and the defendant accused of a serious motoring offence is one of the many puzzling aspects of road accidents and traffic-law infringements which requires further consideration. It is difficult to believe that a fellow-feeling for the accused is the sole factor responsible for this phenomenon, and the whole matter may well be bound up with a deep-seated feeling for personal rights and liberties whose assertion on the road is not regarded by many members of the public as a criminal offence. Whatever the cause might be, there can be little doubt that a good many law-abiding citizens appear to have more sympathy for the dangerous driver than for his victim. The well-known antagonism between driving public and police is yet another phenomenon suggesting that in the minds of most persons conventional crime and road accidents have very little to do with one another.

Some of these points have been discussed by Ross (1960), who, after noting the popular attitudes to road offences, wrote: 'Traffic law violations are a costly and widespread form of criminal behaviour.' He found in America that the proportion of white-collar workers is higher in traffic crimes than in non-traffic crimes and that violations of traffic laws are usually condoned by public opinion. These observations may not be generally applicable for, as far as Great Britain is concerned, serious infringements of the road-traffic regulations occur more commonly among manual workers than among the more affluent sections of the community. Despite this, until recent times it has been widely believed that the majority of persons summoned to appear before Courts for traffic offences came from the wealthier classes who, because of their position, were more likely to be car-owners than those in the lower socio-economic sections of the community. Such persons, of course, would be judged by their social equals in Magistrates' Courts, and this seems to have led to a more tolerant attitude being shown towards this class of offence. Indeed, in some Courts preferential treatment was given to these offenders as, often, they were segregated from the non-traffic offenders in a manner implying that they were certainly not to be regarded as ordinary prisoners in the dock. Baroness Wootton has commented with characteristic pungency on what are sometimes referred to as 'white-collar crimes', but since the publication of her book (*Social Science and Social Pathology*, 1959) a number of studies have drawn attention to the criminal propensities of a proportion of persons involved in road accidents or infringement of traffic laws.

Selling (1940) noted that aggressive driving by juveniles and Negroes in America was associated with a record of delinquency. One can safely assume that driving of this kind would also result in a fair number of accidents. One particular class of traffic offender, the hit-and-run driver, was also examined by Selling (1941), who showed that a high proportion of these men were unskilled labourers manifesting signs of psychopathic personality complicated by heavy drinking. Eighty per cent had previously been convicted for motoring offences, and 38 per cent for non-traffic criminal offences. Canty (1956) compared a group of traffic violators with persons convicted of non-traffic criminal offences. Both groups had been referred by the Courts to the Detroit Clinic largely because of suspected alcoholism, previous mental illness, or a long list of former convictions. Consequently, it would be unwise to draw too many conclusions from these selected groups. Both traffic and non-traffic offenders had in their ranks a large proportion of disturbed and unstable persons and, as far as the traffic offenders were concerned, some 90 per cent were regarded as showing some form of psychiatric disturbance. In the absence of exact diagnostic criteria, it is difficult to assess this finding, even though one might suspect that psychopathic disorder of the aggressive and/or antisocial kind would be a feature common to both classes of repeated offenders. Larsen (1956) found that the higher the number of charges for traffic violations by juveniles, the greater the likelihood that these offenders would have a past criminal record, while Jeffcoate (1962) also commented on the association between delinquency and death on the road in youths born between 1939 and 1945 in Great Britain. Dunbar (1958-9), on clinical evidence, had also noted an association between high accident rates and delinquency in teenagers. However, before accepting these findings as indicative of a casual connection between the two classes of phenomena, one has to consider the possibility that the association is a chance one due to the common occurrence of criminal behaviour and dangerous driving in the same male age-group. Such an association between adolescent crime and road accidents may be co-incidental, although it seems likely that there is a causal relationship between these two classes of behaviour.

In Great Britain, Clarke (1949) examined the records of a number of drivers in transport companies of the Royal Army Service Corps. One hundred and sixty-eight drivers had experienced one or more accidents, and of this group 66 per cent had been found guilty of one or more military offences. Further evidence for the association between road accidents and motoring offences was provided by Minden (1964) when he showed that individuals who had been convicted by the Courts had a higher insurance claim rate than those who had not been charged with traffic offences. The Chief Constable of Cambridge (see Willett, 1964) found among traffic offenders who had had repeated accidents a substantial number who also had previous criminal records. Porterfield (1960), using United States statistics of violent deaths, was able to correlate the incidence of male deaths by homicide with male road-death rates. There was a significant association in 39 metropolitan areas of the United States between these two forms of violent death. In Germany, Handel (1962) compared 1,000 drivers convicted of drunken driving with 1,000 sober drivers convicted of other offences. The alcoholic group showed a higher incidence of previous convictions for non-traffic offences, mainly assault. A further study from West Germany (Middendorff, 1963) indicated that persons convicted of ordinary criminal offences had broken the traffic laws far more frequently than had non-criminals. This suggested that the criminality and traffic misconduct had common roots in the personalities of the offenders.

Two of the most important studies in this field were carried out by Tillman and Hobbs (1949) in Canada, and by Willett (1964) in England. Reference has already been made to the Canadian study, which showed that taxi-drivers involved repeatedly in accidents manifested more frequently sociopathic traits, poor control of aggression, and a higher incidence of previous non-traffic offences for which they had been charged in the Courts. Willett examined the records of 653 persons found guilty of serious traffic offences. As usual, men greatly outnumbered women and the majority of the offenders, contrary to expectations, were classed as manual workers. Twenty-three per cent of the group had been convicted previously for non-motoring offences. As Willett himself wrote, 'This proportion is substantially in excess of even the most pessimistic estimate of the proportion of persons that could be expected to have criminal records in a random sample of the population of England and Wales.' Furthermore, an additional proportion of the group were known to the police as suspected persons and, if these were added to the numbers previously convicted for non-traffic offences, one finds that one-third of the serious traffic offenders were either suspected persons or had received previous non-traffic convictions. Unfortunately, Willett was not able to discover to what extent the serious motoring offender was likely to have had repeated accidents in the past, but information from other sources certainly suggests that repeated traffic violations and repeated accidents go hand in hand.

Steer and Carr-Hill (1967) have suggested that Willett's sample of traffic offenders was a biased one, and it is not easy to say how far his findings would be applicable to other countries. These authors point out that the young motor-cyclists with criminal records are predominantly convicted of 'dishonest' traffic offences, i.e. riding while disqualified or uninsured. In contrast, the older motorists, with a lower rate of previous convictions for non-traffic offences, are predominantly convicted – in Willet's study – of driving infringements that included dangerous driving, causing death by dangerous driving, driving while under the influence of liquor, and failing to stop after an accident. Furthermore, 73 per cent of the 'driving' offenders were detected after an accident whereas only 4 per cent of the 'dishonest' offenders came to the notice of the police in this way. Steer and Carr-Hill make the point that, if the 'dishonest' offenders are excluded, the remainder of those examined in Willett's study are not particularly criminal in their non-motoring behaviour. However, they also point out that studies in Canada and the USA show an association between criminal behaviour and serious traffic offences, a finding that is confirmed by a number of Australian studies.

An explanation for these discrepant findings probably lies with the type of vehicle used by the young offenders in Willett's study. Whereas in England young working-class men tend predominantly to ride motor-cycles, this is certainly not the case in Australia, Canada, and the USA, where automobiles are far more widely used by young persons. Admittedly a recent statement (American Medical

Association, 1968) shows that there is an increased use of motor-cycles in the USA, with the inevitable crop of fatalities. Even so, motor-cycles in Australia and the USA constitute only a small part of the total road traffic.

Motor-cyclists are less likely than motorists to be involved in traffic accidents leading to prosecution for dangerous driving, etc. Willett's study supports this by demonstrating the small number of young motor-cyclists convicted of serious traffic offences following an accident. However, had these young offenders been using cars instead of motor-cycles, I have little doubt not only that they would have driven them dangerously but also that they would more frequently have been convicted of dangerous and drunken driving or causing death by dangerous driving. In that case, Willett's young offenders would have more in common with their counterparts in Australia and elsewhere who are involved in accidents, commit serious traffic offences, and show previous criminal records. In short, it would appear that the class of vehicle to a considerable extent determines the type of traffic offence and, although many motor-cyclists undoubtedly drive dangerously, should a serious accident occur this will probably be fatal to the rider or result in serious injuries to himself. In such circumstances police action for dangerous driving is less likely to follow than would be the case when a motorist has an accident as a result of dangerous driving, even though this does not necessarily lead to a serious injury or death.

Certainly there seems to be a clear indication in England and Wales that a strong association exists between convictions for dangerous driving and other forms of criminal behaviour. Raphael (1967) has stated that, among persons convicted of dangerous driving, males outnumbered females by twenty to one and had five times the expected number of convictions for breaking and entering. Wolf (1964) in Denmark and Desmarez *et al.* (1965) in Belgium have also found an association between criminality and traffic offences.

MacDonald (1964) in Colorado showed that 10 of 40 patients discharged from a psychopathic hospital had attempted homicide by automobile. Seven of this group had also attempted suicide. A further English study quoted by Willett (Hood, 1966) discovered that 28 per cent of persons found guilty of serious motoring offences had been convicted for indictable non-motoring offences and that 20 per cent of 300 persons convicted of minor traffic infringements had a record of previous criminal acts. In Brisbane, Tweddell (1968) examined 100 persons found guilty of reckless driving and compared them with a control group. The reckless drivers showed qualities of psychopathy, had experienced more injury-producing accidents, had more convictions for speeding, drunken driving, and other traffic violations, and had a larger number of previous criminal non-traffic offences.

It may be objected that the demonstration of an association between crime and traffic offences does not necessarily imply that such an association also exists between crime and road accidents. However, it has been shown that persons involved in repeated accidents have often appeared before the Courts for previous traffic violations. In a study by McFarland and Moseley (1954) in which 57 accident-free drivers were compared with a control group of 57 accident-repeaters it was found that the accident-repeaters had significantly higher Court records of previous automobile offences and offences against the person. Preston and Harris (1965) also showed that persons involved in serious accidents had higher rates of convictions for traffic violations, while Schuman and his colleagues (1967) found that although accident rates affecting young men fell after the age of 20, infringements of traffic regulations did not decline until a further three years had elapsed. These authors noted how young men aged 16–18 tended to use motor vehicles to express their feelings and to 'blow off steam' after rows. Usually these men came from working-class backgrounds.

In general, therefore, the evidence supports a statistical association between road-accident rates, aggressive driving, and other forms of criminal behaviour. Furthermore, only a small part of this criminal behaviour will be of a violent kind, since crimes of this nature constitute only a small part of all indictable offences committed by young persons (see West, 1967). Some of the papers referred to specifically mention offences against the person among the crimes committed by those who repeatedly infringe the traffic regulations, but there is no reason to believe that violent crime in general is the commonest class of offence carried out by these individuals. One can, of course, look on all predatory antisocial acts as examples of aggressive behaviour, but most persons would consider physical assault as more violent than simple larceny. Unfortunately, the more widespread the offence is, the less reliable and comparable are the statistics. Homicide and forcible rape are fairly easily identifiable whereas the true incidence of theft may bear only a very slight relationship to the official figures for this offence.

The personality structure of those convicted of crimes of violence will often show features of aggressive psychopathy. The association of this class of personality with excessive drinking, paranoid ideation, hostile attitudes towards authority, and suicidal tendencies, seems at times to be expressed with devastating consequences on the public highway. The problem of the accident-repeater and the violator of traffic regulations may in part be due to the aggressive behaviour of the psychopath on the roads. Such individuals we know make significant contributions to the sum total of violence in society, and violence can be expressed in many different ways. In a society which sets a high value on the ownership and use of motor vehicles, it seems all too probable that those who have the greatest difficulty in controlling their aggressive propensities will be those most likely to manifest these tendencies through the driving of automobiles.

REFERENCES

AMERICAN MEDICAL ASSOCIATION (Committee on Medical Aspects of Automotive Safety). 1968. Medical aspects of motorcycle safety. *J. Amer. med. Assoc.* **205,** 290–1.

CANTY, A. 1956. Problem drivers and criminal offenders: a diagnostic comparison. *Canad. Services med. J.* **12,** 137–43.

CLARKE, B. 1949. Quoted in T. C. Willett, *Criminal on the road.* London: Tavistock, 1964.

DESMAREZ, J. J., BIERLAEN, R., and BERVLOET, J. R. 1965. A critical study of various social, medical and psycho-technical investigations aimed at detecting a propensity toward traffic delinquency. *Acad. roy. med. Belg.* **5,** 529–69.

DUNBAR, F. 1958. Homeostasis during puberty. *Amer. J. Psychiat.* **114,** 673–83.

—— 1959. *Psychiatry in the medical specialities,* p. 350. New York: McGraw-Hill.

ELLIOTT, D. W., and STREET, H. 1968. *Road accidents.* Harmondsworth: Penguin Books.

HANDEL, K. 1962. Personality of the alcohol intoxicated driver. *Proc. 3rd Internat. Conf. Alc. and Road Traffic.* London: BMA, 1963.

HOOD, R. Quoted in T. C. Willett, The motoring offender as a social problem. *Med. Legal J.* (1966) **34,** 146–52.

JEFFCOATE, G. O. 1962. The chance of being killed in a road accident for people born during different years. *J. roy. stat. Soc.* (A) **125**, 583–7.

LARSEN, J. C. 1956. Rehabilitating chronic traffic offenders. *J. crim. Law, Criminol., Police Sci.* **47**, 46–50.

MACDONALD, J. M. 1964. Suicide and homicide by automobile. *Amer. J. Psychiat.* **121**, 366–70.

MCFARLAND, R. A., and MOSELEY, A. L. 1954. *Human factors in highway transport.* Boston: Harvard School of Public Health.

MED. J. AUSTRALIA 1968. Driving and the demon drink. Editorial in Part ii, p. 443.

MIDDENDORFF, W. 1963. Traffic criminology. 12th International Course in Criminology. Jerusalem.

MINDEN, J. M. 1966. Accident rates of car drivers by age. *Internat. Rd Safety and Traffic Rev.* **14**, 28–9.

PORTERFIELD, A. L. 1960. Traffic fatalities, suicide and homicide. *Amer. social. Rev.* **25**, 897–901.

PRESTON, C. E., and HARRIS, S. 1965. *Psychology of drivers in traffic accidents. J. appl. Psychol.* **49**, 284–8.

ROSS, H. L. 1960. Traffic law violation: a folk crime. *Social Problems* **8**, 231–41.

SCHUMAN, S. H., PELZ, D. C., EHRLICH, N. J., and SELZER, M. L. 1967. Young male drivers, impulse expression, accidents and violations. *J. Amer. med. Assoc.* **200**, 1026–30.

SELLING, L. S. 1940. Personality traits in automobile drivers. *J. crim. Psychopathol.* **1**, 258–63.

—— 1941. The psychopathology of the hit and run driver. *Amer. J. Psychiat.* **98**, 93–8.

STEER, D. J., and CARR-HILL, R. A. 1967. The motoring offender: who is he? *Crim. Law Rev.* 214.

TILLMAN, W. A., and HOBBS, G. E. 1949. The accident-prone automobile driver. *Amer. J. Psychiat.* **106**, 321–31.

TWEDDELL, S. 1968. Personal communication.

WEST, D. J. 1967. *The young offender.* London: Duckworth; New York: International Universities Press.

WILLETT, T. C. 1964. *Criminal on the road.* London: Tavistock.

WOLF, P. 1964. The myth of the virtuous traffic offender. *Social Meddelelser* **9**, 73–7.

WOOTTON, B. 1959. *Social science and social pathology.* London: Allen & Unwin.

6 · Illness, suicide, and road accidents

> Boswell: *Do you think Sir, that all who commit suicide are mad?*
> Johnson: *Sir, they are often not universally disordered in their intellects, but one passion presses so far upon them that they yield to it, and commit suicide as a passionate man will stab another.*
>
> JAMES BOSWELL, *Life of Johnson*

> *The Dead ride fast.*
>
> G. A. BÜRGER, *Leonore*

Persons working for large transport organizations are usually required to undergo regular medical examinations in order to detect any physical or mental disability which could impair their competence as drivers, pilots, or navigators. Medical examination before employment will eliminate some of the potential accident risks from the transport services and in recent times a number of papers have suggested that inquiries of a similar nature should be carried out on those seeking or renewing driving licences. Some insurance firms will give full cover only if satisfactory medical certificates of health can be provided, a requirement more likely to be imposed on elderly drivers or those known to suffer from a serious disability.

This aspect of road safety needs to be looked at carefully, but whatever the facts might be it has always to be remembered that the highest road-casualty rate is sustained by the healthiest section of the community – young men; and that regular medical checks of ostensibly healthy persons are apt to be of a superficial and perfunctory nature. Such examinations will probably fail to detect early changes of serious disease and almost certainly will be quite inadequate for the accurate diagnosis and assessment of emotional and personality disorders which contribute significantly to the causes of road accidents. Minor impairment of health due to infection, drugs and alcohol, emotional upsets, and fatigue, will probably pass unnoticed.

Health in fact cannot be considered separately from the age and experience of the driver. Youth, temperament, and lack of experience are important variables conducive to high death and injury rates on the roads. In Australia in 1966, young men aged 17–29, who comprise 18·9 per cent of the male population, provided 48·3 per cent of driver deaths and 71·2 per cent of motor-cycle deaths for all men killed in these circumstances. In this age-group were 48·2 per cent of male passengers, but only 11 per cent of male pedestrians, killed in road accidents. The reasons for these figures may not differ greatly from those offered by United States commentators.

MacFarland and Moore (1960) have made observations on the influence of the automobile on American youth, noting that a car is an essential item of existence enabling him to compete in the social customs of dating and other activities. At the same time, the vehicle is a useful instrument for acting out tensions and latent aggression. One particular group of young men known as 'hot rodders' were remarkable for their physical development, an early interest in automobiles, and their skill as drivers. They originated from middle-class homes, showed some features of emotional deprivation, and their temperaments were predominantly aggressive with alternating moods of boredom relieved by excessive stimulation attained by wild and fast driving. Because of their driving ability these young men managed to avoid serious accidents. However, this seems to have been a special group, since Munden and Quenault (1966) found in Great Britain that youths aged less than 20 years had 7–8 times the casualty rates of men in their middle 50s, who showed the lowest rates. These authors felt that lack of driving experience and excessive speed leading to dangerous skidding were responsible. Although young men were infrequently convicted of driving under the influence of alcohol, when liquor was taken the subsequent accident rate was high. Experience and its lack can obviously show themselves in many different ways, and Austin (1966) has commented that the motor-cyclist with less than six months' experience has twice as many accidents as those who have been riding for longer periods. Unfortunately, experience is not the sole deciding factor in road mortality for, although it is known that the middle-aged have the lowest incidence of road casualty rates, these rates start to rise in the older age-groups. Furthermore, the middle-aged are conspicuous for their contribution to serious accidents caused by over-indulgence in alcohol (see Waller, 1966). The higher casualty rates for elderly

E

persons are found particularly for pedestrians and, in Australia in 1966, 40 per cent of pedestrians killed were aged 60 or over. These observations suggest that slower reaction times, loss of visual acuity, fatigue, and ill health, more than counteract the experience gained from some decades of fairly safe driving or walking on the roads.

The problem of fatigue in relation to driving has engaged the attention of a number of authorities. Crawford (1961) noted the difficulty in finding a satisfactory definition of fatigue, but stated that continuous emotional arousal induced by exposure to other road traffic could lead to changes in reactivity. This may take the form of a strong reaction to minor irritants or to adaptation to the incoming stimuli, leading to a lowered emotional response. Interpersonal problems and difficulties could also produce changes in emotional tension, causing inappropriate or dangerous responses to the various situations encountered on the road. In those conditions requiring cool and deliberate assessment with maximum alertness, changes of emotional threshold induced by fatigue and habituation could cause wholly inappropriate responses. Needless to say, such transitory states of fatigue and emotional reactivity will pass undetected by routine medical examination, even though psychiatric assessment might enable an observer to predict those who will be most susceptible to the influences of these temporary alterations in physical and mental alertness.

The effects of ill health on driver performance are difficult to estimate. The consequences of driving following the ingestion of alcohol and certain classes of drugs are so well known that most countries have laws prohibiting driving while under the influence of drugs of all kinds. In recent years the widespread use of psychotropic preparations, many of which can produce alteration of visual accommodation and emotional arousal, has probably caused a number of accidents. Precise information on this point is not available, but drugs taken to reduce fatigue and somnolence are known to contribute to accidents sustained by long-distance lorry-drivers. The effect of amphetamine-taking by these men is well known, and undoubtedly a number of serious accidents have occurred owing to the altered perceptions and hallucinations induced by this group of drugs.

More information is available on the effects of physical and mental ill health on driving ability. Surprisingly, physical ill health is not a major factor in the causation of accidents. Selzer *et al.* (1968)

estimate that although 80 per cent of road-traffic deaths in the United States of America are due to driver-error, except for sudden and severe illness other physical disabilities are not important. Nevertheless, Eriksen and Waller (1962), working in California, noted high accident rates for persons suffering from epilepsy, cardio-vascular disease, diabetes, and mental illness, while MacFarland (1962) estimated that 8·2 per cent of 355 persons admitted to hospital following road-traffic accidents had pre-existing disease responsible for the accident. However, West (1963), also working in California, estimated that there were some 1,700,000 persons with impairment of physical health driving on the roads but that the highest accident rates were shown by the alcoholic and by the healthy young male. Along with a number of other authors he disputed the value of regular medical check-ups for ordinary drivers as a measure designed to reduce accidents caused by physical ill health. In a more recent paper (1968) West and his colleagues found that for 15 per cent of 1,026 drivers dying within 15 minutes of a single-vehicle accident, pre-existing disease was responsible for the deaths. Ninety-six per cent of the drivers were male with an average age of 60, and of those dying from natural causes 94 per cent suffered from cardiac disorders. Only 60 per cent of these men were aware of their heart disease before the fatal accident. Of the 1,026 drivers, 74 per cent had high blood-alcohol concentrations with an average of 190 mg per 100 ml of blood. To what extent these cardiac deaths were precipitated by excessive drinking is uncertain. It is interesting to note that carbon monoxide poisoning and drug intoxication made little contribution to these deaths.

In Pennsylvania (Brandaleone and Sim, 1966), where examination for fitness to hold a driving licence has been instituted, 1·7 per cent of applicants have been refused on medical grounds. The largest number was in the 61–92 age-group. A thorough survey by Snedby and Ysander (1966) found that out of 44,255 road accidents 41 were caused by epilepsy or myocardial infarction. In only 19 of the 41 would prior medical examination have led to the withdrawal of a certificate of fitness to drive. These authors estimated that sudden physical disease as a cause of accidents occurred in only 2 per 1,000 accidents in Great Britain and the United States of America. In a recent paper, Gratton and Jeffcoate (1968) determined the frequency of medical factors as causes of road-traffic accidents. Sudden illness preceding accidents resulting in injuries of all kinds occurred in 1·5 per 1,000 accidents and 4 per 1,000 accidents with serious injuries. These authors also examined the problem of chronic disease and found that 5 of every 1,000 accidents resulting in serious injuries were associated with chronic medical conditions which might have contributed to the mishap. Among the conditions listed were coronary heart disease, cerebrovascular disease, epilepsy, and hypoglycaemia.

There seems good reason to suppose that of all the acute and chronic disorders affecting a car-driving population diseases of the cardiovascular system are the most important. Even so, their contribution is, on the available evidence, very small compared with the total number of accidents sustained. Hartmann (1966), reporting from the State of Ohio, claimed that sudden heart failure during, immediately before, or after car-driving, occurred in 0·02 per cent of the driving population. Only about 37 per cent of the incidents resulted in an accident and nobody apart from the driver was hurt. Practically all the drivers were men and the highest incidence of heart failure occurred in the 45–70 age-group.

In Australia (1968) sudden heart disease is regarded as a rare cause of road accidents, and it was noted that in Sweden only 7 cases of myocardial infarction occurred in 44,255 accidents. In Minnesota it has been estimated that out of 82,000 accidents in 1966, 159 were due to illness, of which only a small proportion were due to heart failure. Nevertheless, recent investigations of the effect of car-driving upon the electrocardiographic records shows that significant changes in heart rate and function can occur. Apparently it is not so much the stress of driving but the reaction to that stress which is responsible for these changes. Waller (1967) examined the driving record of elderly subjects, some of whom were fit while others suffered from cardiovascular disease with or without evidence of 'senility'. They were compared with a group of men aged 30–59. The healthy older men did not differ from the younger drivers in terms of accident or traffic violation rates but the older subjects showing impairment had higher rates for these incidents. The violations were mainly acts of omission such as failure to observe signals and traffic lights.

Norman (1962) found that myocardial infarction was a cause of one-third of all motor accidents brought about by sudden loss of consciousness of the driver. Nevertheless, such incidents were rare, occurring only once in 280 million vehicle-miles travelled by drivers of London Passenger Transport Board vehicles. In the United Kingdom in 1958 it was estimated that 0·6 per cent of personal injury accidents involving a motor-vehicle driver or a cyclist were contributed to by injury or physical defect.

In connection with traffic violations Crancer and McMurray (1968) showed that subjects suffering from diabetes, epilepsy, fainting attacks, and other medical conditions had higher rates of accidents and infringements of the traffic laws. Interestingly, subjects with cardiac conditions had significantly lower rates for infringements and their accident rates were only slightly higher than those of the controls. It is worth mentioning in this connection that, although applicants for driving licences are asked to state whether they suffer from epilepsy, accidents caused by epileptic fits are comparatively infrequent.

These findings suggest that sudden or chronic physical illness are not important factors in the aetiology of road deaths and injuries and one might – leaving aside the economics of the procedure – question the value of regular medical check-ups as a prophylactic measure. The most one can do is to take note of variations in health while appreciating the possible effects of such variations on emotional stability, vigilance, and reaction time. A minor illness such as influenza might be more significant as a cause of emotional disturbance leading to an accident than a good many more serious or chronic disorders. Clearly, it would be impossible to prevent everyone suffering from minor ill health from driving on the roads, and even major medical emergencies cannot be foreseen in more than a small proportion of subjects.

However, before dismissing physical illness as a major hazard on the road it would be essential to know how often such illnesses are concealed at the time of an accident. Hoff (1967) believed that internal disease was a commoner cause of accidents than was generally supposed and that drugs could have impaired driving ability in 12·6 per cent of a group of persons who had been involved in accidents. Yet when alcohol and drugs are removed from the list of causes of physical impairment, one is left with only a small number of drivers whose poor health has been directly responsible for the accident sustained.

When one turns to mental illness – excluding alcoholism and drug dependence – there is reason to believe that past or present psychiatric disorders are potential causes of road accidents. Admittedly

Trüeb (1966) found that schizophrenic patients fared no worse on the roads than mentally normal drivers, but Buttiglieri and Guenette (1967) showed in California that male drivers who subsequently developed mental illness had higher accident rates in the three months preceding hospital admission. It seems reasonable to assume that if psychological factors are all-important in the causation of motor accidents, major disturbances of psychological function are likely to be all the more devastating, a point stressed by Selzer and his colleagues (1968) when attempting to relate fatal accidents to the psychopathology of drivers. Even minor degrees of emotional disturbance could be contributory and Dalton (1960) found that women drivers were involved more frequently in road accidents four days before or during menstruation. If the premenstrual tension syndrome occurs as commonly as is believed, this might be a partial explanation of this particular phenomenon. However, Weist (1967) was unable to support Dalton's findings.

Pond (1967), who was of the opinion that only a small number of accidents were due to severe mental illness, also made the pertinent observation that routine driving-licence inquiries into mental illness were quite useless as a means of detecting such disorders. In Great Britain epilepsy, mental disorder, and severe subnormality are included among disabilities which may prevent an applicant from being granted a driving licence. As Elliott and Street (1968) remark, the list is not comprehensive enough and should include drug and alcohol dependence and diabetes. One difficulty so far as drug and alcohol dependence are concerned is the subject's unwillingness to acknowledge his illness. Furthermore, truthfulness about alcohol consumption is not one of the most notable characteristics of those known to have drinking problems.

Waller (1965) estimated that in California persons suffering from mental illness had twice the expected number of road accidents per million vehicle-miles and 1·8 times the expected number of traffic violations. 9 per cent of drivers incurring accidents contributed to by medical conditions were said to be suffering from mental illness. Waller noted that disturbances of consciousness due to epilepsy were rare causes of road accidents, but stated that 25 per cent of persons with mental illness involved in accidents were suffering from hysterical fugue states. There seems little enough reason to classify such conditions under the heading of 'loss of consciousness' and it may well be that some of the hysterical symptoms were the result of an accident – with or without head injury (see Whitlock, 1967) – rather than its cause.

Needless to say, the presence of mental disorder in a person who has had a road accident does not necessarily imply that the illness was the cause of the mishap. However, if it could be shown that persons suffering from serious mental illness had significantly higher death rates on the road than the normal population one might seriously consider the role of the illness as a major cause of the fatality. Unfortunately, it is very difficult to obtain adequate information on the causes of death of persons suffering from major psychiatric disorders while living outside institutions at the time of their demise. In one recent study from Finland (1967) Achté found that, during a five-year follow-up of 200 schizophrenic patients, 5 had died from suicide and 2 in traffic accidents, giving a road-accident death rate per 100,000 per annum of 200. If the full series of 513 from which the 200 follow-up patients were selected is taken as the basis for calculation of traffic-accident rates, one obtains a death rate of 78 per 100,000 per annum which is over four times greater than that of the general population. It would be unwise to read too much into these figures, but as 40 per cent of the 200 patients either took their lives, attempted suicide, threatened suicide, or admitted to suicidal thoughts, one might reasonably ask to what extent the two road-traffic deaths in this series represented suicide rather than accident.

In fact, suicide as a cause of road deaths and accidents has only recently come to the notice of legal and medical writers and the matter has received most attention in the United States. I have treated a number of patients in Australia who have deliberately crashed their cars or who have contemplated acts of this nature when in states of depression coloured by suicidal ideation. Nevertheless, as yet, as far as Great Britain and Australia are concerned, it is difficult to demonstrate that suicide by automobile is a particularly common event. In America (Rawlings, 1964) a doctor working at a Marine Base in California observed that 70 per cent of men who were troubled with suicidal thoughts considered suicide by automobile as the most likely method. In all probability the majority of these men were thinking of carbon monoxide poisoning from exhaust fumes rather than deliberate crashes and in a five-year survey in King County, Washington, of 109 known suicides by automobile, 106 were due to carbon monoxide poisoning whereas only three were the results of deliberately contrived car crashes. In this monograph we are concerned only with persons who die or are injured on the roads as a consequence of a consciously or unconsciously formed suicidal intent. Among this group will be included pedestrians who can and do throw themselves deliberately in front of moving traffic and those persons who deliberately incur accidents in order to kill themselves. McDonald (1964) has reported on 40 patients who made suicidal and/or homicidal attempts by automobile, following discharge from the Colorado Psychopathic Hospital. In all probability, the inmates of this hospital constituted a special group with markedly aggressive tendencies, but McDonald calculated from his findings that the suicide rate of patients discharged from this hospital was 34 times greater than that of the general population.

Since Menninger wrote on the topic (1938) there have been a number of papers correlating suicide and suicidal impulses with other forms of behaviour of an allegedly self-destructive kind. Among these were included repeated accidents, alcoholism, and multiple surgical operations. Selzer and Payne (1962a, b) were able to show that the patient with suicidal ideas had experienced more road accidents than non-suicidal psychiatric patients, and Tabachnick and his colleagues (1966) noted a number of similarities between persons who had died in road-traffic accidents and persons who had died by their own hand. In a recent study, Whitlock and Broadhurst (1968) found that a group of patients who had made suicidal attempts had, compared with non-suicidal psychiatric and healthy controls, experienced more frequently road accidents and other forms of accidental injury. Muller (1965) in Germany observed that suicide by pedestrians was not uncommon and, in this connection, I have recorded a female patient who had made five suicidal attempts in the past, who had sustained minor injuries in three car accidents, and who on the occasion of her most recent hospital admission had run out into the road with complete disregard for the traffic. She was hit by a vehicle but fortunately received only minor injuries. She denied conscious suicidal intent, but in this particular patient suicidal ideation was rarely far from the surface of her mind and it could be inferred that this was yet a further attempt upon her own life.

To what extent serious mental illness contributes to suicide on the road cannot at present be determined. In a two-year follow-up of 630 persons admitted to hospital in Brisbane, following a suicidal attempt, Dr John Edwards (1968) found that 2 had been killed in road accidents and 23 had succeeded in taking their lives. Undoubtedly, such a group of patients constitute a special problem but the very high road-death and suicide rates of these patients suggests that the two phenomena were interrelated. Alcoholics as a group carry a high risk of suicide, and undoubtedly a percentage of the drinking drivers who die will be examples of consciously or unconsciously willed death. The matter has been discussed by Selzer and his colleagues in a number of papers, in one of which (1966) they compared 50 alcoholic accident drivers with 50 psychiatrically ill non-alcoholic drivers. The alcoholics showed evidence of suicidal preoccupation and attempts, a finding confirmed in another study (1962a, b). In this investigation, 30 non-alcoholic psychiatric patients were compared with 30 alcoholics. Thirty-three patients admitted suicidal acts or ideas and 27 denied such preoccupations. The 33 suicidal patients were responsible for 89 traffic accidents, that is 2·7 per person, whereas the 27 non-suicidal had experienced only 1·3 accidents per person. In 1966, this group of investigators showed that alcoholic subjects had twice the number of accidents and traffic offences compared with the non-alcoholic psychiatric male population and, once again, thoughts of self-destruction, serious suicidal preoccupations, or previous attempts were noted. Spain and his colleagues (1951) commented on the association between alcohol and violent death. Fifteen of 78 persons who took their lives had taken alcohol and there was evidence of alcohol in 36 of 78 fatal motor-vehicle accidents.

Persons involved in repeated accidents and persons who make suicidal attempts are similar in respect of their extra- and intra-punitive tendencies as measured by the Rosenzweig Picture Frustration Test (Preston, 1964). However, this view of suicidal acts as examples of inwardly directed aggression has not been supported by all investigators, as Lester (1967) was not able to demonstrate any differences between suicidal and non-suicidal subjects so far as their preference for methods of showing aggression was concerned. Highly significant correlations between road-death rates and suicide in the United States were demonstrated by Porterfield (1960), who wrote, '. . . it may be predicted that drivers who have little regard for their own lives or the lives of others or both . . . will have higher rates of accidents than drivers who place a high value on human life'. Some of the qualities which appear to be associated with this disregard for lives and rights of others on the road have already been mentioned, and there are close similarities between the personality traits of the persons killed in single car accidents and the psychopathic subjects who make repeated suicidal attempts (see Litman and Tabachnick, 1967).

Ford and Moseley (1963) described a number of drivers and pedestrians who attempted suicide or took their own lives. The present author has seen recently four patients in whom suicidal intent and dangerous driving were closely associated. Two were men who deliberately crashed their vehicles and sustained, in one case, serious injuries. The other two patients were women, one of whom took an overdose of barbiturates but admitted that beforehand she had contemplated driving her car into the path of some on-coming vehicle. Fortunately, she was deterred by concern for other persons who might have been injured in her attempt at self-destruction. It is to be regretted that not all suicidal drivers show such consideration for the safety of others on the road.

It might be objected that whereas suicide is an act most often carried out by the middle-aged and elderly, road deaths have their peak incidence in youth. However, age-specific suicide rates can be somewhat misleading. Although suicide *rates* go up in middle and old age for both sexes in those countries studied, the *proportion* of deaths from this cause declines. In fact one might challenge the accepted statement that elderly persons are more prone to suicide than the young, for in youth suicide is the third commonest cause of death whereas in middle and old age the contribution of suicide to the total death rate is small. What one does observe among young persons in Australia and other Western countries is a high proportion of deaths due to violence – notably road accidents, other accidents, and suicide. Among males aged 15–24 three-quarters of the deaths were due to violence and nearly half followed road accidents. Among women in this age-group half the total deaths were due to violence but only one-third resulted from road accidents. Needless to say, suicide death *rates* are higher in males than in females in this age-group, a finding that is shown by the majority of the countries studied.

Somewhat similar findings could be provided by a number of countries, notably the United States of America, where again about three-quarters of the deaths of young men aged 15 to 24 are caused by violence. In 1964, road deaths accounted for 42·4 per cent and other accidents for 19·3 per cent of all deaths, while deaths by suicide (5·9 per cent) were exceeded by those due to homicide (6·4 per cent). In Japan, suicide accounts for 17·5 per cent of male deaths in this age-group, while 31·1 per cent of deaths were due to road accidents. Figures of this kind at least indicate that death by violence far exceeds other causes of death of young men; and that the manner in which violence is expressed will depend upon the society, the use of the motor vehicle, and a number of other factors. In all probability, therefore, road deaths in youth often conceal a suicidal intent, and one could predict that the more closely some of these traffic fatalities are examined, the more frequently one would discover evidence of self-destructive motives.

REFERENCES

ACHTÉ, K. A. 1967. On prognosis and rehabilitation in schizophrenia and paranoid psychoses. *Acta Psychiat. Scand.* **43**, Suppt 196.

AUSTIN, M. 1966. *Accident black spot.* Harmondsworth: Penguin Books.

BRANDALEONE, H., and SIM, R. P. 1966. Medical aspects of driver licencing. *New York J. Med.* **66**, 602–8.

BUTTIGLIERI, M. W., and GUENETTE, M. 1967. Temporal relationship between automobile accidents and psychiatric hospitalisation. *Perceptual Motor Skills* **24**, 1327–32.

CRANCER, A., and MCMURRAY, L. 1968. Accidents and violation rates of Washington's medically restricted drivers. *J. Amer. med. Assoc.* **205**, 272–6.

CRAWFORD, A. 1961. Fatigue and driving. *Ergonomics* **4**, 143–54.

DALTON, K. 1960. Menstruation and accidents. *Brit. med. J.* ii, 1425–6.

EDWARDS, J. E. 1968. Attempted suicide in Brisbane. (Personal communication.)

ELLIOTT, D. W., and STREET, H. 1968. *Road accidents.* Harmondsworth: Penguin Books.

ERICKSEN, H. M., and WALLER, J. A. 1962. *Proc. Nat. Conf. on Medical Aspects of Driver Safety and Driver Licencing.* Chicago.

FORD, R., and MOSELEY, A. L. 1963. Motor vehicle suicide. *J. crim. Law, Criminol., Police Sci.* **54**, 357–9.

GRATTON, E., and JEFFCOATE, G. O. 1968. Medical factors in road accidents. *Brit. med. J.* i, 75–9.

HARTMANN, H. 1966. Sudden death at the wheel of an automobile. *Postgrad. Med.* **39,** A68–76.

HOFF, F. 1967. Impairment of driving ability by disturbances of consciousness due to internal diseases. *Med. Welt* **31,** 1761–7. Stuttgart.

LESTER, D. 1967. Suicide as an aggressive act. *J. Psychol.* **66,** 47–50.

LITMAN, R. E., and TABACHNICK, N. 1967. Fatal one-car accidents. *Psychoanal Quart.* **36,** 248–59.

MCDONALD, J. M. 1964. Suicide and homicide by automobile. *Amer. J. Psychiat.* **121,** 366–70.

MacFARLAND, R. A. 1962. *Proc. Nat. Conf. on Medical Aspects of Driver Safety and Driver Licencing.* Chicago.

——, and MOORE, R. C. 1960. *Youth and the automobile.* Golden Anniversary White House Conference on Children and Youth Inc.

MENNINGER, K. A. 1938. *Man against himself.* New York: Harcourt; London: Harrap.

MULLER, E. 1965. Traffic accidents and suicide. *Arch. Kriminal.* **135,** 61–8.

MUNDEN, J. M., and QUENAULT, S. W. 1966. The young driver in Great Britain. 8th Internat. Study Week on Traffic Engineering and 1966 Internat. Rd Safety Congress. Barcelona.

NORMAN, L. G. 1962. *Road traffic accidents.* Public Health Paper No. 12. Geneva: WHO.

POND, D. 1967. Mental disturbances. *Med. Sci. Law* **7,** 28.

PORTERFIELD, A. L. 1960. Traffic fatalities, suicide and homicide. *Amer. sociol. Rev.* **25,** 897–901.

PRESTON, C. E. 1964. Accident proneness in attempted suicide and automobile accident victims. *J. consult. Psychol.* **28,** 79–82.

RAWLINGS, J. 1964. Suicide on the highway: how frequent? *Traffic Dig. Rev.* **12** (2), 4–6.

SELZER, M. L., and PAYNE, C. E. 1962a. Automobile accidents, suicide and unconscious motivation. *Proc. 3rd Internat. Conf. Alc. and Road Traffic.* London: BMA, 1963.

——, —— 1962b. Automobile accidents, suicide and unconscious motivation. *Amer. J. Psychiat.* **119,** 237–40.

——, ——, QUINN, J., and WESTERVELT, F. H. 1966. A depression–aggression syndrome related to accidents caused by alcoholic drivers. *Proc. 4th Internat. Conf. Alc. and Traffic Safety.*

——, ROGERS, J. E., and KERN, S. 1968. Fatal accidents: the role of psychopathology, social stress and acute disturbances. *Amer. J. Psychiat.* **124**, 1028–36.

——, and WEISS, S. 1966. Alcoholism and road traffic fatalities. *Amer. J. Psychiat.* **122**, 762–7.

SNEDBY, H. P., and YSANDER, L. 1966. Sudden illness as a cause of motor vehicle accidents. *Brit. J. indust. Med.* **23**, 37–41.

SPAIN, D. M., BRADESS, V. A., and EGGSTON, A. A. 1951. Alcohol and violent death. *J. Amer. med. Assoc.* **146**, 334–5.

TABACHNICK, N. *et al.* 1966. A comparative study of accidental and suicidal death. *Arch. gen. Psychiat.* **14**, 60–8.

TRÜEB, M. 1966. Schizophrenia and competence to drive. *Dtsch Z. ges. gerichtl. Med.* **57**, 326.

WALLER, J. A. 1965. Chronic medical conditions and traffic safety. *New Eng. J. Med.* **273**, 1413–20.

—— 1966. Use and misuse of alcoholic beverages as a factor in motor vehicle accidents. *US Pub. Hlth Rep.* **81**, 591–7.

—— 1967. Cardiovascular disease, ageing and traffic accidents. *J. Chron. Dis.* **20**, 615–20.

WEIST, H. J. 1967. Accidents and the menstrual cycle. Abstract in *Excerpta criminol.* **7**, 171.

WEST, I. 1963. The impaired driver. *Calif. Med.* **98**, 271–4.

——, NIELSEN, G. L., GILMORE, A. E., and RYAN, J. R. 1968. Natural death at the wheel. *J. Amer. med. Assoc.* **205**, 266–72.

WHITLOCK, F. A. 1967. The aetiology of hysteria. *Acta Psychiat. Scand.* **43**, 144–62.

——, and BROADHURST, A. 1968. Attempted suicide and the experience of violence. *Journal of Biosocial Science* **1**, 353–68.

7 · Alcohol and road accidents

> '*Drive carefully*', *he said as he opened the front door*, '*this is a Christian country and it's the Saviour's birthday. Practically everybody you will see will be drunk.*'
> ALDOUS HUXLEY, *The Genius and the Goddess*

> *Before the Roman came to Rye or out of Severn strode,*
> *The rolling English drunkard made the rolling English road.*
> G. K. CHESTERTON

In recent years so much has been writen on the relevance of alcohol and alcoholism to the road-death and injury rates that a full examination of this topic would be superfluous. A number of international conferences on alcohol and road safety, and a recent review (*Quart. J. Stud. Alc.*, 1968) adequately cover all aspects of the subject. However, any survey of the road-accident epidemic must, of necessity, examine some of the consequences of driving while intoxicated and, bearing in mind the main thesis of this monograph, it will be equally important to inquire into the contribution of alcohol to violence in general and violence on the road in particular.

One of the more interesting features of the whole subject is our ambivalent attitude to drinking and driving. Many countries and states have introduced legislation designed to prevent persons driving when their competence to do so is impaired by liquor. There have been very few occasions when these proposals have not encountered the most strenuous opposition from groups and individuals who have little in common beyond the wish to drink and drive. Without hesitation, most persons agree that anyone in charge of a public transport vehicle, locomotive, aircraft, or ship should stay absolutely sober while on duty. We usually demand that persons engaged in road haulage – whether local or long-distance – should avoid alcohol while driving. Yet when it comes to the private car-owner, another set of principles seems to apply; although it is hard to see in what way a man in his own car differs from the lorry-driver in respect of his competence to drive after heavy drinking. More will be said about this phenomenon later, but in the meantime the double standard should be remembered, for little attempt has been made to explain its origin.

As already mentioned, a good deal is already known about the effects of alcohol on driving. The epidemiological and social features of the drinking driver have been investigated in North America, Great Britain, and Australia with singular uniformity of findings. What is surprising is the sheer quantity of alcohol consumed by many of the drivers arrested for drunken driving or killed in road crashes. In Australia, for example, Pearson (1957) examined 218 road fatalities and found that 86 (39·4 per cent) had blood-alcohol concentrations greater than 0·1 per cent. In 53 (24·3 per cent) cases the blood-alcohol concentrations exceeded 0·2 per cent. Birrell, in a number of papers (1964, 1965a, 1967b,) has found that accidents more frequently involve persons with blood-alcohol concentrations greater than 0·05 per cent. Whereas most normal social drinking gives blood-alcohol levels below this figure, the average finding in drunken drivers is over four times higher (0·22 per cent). In a study in Victoria, it was found that suspected drinking drivers had blood-alcohol concentrations ranging from 0·0 to 0·46 per cent, and that persons killed in road accidents had very low blood alcohols or none, or very high concentrations. In a further study of 25 automobile drivers involved in fatal accidents following collisions with tramcars, 22 had significant alcohol concentrations in their blood and 32 per cent of the group were known alcoholics.

In Adelaide, Robertson and his colleagues (1966) found that 56 per cent of pedestrians killed on the roads and 12·5 per cent of drivers involved in accidents had taken alcohol beforehand. The pedestrians in this survey were predominantly in the 35 to 64 age-group. In Brisbane, Jamieson and Tait (1968) examined the findings in 1,000 consecutive deaths from 822 road accidents occuring in 1962 to 1963. There were 267 drivers and 243 pedestrians. Eighteen of 53 dead drivers and 25 of 78 dead pedestrians had blood-alcohol concentrations greater than 0·1 per cent, and 32·9 per cent of all motorists were driving under the influence of alcohol. Findings resembling these, noted elsewhere in Australia, were presented at the Second Summer School of Alcohol Studies (1967a), when Birrell showed that 60 per cent of drivers killed in single-vehicle accidents had blood-alcohol levels greater than 0·1 per cent. In a more recent paper, Jamieson (1968) in Brisbane, found that 40 per cent of drivers taken to hospital as a result of traffic accidents had blood-alcohol levels greater than

0·05 per cent. Drinking drivers tended to be older, were mostly male, and came predominantly from the lower occupation groups.

Somewhat similar figures have been presented by investigators in Great Britain (Jeffcoate, 1958; Norman, 1962), and studies from the Road Research Laboratory of the Ministry of Transport generally support the findings from other parts of the world. Older and Sims (1966) examined the blood-alcohol findings in 733 fatal accidents in England and Wales and 71 in Scotland occurring during the two months of December 1964 and January 1965. Forty-one per cent of the drivers had been drinking; 34 per cent had blood-alcohol concentrations greater than 0·05 per cent. Drivers who had been drinking were most frequently involved in single-vehicle accidents, a finding which confirmed Collister's observation (1962). Nineteen per cent of the dead drivers and pedestrians in England and Wales had blood-alcohol concentrations greater than 0·1 per cent. Compared with other groups, the 30 to 39 age-group had the highest alcohol content in their bloods (greater than 0·15 per cent). A further study by Rutley (1966), in which blood samples were taken from 281 road-users fatally injured in an area of London between 1963 and 1964, showed that, of 11 drivers involved in single-vehicle fatalities, 45 per cent had taken alcohol and 36 per cent had concentrations greater than 0·1 per cent. A quarter of 24 drivers killed in multi-vehicle accidents had taken alcohol beforehand, and half of these had blood-alcohol levels in excess of 0·1 per cent.

In North America, studies on the relationship between alcohol and road accidents are numerous and convincing. Particular mention should be made of the work of Haddon, Selzer, and Waller in the United States of America and Schmidt and Smart in Canada. Reference to some of their findings will be made in the following section.

Berry (1945) observed that in the United States of America in 1943, 13 per cent of drivers and 20 per cent of pedestrians killed on the road had been drinking beforehand. The author felt that this was probably an underestimate of the true facts, since in one study to which he referred half of the drivers involved in accidents causing death or injury had been drinking and one-third were intoxicated. In a further study carried out in Minnesota, 28 per cent of those killed in road accidents had blood-alcohol concentrations greater than 0·15 per cent. A study of violent death carried out by Spain and his colleagues (1951) estimated that half the persons killed in motor-vehicle accidents had taken alcohol, a finding which was compared with the figure of 27 per cent for all other forms of violent death studied. An important study by Haddon and Bradess (1959) showed that of 83 drivers involved in fatal single-vehicle accidents, 49 per cent were found to have blood-alcohol concentrations greater than 0·15 per cent, while a further 20 per cent had concentrations between 0·05 and 0·15 per cent. McCarroll and Haddon (1962) carried out a controlled study of fatal car accidents in New York. Of the drivers considered responsible for their accidents, 73 per cent had been drinking and 46 per cent had blood-alcohol concentrations greater than the unusually high figure of 0·25 per cent. The authors concluded that alcoholism rather than social drinking was responsible for this finding. A further study of pedestrian deaths by Haddon and his associates (1961) demonstrated that these individuals came from the older section of the population (mean age 58·8 years) and that 47 per cent had blood-alcohol concentrations greater than 0·05 per cent. Fort (1962) estimated that, in California in 1961, 1,000 of 3,839 road deaths were due to drunken driving, while McFarland (1964) came to the conclusion that alcohol was a factor in half of all road-traffic fatalities in the United States. In a survey of 11 studies carried out between 1941 and 1961, Fox and Fox (1963) noted great variations in blood-alcohol findings in road fatalities; 22·5–80 per cent of subjects killed on the road were shown to have taken liquor beforehand.

A noteworthy study into drunken driving was carried out by Borkenstein and his associates in their Grand Rapids Survey (1966). Of 5,985 drivers involved in accidents who were examined, 377 (6·2 per cent) had blood-alcohol concentrations greater than 0·1 per cent. A significantly large number of drivers with high alcohol content were involved in single-vehicle accidents. This group was predominantly male and middle-aged, and its drinking habits suggested that a proportion at least were alcoholics rather than normal social drinkers. One of the more controversial findings of this study was the conclusion that drivers who had consumed *small* amounts of alcohol (BAC < 0·05 per cent) drove better than those who had not taken liquor. However, this finding has been criticized on methodological and statistical grounds by Allsopp (1966). Needless to say. Borkenstein and his colleagues confirmed the general opinion that rising blood-alcohol concentrations are inconsistent with safety on the road.

F

A more recent publication (*Quarterly Journal of Studies on Alcohol*, Supplement 4, 1968) analyses some of the Grand Rapids findings. Hyman considers that persons aged less than 25 or over 70 were more at risk on the road than middle-aged persons, although this last group, if involved in accidents, had higher concentrations of alcohol in their blood. Liquor and accidents were associated more often in the divorced and the separated. In a second paper, Hyman looked at the social characteristics of drunken drivers. The ethnically and socially deprived groups were more commonly arrested, and of those arrested one-third had been involved in accidents. Zylman confirmed the age distribution of drunken drivers and found that persons in the less privileged socio-economic classes had higher blood-alcohol concentrations, but that this finding was observed in both those examined after accidents and also in the accident-free control group. Married persons with blood-alcohol concentrations below 0·04 per cent had fewer accidents, and those who drove less than 1,000 miles each year had higher accident rates than those driving more than 15,000 miles per annum. Clearly, experience counts. Casper and Mozensky found that persons in the age-group 20–29 were most likely to be drivers and drinkers, and that the relationship of drinking variables to age was a complex one. Young drivers drink heavily but episodically, whereas the older motorists drink more continuously. The young men use drink to work through their emotional problems; the older men appeared to drink in order to get drunk. The authors concluded that excessive drinking rather than sporadic drinking was most likely to figure in drunken-driving accidents. Waller estimated that 6·5 per cent of all drivers in California were alcoholics and were responsible for 41–62 per cent of all accidents associated with alcohol. Alcoholics were liable to incur six times as many accidents and traffic violations as healthy drivers or drivers affected by medical illnesses uncomplicated by alcohol. The alcoholics were four times less likely than the healthy drivers to be innocent 'victims' in road accidents; and, as usual, the alcoholics were more often responsible for single-vehicle accidents.

In an earlier study, Waller (1965) found that alcohol was related to road-traffic accidents in 30–70 per cent of instances. Persons driving under the influence of liquor, who were regarded as alcoholics, crashed their cars at higher speeds than did social drinkers. In a later paper (1966) he noted that simple driving skills became impaired when blood-alcohol concentrations exceeded 0·1 per cent. In fact, there is plenty of evidence to support the opinion that considerably lower blood-alcohol concentrations lead to some impairment of driving ability (Bjerver and Goldberg, 1950; Drew *et al.*, 1958; Cohen *et al.*, 1958). Waller estimated that one-third of the adult population in California both drove and drank and that the majority of such persons drove with blood-alcohol concentrations greater than 0·5 per cent. Accidents involving alcohol are usually severe, since substantial numbers of drivers in accidents complicated by previous drinking had blood-alcohol levels greater than 0·15 per cent. Thirty-seven per cent of persons aged 25 years or older who had been killed in road-traffic accidents had been drinking beforehand; and of this group 72 per cent had blood-alcohol concentrations greater than 0·15 per cent while two-thirds of these showed post-mortem signs of fatty or cirrhotic livers suggesting damage due to prolonged misuse of alcohol. Only 15 per cent of the dead drivers who had not been drinking showed these changes. Waller concluded that the real problem of alcohol and road accidents was the driving drinker rather than the drinking driver.

Support for this belief comes from a number of sources. In Canada Schmidt *et al.* (1962) found that 28 per cent of all drivers convicted of drunken driving were alcoholics, while Smart (1965) noted that alcoholics who had repeated accidents were less concerned with careful driving after moderate or heavy intake than were those alcoholics who managed to stay out of trouble. The accident-repeater alcoholic was more prone to believe that liquor had no effect on his competence to drive. Smart and Schmidt (1967) later confirmed their earlier observations that excessive drinkers were largely responsible for accidents caused by alcohol.

This conclusion was also supported by Waller and Turkel (1966) and Waller (1966), who recorded the high incidence of hepatic cirrhosis and fatty degeneration of the liver among traffic fatalities. Those with these diseases had higher post-mortem blood-alcohol levels, a finding which pointed to the likelihood that these accident victims were not normal social drinkers.

Campbell (1967), too, concluded that many drinking drivers are serious alcoholics or pre-alcoholics, since he found in the USA that drinking drivers responsible for fatal accidents had higher blood-alcohol concentrations than those involved in non-fatal accidents. As far as single-car accidents were concerned, 70 per cent of the drivers who were killed had been drinking beforehand.

European investigations tend to support most of these observations. In Romania, for example (1967), it was found that 128 of 457 drivers suspected of driving under the influence of liquor had been involved in accidents, and Vamosi in Czechoslovakia (1960) concluded that persons with blood-alcohol concentrations greater than 0·15 per cent had a 124-fold greater risk of being involved in accidents when compared with those with lower alcohol levels in their blood. Alha (1965) in Finland estimated that 14·6 per cent of 964 road deaths were due to alcohol, and in Poland in 1961 the proportion was 19 per cent, falling to 15 per cent by 1964. Andreasson and Bonnicksen in Sweden (1965) noted a sharp fall in accident rates in 1963 when, for two months, a strike in the liquor trade led to restricted supplies. Once these supplies were reinstated there was an equally sharp rise to former rates. These findings are all the more remarkable when one considers the stringent Swedish traffic laws which forbid a person to drive after drinking, however small the quantity of alcohol consumed. A German study (Weyrich, 1957) supported the American investigations in finding that single-vehicle accidents were more frequently caused by drinking drivers.

Some of the characteristics of persons who take liquor and drive will already have been gleaned from the data presented. In the vast majority of instances, the subject will be male and more commonly in the 30–60 age-group. It is well known that the peak age-period for road fatalities among drivers lies between 15 and 25, and, although this particular group does not contribute so seriously to the drink–driving statistics, Collister in her study found that, as far as car occupants were concerned, drinking most commonly occurred in the 15–24 age-group. It is not entirely clear whether this figure refers only to drivers or to drivers and passengers. In any case, the numbers were comparatively small and were not subject to a statistical analysis. However, Birrell (1968) recently claimed that in Victoria, Australia, men aged 18–24 charged with traffic offences had three times the permitted quantity of alcohol in their bodies. Possibly the pattern of drinking and driving is changing, for Willet (1964) observed that in England the subject charged with drunken driving came from the older age-groups as compared with persons charged with other serious traffic offences. In their study in New York, McCarroll and Haddon also noted that persons responsible for the most severe accidents, often of the single-vehicle variety, were older and had higher blood-alcohol concentrations. McFarland and Moore (1960), who examined the characteristics of young men involved in repeated car accidents, did not mention alcohol as a major factor contributing to the high accident rate in this age-group. However, in one study of young airmen (Barmack & Payne 1961), two-thirds of those involved in accidents had been drinking beforehand. To some extent members of the armed forces must be regarded as a special group in which heavy drinking in off-duty periods is expected and tolerated. Certainly, there is no particular reason to believe that these men were pathologically heavy drinkers. The situation is very different from that prevailing in Sweden (Bjerver *et al.*, 1955), where heavy or pathological drinkers, usually in the older age-groups, contribute strongly to drink–driving statistics. Likewise in France (Truchet *et al.*, 1966) it was noted that, as far as drinking drivers and pedestrians injured in road accidents were concerned, the higher blood-alcohol concentrations occurred in the older age-groups. The finding by Waller (1967) that 64 per cent of motorists arrested for driving while under the influence of liquor were in the 30–59 age-group, emphasizes the importance of the relationship between age and drunken driving. Alcoholism – particularly when complicated by mental and physical illnesses due to the addiction – is more frequently an affliction of the middle-aged, a clinical factor of fairly universal occurrence.

The relationship between the time of an accident and drunken driving has been well attested by a number of studies, particularly in Great Britain (Jeffcoate, 1958; Collister, 1962; Preston, 1958). The highest accident rates occur at weekends after 10 p.m. when licensed premises close, a finding which has been taken as good evidence that alcohol is an important factor, although the effects of fatigue and darkness cannot be neglected. Jeffcoate, in particular, found that 50 per cent of drivers and 60 per cent of pedestrians involved in fatal accidents in Great Britain between the hours of 10 p.m. and 4 a.m. had been drinking.

An interesting aspect of the drinking-driver problem is the demonstration that many of these individuals in the past have been subject to criminal proceedings not necessarily resulting from infringement of road-traffic regulations. Willett's study (1964) is one of the best-known contributions to this topic, but a number of other investigators have repeatedly confirmed his findings. Waller (1967) noted that a considerable proportion of persons charged with drunken driving or hit-and-run offences had been convicted of theft or violence against the person and that about one-third had been in the care of the probation services.

Although Seales (1957) believed that the person most commonly responsible for drunken-driving accidents and violations was the normal social drinker, a number of studies, notably from Sweden and the United States, have since thrown doubt upon this statement. Bjerver and his colleagues (1955) found that 32·5 per cent of persons injured or killed in road accidents in Sweden had serious drinking problems compared with 13·7 per cent in the general population. A second study (Goldberg, 1955), of 2,000 men convicted of drunken driving, showed that 45·4 per cent were alcohol misusers or addicts compared with 8·8 per cent in the rest of the population. Popham (1956) concluded that the problem of the drinking driver was essentially one of alcoholism, and a series of papers by Selzer and his colleagues (1962, 1963, 1966) have repeatedly supported this opinion. In one paper (1962) they commented particularly on the personality traits of drinking drivers and the associations between alcoholism, crime, and suicide. The alcoholic driver carries his problems with him onto the road, and understandably they influence his behaviour and safety. In 1963 Selzer and his associates showed that, of 67 drivers referred by the Courts for psychiatric assessment following conviction for drunken driving, 57 per cent were definitely alcoholic, 15 per cent were probably alcoholic, and a further 6 per cent were problem drinkers in the pre-alcoholic stage. The alcoholic and pre-alcoholic groups had much higher frequencies of previous accidents, arrests for drunken driving, and other traffic violations. In a later study (1966), the authors examined 72 drivers responsible for fatal accidents. Half of this group were alcoholics or pre-alcoholics, and once again the higher incidence of previous accidents and traffic violations was observed. In general, compared with non-alcoholic psychiatric patients, alcoholics had twice the number of traffic offences and to a remarkable degree showed paranoid ideation, suicidal thoughts, and aggressive behaviour. Selzer and his colleagues concluded that dangerous driving was a way of expressing rage, an underlying tendency which was released by alcohol.

The high suicide rate of alcoholics is a well-known phenomenon. It would be surprising, therefore, if the motor vehicle was not used by this group of patients as a means of self-destruction. At times the intent is clearly expressed beforehand; at other times one can safely infer that the suicidal impulse was not far from the surface of the driver's mind. On the evidence presented from a number of sources, it is reasonable to conclude that the single-vehicle accident more frequently than any other type is the result of excessive drinking combined with self-destructive thoughts. For obvious reasons this variety of suicide is not included in official mortality statistics.

One of the more interesting features of the drink/driving problem is the remarkable absence of popular disapproval of persons who drive when intoxicated, a phenomenon to which Cisin (1963) has drawn attention. The absence of condemnation can be explained in a number of ways, among which should be included a feeling of identification with the drinking driver and the belief, in some quarters, that alcohol can improve one's competence as a driver.

The role of alcohol in crimes of violence has been known since the earliest times. Homicide, serious or less serious assault, and violent sexual offences have all been shown to occur when the aggressor, his victim, or both have been drinking. Numerous studies quoted in this chapter not only indict the male as the principal offender in drink/driving cases but also show that such persons make notable contributions to other criminal statistics. The psychopathic offender who drinks is likely, should he drive a car, to manifest his personality traits on the highway with disastrous consequences both for himself and others. His inability to learn from these experiences – should he survive them – was well shown by one of my patients, who in two years of motor-cycling had sustained serious injuries in three accidents. As usual in these cases, everyone but himself was blamed, and despite the degree of damage incurred he proposed to continue to ride his motor-cycle without wearing a crash helmet. He was remarkable for his police record, his aggression, and his misuse of alcohol. Such clinical findings could be mulitiplied by any number of observers, and they provide impressive and vivid support for the statistical data so laboriously accumulated by the investigators quoted in this chapter.

The role of alcohol in crime and driving accidents is clearly not a simple one. Is the excessive drinking the main cause of these tragedies or is it but one attribute of offender and victim which combines with those other qualities of violence, antisocial behaviour, rage, paranoid feelings, and an underlying wish to kill or be killed? There is no easy answer to this question, but the association of these qualities in a proportion of those who drive when intoxicated seems to be one of the better-established facts.

Increasing use of the motor vehicle by those engaged in criminal acts is also a problem that concerns law-enforcement agencies in a number of countries. In Australia, forcible rape seems often to require an automobile in which to transport the victim to some secluded area. Mr Paul Wilson (personal communication) has noted the personality, age, social class, and other qualities of men committing such offences, and once again there is a striking resemblance between this group and the psychopathic offenders who drink and drive. In fact, a high percentage of offenders in rape cases are intoxicated at the time or have been drinking beforehand.

There can be little doubt that death on the road and the drinking driver are closely associated phenomena; and that as casualty rates in the United States have gone up so has the proportion of accidents involving alcohol (35 per cent in the 1940s, 50 per cent in the 1960s, according to Bacon, 1968). Similarly, when prohibition was repealed in the United States there was a fairly rapid increase in road deaths (Campbell, 1967). Nevertheless, alcohol can be only one among many variables associated with traffic accidents. For the time being at least, the motorist most at risk is the young male aged 17–25. Generally speaking, this age-group includes only a minority of alcoholic drivers. Needless to say, a proportion of these young men have been drinking before they are killed, but the pattern of drinking differs from that of older men. Inexperience, too much to drink, and strong aggression, may all make an important contribution to fatal driving accidents involving young men, but apart from the study in Victoria by Birrell, the drunken youth at the wheel seems to be not quite as serious a menace as his older counterpart.

Finally, whatever might be said about alcohol and driving, it has to be remembered that a considerable proportion of road casualties are pedestrians. The majority of pedestrians killed on the road are elderly citizens, a number of whom have been drinking, or children. No doubt alcohol intake has caused the older pedestrian to neglect normal safety precautions on the road, but one can hardly indict aggression as fundamental to this form of behaviour, unless, of course, suicidal impulses are a frequent accompaniment of pedestrian deaths: a possibility that, as yet, has not been demonstrated. As an aspect of road deaths it can hardly be ignored, but clearly it is of less significance than the behaviour of the alcoholic at the wheel, who is responsible for so much death and destruction on the road.

REFERENCES

ALHA, A. 1965. Advance prevention of drunken driving. *Proc. 4th Internat. Conf. Alc. and Traffic Safety.* Indiana, 1966.

ALLSOPP, R. E. 1966. *Alcohol and road accidents.* Road Research Laboratory, Ministry of Transport Report 6.

ANDREASSON, R., and BONNICKSEN, R. 1965. The frequency of drunken driving in Sweden during a period when the supply of alcoholic drink was restricted. *Proc. 4th Internat. Conf. Alc. and Traffic Safety.* Indiana, 1966.

BACON, S. D. (ed.) 1968a. Studies of drinking and driving. *Quart. J. Stud. Alc.* Suppt 4.

—— 1968b. Traffic accidents involving alcohol in the USA. *Quart. J. Stud. Alc.* Suppt 4.

BANCUI, D., and DIACONITA, G. 1957. Romanian road–alcohol statistics. *Rev. Hug. med. Soc.* **5**, 311.

BARMACK, J. E., and PAYNE, C. E. 1961. Injury-producing private motor vehicle accidents among airmen. *US Highway Res. Board Bull.* **285**, 1–22.

BERRY, D. S. 1945. Alcohol and traffic. In *Alcohol, science and society.* Laboratory of Applied Physiology, Yale University, New Haven.

BIRRELL, J. H. W. 1964. Alcohol and road accidents. *Med. J. Australia* i, 265–9.

—— 1965a. Blood alcohol levels in drunk drivers, drunk and disorderly subjects and moderate social drinkers. *Med. J. Australia* ii, 949–53.

—— 1965b. Public education and mass communication aspects. *Proc. 4th Internat. Conf. Alc. and Traffic Safety.* Indiana, 1966.

—— 1967a. Alcoholism and social drinking in drivers and pedestrians. 2nd Summer School of Alcohol Studies, University of Melbourne.

—— 1967b. A note on automobile–tram (streetcar) fatal accidents and alcohol in the City of Melbourne. *Med. J. Australia* ii, 1–4.

—— 1968.
Australian, 17 August.

BJERVER, K., and GOLDBERG, L. 1950. The effects of alcohol ingestion on driving ability. *Quart. J. Stud. Alc.* **11**, 1–30.

BJERVER, K., and GOLDBERG, LINDA. 1955. Blood alcohol levels in hospitalized victims of traffic accidents. 2nd Internat. Conf. Alc. and Road Traffic, Toronto.

BORKENSTEIN, R. M. *et al.* 1966. In A. Dale (ed.), The role of the drinking driver in traffic accidents. *Proc. 4th Internat. Conf. Alc. and Traffic Safety.* Indiana University.

CAMPBELL, H. E. 1967. Traffic deaths go up again. *J. Amer. med. Assoc.* **201,** 861–4.

CASPER, R., and MOZENSKY, K. 1968. Social correlates of drinking and driving. *Quart. J. Stud. Alc.* Suppt 4.

CISIN, I. H. 1963. Social-psychological factors in drinking/driving. In B. H. Fox and J. H. Fox (eds.), *Alcohol and traffic safety.* US Dept of Health Education and Welfare, Maryland.

COHEN, J., DEARNALEY, E. J., and HANSEL, C. E. M. 1958. The risk taken in driving under the influence of alcohol. *Brit. med. J.* i, 1438.

COLLISTER, R. M. 1962. The incidence of alcohol in road traffic accidents. *Proc. 3rd Internat. Conf. Alc. and Road Traffic.* London: BMA.

DREW, G. C., COLQUHOUN, W. P., and LONG, H. H. 1958. Effect of small doses of alcohol on a skill resembling driving. *Brit. med. J.* ii, 993–9.

FORT, J. 1962. Drinking and driving in California and the USA. *Proc. 3rd Internat. Conf. Alc. and Road Traffic.* London: BMA.

FOX, B. H., and FOX, J. H. (eds.) 1963. *Alcohol and traffic safety.* US Dept of Health Education and Welfare, Maryland.

GOLDBERG, L. 1955. The drinking driver in Sweden. 2nd Internat. Conf. Alc. and Road Traffic. Toronto.

HADDON, W., and BRADESS, V. A. 1959. Alcohol in the single vehicle accident: experience in Westchester County, New York. *J. Amer. med. Assoc.* **169,** 1587–93.

——, VALIER, R., MCCARROLL, J. R., and UMBERGER, C. J. 1961. A controlled investigation of the characteristics of adult pedestrians fatally injured by motor vehicles in Manhattan. *J. Chron. Dis.* **14,** 665.

HYMAN, M. M. 1968a. Accident vulnerability and blood alcohol concentrations of drivers by demographic orientation. *Quart. J. Stud. Alc.* Suppt 4.

—— 1968b. Social characteristics of drunken driving. *Quart. J. Stud. Alc.* Suppt. 4.

JAMIESON, K. G. 1968. Alcohol and driving: the breathalyser bogey. *Med. J. Australia* ii, 425–33.

——, and TAIT, I. A. 1967. Traffic injury in Brisbane. NHMRC Special Report Series No. 13. Canberra.

JEFFCOATE, G. O. 1958. An examination of reports of fatal road accidents in three police districts from the point of view of the effect of alcohol. *Brit. J. Addict.* **54**, 81.

MCCARROLL, J. R., and HADDON, W. 1962. A controlled study of fatal automobile accidents in New York City. *J. Chron. Dis.* **15**, 811–26.

MCFARLAND, R. A. 1964. Alcohol and highway accidents. *Traffic Dig. Rev.* **12** (5), 30–2.

——, and MOORE, R. C. 1960. *Youth and the automobile.* Golden Anniversary White House Conference on Children and Youth Inc.

MED. J. AUSTRALIA 1968. Driving and the demon drink. Editorial in Part ii, p. 443.

NORMAN, L. G. 1962. *Road traffic accidents.* Public Health Paper No. 12. Geneva: WHO.

OLDER, S. J., and SIMS, M. 1966. *Blood alcohol levels in road accident fatalities in Great Britain during Dec. '64 and Jan. '65.* Road Research Laboratory, Ministry of Transport Report 32.

PEARSON, A. T. 1957. Alcohol and fatal traffic accidents. *Med. J. Australia* ii, 166–7.

PFEIFFER, J. 1963. The anti-alcohol programme for road traffic safety in Poland. In B. H. Fox and J. H. Fox (eds.), *Alcohol and traffic safety.* US Dept of Health Education and Welfare, Maryland.

POPHAM, R. E. 1956. Alcoholism and traffic accidents. *Quart. J. Stud. Alc.* **17**, 225–32.

PRESTON, B. 1958. Alcohol and road accidents. *New Scientist* **4**, 1543.

QUARTERLY JOURNAL OF STUDIES ON ALCOHOL 1968. Suppt 4, May.

ROBERTSON, J. S., MACLEAN, H. A., and RYAN, G. A. 1966. *Traffic accidents in Adelaide, South Australia, 1963–64.* Australian Road Research Board, Special Report 1.

RUTLEY, K. S. 1966. *The incidence of alcohol in the blood of some fatally injured road users.* Road Research Laboratory, Ministry of Transport Report 18.

SCHMIDT, W. S., SMART, A. G., and POPHAM, R. E. 1962. The

role of alcoholism in motor vehicle accidents. *Proc. 3rd Internat. Conf. Alc. and Road Traffic.* London: BMA. Also in *Traffic Safety Res. Rev.* No. 6, 21–7, 1962.

SEALES, T. A. 1957. The drinking driver. *Traffic Safety Res. Rev.* **1**(3), 80–93.

SELZER, M. L., and PAYNE, C. E. 1962. Automobile accidents, suicide and unconscious motivation. *Amer. J. Psychiat.* **119,** 237–40.

SELZER, M. L., PAYNE, C. E., GIFFORD, J. D., and KELLY, W. L. 1963. Alcoholism, mental illness and the drunk driver. *Amer. J. Psychiat.* **120,** 326–31.

——, and WEISS, S. 1966. Alcoholism and traffic fatalities. *Amer. J. Psychiat.* **122,** 762–7.

SMART, R. G., and SCHMIDT, W. S. 1967. Responsibility, alcoholism and traffic safety. *Traffic Safety Res. Rev.* **11,** 112–16.

SPAIN, D. M., BRADESS, V. A., and EGGSTON, A. A. 1951. Alcohol and violent death. *J. Amer. med. Assoc.* **146,** 334–5.

TRUCHET, P., JACQUEMEND, D., and BENEZET, L. 1966. A statistical study of alcohol levels in the injured admitted to a surgical service. *Lyon Méd.* **215,** 903–17.

VAMOSI, M. 1960. Determinations of the amount of alcohol in the blood of motorists. *Traffic Safety Res. Rev.* **57,** 8–11.

WALLER, J. A. 1965. Implications of shifting emphasis on alcohol, youth and traffic accidents. *Proc. 4th Internat. Conf. Alc. and Traffic Safety.* Indiana, 1966.

—— 1966. Use and misuse of alcoholic beverages as a factor in motor-vehicle accidents. *US Pub. Hlth Rep.* **81,** 591–7.

—— 1967. Identification of problem drinking among drunken drivers. *J. Amer. med. Assoc.* **200,** 114–20.

—— 1968. Patterns of traffic accidents and violations related to drinking and some medical conditions. *Quart. J. Stud. Alc.* Suppt 4.

——, and TURKEL, H. W. 1966. Alcoholism and traffic deaths. *New Eng. J. Med.* **275,** 532–6.

WEYRICH, G. 1957. Alcohol and road traffic accidents in South Baden. *Dtsch med. Wochschr.* **82,** 1100–3.

WILLETT, T. C. 1964. *Criminal on the road.* London: Tavistock.

WILSON, P. 1968. Rape and attempted rape in Australia. (Personal communication.)

ZYLMAN, R. 1968. Accidents, alcohol and single cause explanations. *Quart. J. Stud. Alc.* Suppt 4.

8 · Methods, sources, and statistics

Now what I want is Facts . . . Facts alone are wanted in Life.
CHARLES DICKENS, *Hard Times*

'*Singularity is almost always a clue.*'
SHERLOCK HOLMES

The review of some of the relevant literature in the previous chapters supports in general the finding in Australia, referred to in Chapter 1, that road-casualty rates are related to other forms of social violence. The work carried out in other countries with social and cultural backgrounds similar to those of Australia also sustains the hypothesis. Nevertheless, some more exact assessment of social violence was necessary before assuming that the Australian findings were generally applicable. To accomplish this, every effort was made to obtain reliable statistics of populations, road-casualty and accident rates for other forms of violent death, data on violent crime, rates of offences committed with alcohol, and information on road-transport figures. In addition, in order to test the possibility that 'non-violent' social pathology was equally significant, inquiries were made into the incidence of such factors as divorce, illegitimacy, and industrial disputes, and into prison and mental hospital admission statistics and the prevalence of alcoholism in the various communities that were studied. The extent to which one can regard some of these forms of social pathology as non-violent is debatable. Certainly, industrial disputes have been characterized in the past by notable outbursts of physical violence (Taft, 1966), while deaths from alcoholism often imply a good deal of violence in the lives of the deceased.

Once a decision had been made to examine these variables, certain problems of selection had to be solved. The main part of the study was carried out in the latter part of 1967. Ideally, 1966 would have been the best year for study, because it should have provided data closest to the author's knowledge of the current social scene.

Unfortunately, except for a few countries, statistical information for 1966 was far from complete. The most recent year for which fairly comprehensive data were available was 1964, which was finally chosen as the end-point for the study.

The next problem was the selection of the preceding years to be surveyed. Initially, it was intended to examine all years from 1946 onwards. For obvious reasons the end of the Second World War in 1945 set a limit to the period to be surveyed. Following the war, social chaos in Europe and years of reconstruction elsewhere introduced a list of variables – including civil wars – which probably contributed more to violence than any number of road accidents in more recent times. It was essential, therefore, that any country to be included in this study should have recovered from the effects of war and developed a satisfactory level of economic and social security. At the same time it should be free from active hostilities, whether civil or international. The further one went back in time towards 1945, the less reliable or complete were the published statistics. Finally, after taking all these facts into account, 1955 was the year selected for the start of the study.

Ideally, annual statistics for the entire decennium 1955 to 1964 should have been examined. However, in the time available this was not possible and, as a compromise measure, the three years 1955, 1960, and 1964 were chosen, and averages of the figures for the three years were calculated to give a mean score for the whole decennium. In fact, test samples of the entire ten-year period carried out for a limited number of countries did not produce figures differing to any marked degree from the means of the three sample years. Consequently, it was felt that any slight loss in accuracy was hardly sufficient to justify the additional time and work that would have been needed to make a complete study of the ten-year period.

The selection of countries to be surveyed was decided largely by the availability and reliability of published annual statistics and by the freedom of the countries concerned from warfare of all kinds. Preference was shown for those countries having a shared cultural pattern and, for obvious reasons, the states whose cultural origins are based largely on the Graeco-Latin culture of the Mediterranean civilization and Western Europe were considered most suitable for study. Consequently, African and Asian nations, having totally different backgrounds and degrees of economic development, were excluded. The author's intention initially, at least, was to include the countries of South and Central America, but unfortunately it was not possible to obtain satisfactory statistics for most of these countries, which consequently were omitted. The English-speaking countries of the United Kingdom, the Republic of Ireland, Australia, New Zealand, Canada, and the United States of America were easy choices, not only because of the satisfactory nature of their published statistics, but also because of accessibility of information and some understanding on my part of their cultural background. At first, the Republic of South Africa was included, but unfortunately the year-books for that country provide separate statistical information for the various racial groups of the community. For this reason South Africa was omitted, since it was very difficult to make adequate comparisons between that country as a whole and the other states included in the survey. The final choice, therefore, was limited to the English-speaking countries already mentioned, the countries of Western Europe, Scandinavia, and the Mediterranean seaboard, and certain Eastern European states whose annual statistics were available. The Soviet Union was excluded mainly because of my inability to read Russian, but also because of the diverse cultural background of that country. In the end, 27 countries providing reliable statistical information were selected for more intensive examination.

The sources from which this information was obtained have been listed in Appendix I. The initial choice of the United Nations and World Health Organization statistical and demographic publications was prompted by the belief that the information in these volumes would be reasonably comprehensive, up to date, and reliable. In fact, major difficulties were encountered immediately, since some of the WHO mortality statistics differed quite markedly from the data obtained from state yearbooks and from other sources. At times this discrepancy was marked; but on the empirical ground that no country is likely to exaggerate the incidence of violent death within its confines, it was decided that when two or more sets of figures for the same piece of information were available the highest figure would be the one selected.

Most of the information concerning road-death rates was derived from WHO statistical yearbooks and the United Nations Council of Europe statistics on road transport in Europe. However, whereas some countries publish two sets of figures – the number of persons killed on the road and the number of accidents producing fatalities – a fair proportion only gave the first class of information. In some respects the second figure would have been preferable. If a solitary motorist crashes his car into a tree and is killed, that is one accident and one fatality, the so-called single-vehicle accident so often associated with alcoholism. If a coach-load of sightseers has been driven off the road into a ravine with the deaths of 20 persons, that also is a single accident, even though the number of deaths is very much greater. However, there seemed to be no way of overcoming this difficulty, and, for the sake of uniformity, the number of *deaths* due to road accidents was recorded rather than the number of fatal accidents. As figures for other violent deaths give the number of persons who died rather than the number of fatal incidents, at least consistency over choice of statistics is being maintained. In some countries and states with small populations, the incidence of road injuries was also estimated, since it was found that, in those countries, quite small changes in the gross number of deaths could, owing to the smallness of the population, lead to marked changes in the calculated rates per 100,000 of the population. Therefore, to obtain further reliability in some small countries and states, data for the whole ten years were obtained so that any major deviations from the average would cancel each other out. In this way, a major departure from the average in one of the three years was corrected by the large number of findings for the whole decennium.

At this stage it was necessary to find some satisfactory method of general applicability for the calculation of road-death rates. These mortality figures can be expressed as numbers per 100,000 of the population, as numbers per 10,000 motor vehicles, or as numbers per million vehicle-miles driven each year. A fourth index of road deaths can be obtained by using Calleja's formula (1965), which estimates the density of traffic on the roads of any given country and then divides the number of road deaths by this quotient, so giving an index of road deaths per vehicle per mile of highway.

The most generally accepted basis for the calculation of road-death rates is the annual vehicle mileage estimated for each state. This statistic takes into account the number of motor vehicles on the road and the average distance travelled by each one per year. This, to some extent, makes allowance for the exposure risk for drivers of motor vehicles but will not wholly account for pedestrian exposure, which in all probability can only be estimated from population density figures in built-up areas. In the United States the vehicle-mile estimates were available for the 1955 to 1964 period for all 48 mainland states. They were also available for 1963 in Australia. A number of countries (Statistical Data: International Road Federation, 1965, Washington, DC) publish figures for the annual vehicle-miles travelled, but these lack uniformity because some countries do not include all motorized vehicles in their calculations. Hence, comparison between countries is impossible. Indeed, at times, one doubts the reliability of the figures. For example, it is difficult to believe that New Zealanders, with less than one-quarter of the population and motor vehicles of Australia, should appear to travel twice as many vehicle-miles as Australians.

In countries such as the United States, Australia, and Canada, it might be permissible to assume that the individual component states or provinces share a common culture and have roughly the same number of automobiles per head of population. Consequently the number of road deaths per 100,000 of the population could be used as a reasonably satisfactory basis for making comparisons between the individual states in these three countries. However, such a method could be misleading if used to make comparisons between countries with different cultures and at varying stages of economic development.

The difficulties of making international comparisons of road-accident statistics have been discussed by Smeed (1949, 1953), Norman (1962), and Carlquist (1966). This last author, after surveying the various methods used for estimating road deaths, concluded that international comparisons were impossible. Without sharing this pessimism, one is bound to admit that the ideally reliable statistic of road-death rates, valid for all countries, is not yet available. Whereas rates for homicide by shooting are not in general based on the number of firearms in the community, it is obvious that a rate of road deaths which does not take into account the number of auto-mobiles on the road would be singularly misleading. If a country is so impoverished that it has no automobiles, quite obviously it is not in a position to record deaths on the road from motor-vehicle accidents. Conversely, those highly developed nations having a large number of automobiles must, all other things being equal, have a larger number of fatal and injurious accidents. For example, it would be quite meaningless to compare the road-death rate per 100,000 of population in the United States of America, which has the highest number of motor vehicles per head of population, with the road-death rate in Greece, which has a much smaller number of

G

vehicles. To make a true comparison it is necessary to take into account not only the size of the human population, but also the number of private cars, commercial vehicles, buses, and motor-cycles on the roads.

Smeed (1949) has shown that a country with a small number of cars will have a small number of deaths per 100,000 of the population but a large number of deaths per motor vehicle, whereas a highly motorized country will have comparatively high rates of road death per 100,000 of the population, but a very much lower rate for every 10,000 motor vehicles. These twin findings were brought together by Smeed in the following formula:

$$D = 0.0003(NP^2)^{1/3}$$

where D equals the number of road deaths per annum to be expected in a given community, N is the number of motor vehicles, and P is the human population.

On the basis of the information available in official publications, this formula was calculated for all the countries and the individual states of countries included in this survey. The figures for the observed numbers of road deaths (O) were divided by the expected number of deaths (E) provided by Smeed's formula, thus giving an index of road deaths for each individual state and country. This index lay between 0.57 and 1.88 for the 27 countries covered by the survey.

This ratio of observed to expected traffic deaths was used as the principal index of road deaths for the purpose of making compari-sons with other variables. In fact its reliability could be tested in Australia and the United States, where figures for the number of vehicle-miles driven annually in each state were available. Product–moment correlations were calculated between the number of deaths per 100 million vehicle-miles and the ratio of observed to expected deaths for the 6 main Australian states and the 48 mainland states of the United States. The figures obtained were:

Australia $r = +0.877$ ($df = 4$; $p < .05$)
USA $r = +0.727$ ($df = 46$; $p < .001$)

The use of Calleja's formula based on road-traffic densities was considered, but it was impossible to obtain uniform data for road lengths in the countries examined. Some states give the mileage of trunk roads only, some exclude smaller streets in the urban areas, while others include all roads, metalled and unsurfaced. Furthermore, the formula has certain drawbacks because it fails to allow for variations in traffic densities in urban and rural areas. Large states with few major cities will have low traffic densities and their road-accident rates per mile will appear higher than would be the case for smaller, more urbanized countries. Calleja's formula was used in the United States, and the derived death rates were correlated with the deaths per 100 million vehicle-miles. A significant positive correlation was obtained ($r = +0.416$: $t = 3.068$, $df = 46$, $p < .01$), but this was less satisfactory than the very much higher correlation obtained between the ratios of observed to expected deaths and the 100 million vehicle-mile death rate.

Countries vary in the way they classify deaths due to road accidents, depending upon the amount of time elapsing between collision and death. Whereas most countries accept that an accident was the cause of death if the victim dies within 30 days of the injury, in Belgium and Portugal such a death is included in official statistics only if the individual dies at the site of the accident. In Austria, Czechoslovakia, France, Luxembourg, Poland, and Spain, deaths are recorded as due to road accidents only if they occur within 24 hours of the mishap. It has been found that 65 per cent of persons dying as a result of car accidents do so within 1 hour of that accident, and 80 per cent within 24 hours. Ninety-seven per cent of all persons who die as a result of injuries received from road smashes do so within 30 days. Consequently, in order to make satisfactory comparisons between countries, it was necessary to multiply the road deaths of Belgium and Portugal by 1·5 and those of Austria, Czechoslovakia, France, Luxembourg, Poland, and Spain by 1·25. This correction was applied before estimating the observed to expected death ratio.

There were difficulties in obtaining satisfactory figures for the numbers of road vehicles in each state. The Council of Europe statistics exclude motor-bicycles and mopeds from the sum total of motor vehicles listed, but as European nations use large numbers of these powered bicycles it was essential to include them in the total of motor vehicles in all states. Motor-cycle accidents are major causes of road deaths of young men, and exclusion of this class of vehicle from the final sum of motor vehicles could lead to considerable error when this figure was applied to the calculation of expected death rates. It was possible to obtain satisfactory figures for the numbers of motor-bicycles and mopeds in all countries except Czechoslovakia.

In that country, data were available for the total number of private, commercial, and public service vehicles but no mention was made of two-wheeled vehicles. It was assumed that the ratio of two-wheeled vehicles to other forms of road transport in Czechoslovakia would not differ very greatly from the known ratios of motor-bicycles to other vehicles in countries adjacent to that state. These ratios were calculated for Austria, East Germany, and Poland, and on this basis it was estimated that 47·2 per cent of all powered vehicles in the mid-European states were motor-cycles or mopeds. Consequently, the numbers of road vehicles in Czechoslovakia were increased by this amount, but possibly this correction does not reflect the true state of affairs.

For the United States, statistics were obtained for the mainland states, except for the District of Columbia and Alaska. Hawaii was also omitted, so the number of states included amounted to forty-eight. As already mentioned the number of vehicle-miles travelled by motor vehicles in each state was known and this was used as the basis for calculation of road deaths in preference to any of the other measures already described.

In Australia, Australian Capital Territory and Northern Territory were excluded owing to the small populations in these states, thus leaving the five major mainland states and Tasmania for consideration. Estimates were made of the road-death rates per 100,000 persons, and the ratio of observed to expected deaths. It was found that the small population figures allowed for very little variation in death rates between the states. To broaden the differences between states, the road-injury rates were calculated and added to the death rates. It was necessary to reduce the injury rates by 21 per cent in South Australia in order to bring the numbers into line with those obtained in other states. In South Australia, all injuries, however trivial, sustained in road accidents are included in the final figures, whereas in other states only those injuries requiring medical or surgical treatment appear in official statistics. From these figures it was possible to calculate death and injury rates per 100,000 of the population. However, in 1963, estimates were made of the vehicle miles travelled in each state. Consequently, instead of using the years 1955, 1960, and 1964, the quinquennium 1960–4 was examined, and all statistics of road deaths, other violent deaths, crime rates, etc. were based on figures for these five years. It was considered that the death and death-and-injury rates per 100 million vehicle-miles in 1963 provided the most satisfactory indices of road violence, but it would have been preferable to have had available vehicle-mile data for all years as was the case in the United States. However, for comparison, the observed to expected road-death ratios were calculated for the five years, as well as the death rates per 100,000 of the population. In the statistical analysis the death rates per 100 million vehicle-miles, the death and injury rates per 100 million vehicle-miles, and the ratio of observed to expected deaths were all used for correlation with the other variables. One could certainly question the reliability of road-death and injury rates based on a single year's estimate of vehicle mileage but, as has already been observed, there was a surprisingly high correlation between this figure and the observed to expected death ratio based on the average for the five years.

After some delay I was able to obtain data for the annual vehicle mileage run in each of the ten Canadian provinces for the years 1955, 1960, and 1964. Initially the figures for road deaths per 100,000 inhabitants and the ratio of observed to expected deaths in each province were calculated and used, because the Canadian Year Book from which these data were obtained did not publish figures for the annual vehicle mileage. However, once this information became available, I decided that the road deaths per 100 million vehicle-miles would be a better basis for further calculation and although the other two measures of road deaths have been included in the tables and correlations, the road-death rates per 100 million vehicle-miles are of greater value, particularly when it comes to making comparisons with the USA. As will be seen, the Canadian findings – initially at least – were markedly at variance with those obtained elsewhere, largely because of the influences of climate and differences in the numbers of vehicles in the five eastern provinces compared with the five central and western provinces.

The basic statistical data for the 27 countries, the United States, Australia, and Canada are set out in Appendix II.

Offences of Drunkenness

The previous chapter showed all too clearly that excessive drinking and road-death rates are closely interrelated. Furthermore, alcohol is often associated with violent crime. Many countries publish figures for convictions for public drunkenness and for driving a motor vehicle under the influence of liquor or for being in charge of a motor vehicle while under the influence of drink or drugs. The theory derived from a study of previous literature that road deaths, violent crime, and drunkenness are capable of being interpreted as aggressive behaviour or as conducing to such behaviour, would lead us to expect some correlation between drunken behaviour, crime, and traffic accidents. Again, one has to bear in mind that social and official attitudes towards public drunkenness will markedly affect the arrests and convictions for this type of offence; a consideration which applies with even greater consequence to the offences of being in charge of or driving a motor vehicle while under the influence of liquor.

In Norway, for example, disapproval of public drunkenness leads to very high arrest and conviction rates which seem strangely at variance with the law-abiding and pacific nature of most other aspects of Norwegian society. In France, on the other hand, tolerance of drunkenness by the authorities seems to be extreme and low conviction rates are recorded in the official statistics. This finding has to be taken in conjunction with the known fact that France has one of the highest death rates in the world from alcoholic cirrhosis of the liver.

However, with these reservations, convictions for public drunkenness and drunken driving were recorded for as many states as possible. Drunkenness rates were expressed as the number of convictions per 10,000 of the population, while drunken-driving convictions corresponded to other criminal statistics – that is the number of convictions per 100,000 population.

An alternative method of estimating alcoholism in a community is based on the number of male deaths from cirrhosis of the liver. The Jellinek formula for calculating the incidence of alcoholism depends largely on the rates of deaths from alcoholic cirrhosis, details of which are published annually by the World Health Organization for the majority of the states included in this study. For the United States, estimates of alcoholism for the year 1960 were also available (Efron and Keller, 1963). Doubts have been expressed about the reliability of the Jellinek method of estimating alcoholism, because the quality and type of alcoholic beverage consumed may be more important as a cause of cirrhosis than actual intemperance. As will be seen, cirrhosis rates and estimates of alcoholism rates in the individual states of the United States correlated significantly but negatively with road-death rates, a finding that to say the least was disconcerting in the face of the repeatedly confirmed statement that half the road deaths in the United States are associated with excessive drinking. This is a matter which will receive more detailed consideration in the next chapter.

An additional source of figures relating to public drunkenness and drunkenness on the roads was provided by the annual reports on traffic offences and offences of drunkenness in the different police districts in England and Wales. These figures were used to estimate rates of road deaths and accidents, prosecutions for drunken driving, and convictions for public drunkenness. It was then possible to investigate whether high road-death rates were associated with high rates of intoxication. As the actual sizes of the populations in the individual police jurisdictions are comparatively small, any results based on a limited number of annual samples could lead to fairly serious fluctuations in the road-death and drunkenness rates. Consequently, five-year and ten-year periods were examined when investigating the relationships of the three variables mentioned. For a number of reasons the county police areas were excluded and the findings were based solely on the reports from the urban police forces. It was felt that, as far as road accidents were concerned, those occurring in urban areas more probably would involve the local inhabitants whereas accidents in the country areas, which contain a number of main transit roads, would not necessarily be caused solely by drivers living in the country. In fact, a test sample for the country areas showed very little variation in accident and drunkenness rates, whereas quite considerable differences existed between the urban areas.

Other Forms of Social Pathology

Although this study is primarily concerned with the various manifestations of social violence, it could not be assumed beforehand that other forms of disturbance of a non-violent kind were irrelevant to road-death rates. From the numerous indicators of social unrest, only a few for which reasonably comprehensive statistics were available could be used. The United Nations Organization publish annual figures for divorce and extra-nuptial birth rates. In the United States mental hospital first admissions and prison admission rates are also given in official publications. Unfortunately, in the United States extra-nuptial birth figures are given by only 32 of the 48 states included in this study.

Industrial disputes constitute another form of social disturbance of a measurable kind, and figures for these were available in Australia and the United States of America. A number of countries supply annual figures of work-days lost through strikes and lockouts which are published in the International Labour Office reports. However, it was difficult to be certain of the reliability and comparability of the figures given, and consequently, industrial dispute rates could not be used in the analysis of the 27 world states.

The extent to which these variables are true indicators of social and domestic unrest depends very much on local cultural, legal, and religious attitudes. In some societies, for example, extra-nuptial pregnancies are of no great consequence, a finding which would make the incidence of such births more an indication of social normality than of deviance. Similarly, divorce rates will depend almost entirely on legal and religious enactments without providing any clear guide to the true incidence of marital disturbances in a society. There are, of course, well-known correlations between divorce and mental illness, suicide, alcoholism, and, for that matter, road accidents. But a law prohibiting divorce clearly negates any possibility of correlating this procedure with any of the variables already examined.

Mental hospital admission rates are very crude indicators of the extent of psychiatric morbidity in the community. So many barriers exist between a patient's illness and the decision to admit him to hospital. One can safely say that admission will depend more on social attitudes to mental illness, the availability of psychiatric beds, and the existence of alternative methods of care than on particular features of an illness that compel immediate removal of the patient from the social scene. Prison admission may reflect greater or lesser degrees of punitiveness rather than a true need to confine an offender. Strikes are governed by so many economic and legal factors that purely sociological considerations may play only a very small part in their origins and duration. It follows, therefore, that these social variables, although incontestably indicators of social restlessness and discomfort, may be affected by a large number of factors other than the violent attitudes of the parties concerned. It remained to be seen whether or not non-violent or less violent social disturbances would coexist and correlate with road deaths. Strongly positive correlations would indicate the need for modification of the original hypothesis; while negative or weak positive correlations would tend to reinforce the belief that traffic casualties are due more to socialized aggression than to other facets of human behaviour.

Divorce rates are expressed as the number of divorces per 10,000 population, and extra-nuptial birth rates as a percentage of total live births. The rates for industrial disputes can be estimated in various ways, but finally it was decided to set out the number of man-days lost as a percentage of total man-days worked per annum. In the United States prison admissions and first admissions to mental hospitals were recorded as the rate per 10,000 of the population. Unfortunately, comparable interstate data for these two variables could not be obtained for Canada and Australia.

Accident, Suicide, and Homicide Rates

Death rates for all accidents other than road-traffic accidents, for suicide, and for homicide were calculated from the figures given in the World Health Organization Demographic Yearbook. Other sources of information were consulted, but for the most part the accidental and suicidal deaths tallied closely with those provided by the World Health Organization. Homicide, on the other hand, was less satisfactory and numbers varied considerably, depending upon the sources. Some State Yearbooks provided homicide death figures differing considerably from those set out in the World Health Organization Yearbooks. An additional variable was introduced by the statistics for homicide provided by Interpol, which were often at odds with the World Health Organization statistics. Much, of course, depends on how homicide is defined and whether manslaughter, negligent or non-negligent, is to be included in the final homicide total. As road deaths have increased, a number of countries have created a second category of serious offence – causing death by dangerous or reckless driving. This offence in the past was included under the headings of negligent or non-negligent manslaughter. With some reservations, therefore, it seemed wisest to use the World Health Organization figures, although one could not assume that absolute uniformity of reporting had been observed.

Should accidental, suicidal, and homicidal deaths be considered as equivalent in terms of violence? Such deaths can be explored in a number of ways, but their final position in a hierarchy of violence will depend upon a number of factors. Among these will probably be included the cause of the death, the extent to which the death was willed by the victim or an assailant, and the degree of responsibility borne by the person or a number of persons for fatalities of this kind. An accidental death by simple drowning is less violent than being eaten by a shark. Suicide by barbiturate overdose is less shocking than self-incineration. Deliberate homicide is always judged as more violent and culpable than either accidental or suicidal death, but, even so, some homicides are less abhorrent to public feelings than others. It follows, therefore, that a person who dies following an accident at work – whatever the mode of death – seems to die less violently than one who takes his own life or dies at the hands of an assailant. Most persons would agree that homicide is more culpable than suicide and that countries with high homicide rates are more violent societies than those with low homicide rates. Consequently, the statistics of accidental, suicidal, and homicidal deaths can be presented as if they were of equal significance or, more logically, with a weighting attached to homicide and suicide leaving accidental deaths unweighted.

The only weighting scale for crime is that developed by Sellin and Wolfgang (1964), who based their findings on the manner in which different groups of individuals in the USA ranked offences committed by juvenile delinquents. The authors found that the age of the offenders made little difference to the assessors' estimates of the seriousness of a crime and, later in their monograph, demonstrated an application of the scale to the *Uniform Crime Reports* of the USA. Unfortunately, there is no weighting given for suicide in this scale, and one was faced by the problem of giving this act an arbitrary weight or, alternatively, equating it with some comparatively minor offence that was included in the Sellin and Wolfgang list of crimes. In some countries suicide and attempted suicide are still regarded as criminal acts and aiding and abetting suicide is a criminal offence in most English-speaking communities. In England and Wales, prior to the Suicide Act (1960), attempted suicide was a misdemeanour punishable by a short term of imprisonment. It appeared that common assault and attempted suicide carried the same degree of legal disapproval and punishment and so, for the purpose of this study, suicide was given the same weighting as common assault in the Sellin and Wolfgang Scale – 4·3. Homicide was given the weighting of 26 and accidental deaths were left unweighted.

Probably the weighting for homicide was too high, since the WHO figures for this form of death include death by negligent manslaughter, an offence that would rate lower than non-negligent manslaughter and deliberate murder. Nevertheless, as it was not possible to calculate a new weighting for the various categories of homicide it seemed better to use the Sellin and Wolfgang figure rather than present all varieties of violent death unweighted. The possible dangers of using this rating scale in this fashion – at least outside the USA – are recognized and for this reason correlations were also carried out between road-death rates and the three forms of violent deaths unweighted, whether presented individually or as the total score of violent death.

Criminal Statistics

The estimation of crime rates in the various communities studied was fraught with many difficulties. Different legal formulae and languages make comparative criminology a hazardous business, and the final figures produced for a limited number of countries must be accepted with considerable caution.

Clearly, if violence as a general feature of a society is a factor in road-death rates, one might expect that violent forms of crime would be high in those societies where road deaths are most frequent. Unfortunately, violent crime is not always easy to define, since it covers the more obvious forms of assault upon the person with consequences varying from death to minor injury, threats of violence, robbery, extortion of money by threats of violence, and some sexual offences. Verbal violence or threats are even harder to define because such acts are sometimes covered by the blanket term 'behaviour liable to lead to a breach of the peace'. In Scandinavian countries violence against official persons is listed separately. Assaults on the police and resisting arrest are also separate forms of aggressive behaviour given special treatment in some criminal statistics. To take all forms of crime as examples of violence would hardly be justifiable, even though it could be argued that every crime is in some respects an aggressive act against society. However, it would obviously be unreasonable to include under this heading such acts as homosexual behaviour between consenting males, fraudulent conversion, or selling of intoxicating liquor outside the prescribed hours. Indeed, some of these offences can exist only in countries which have special prohibitions on certain forms of sexual behaviour or restrictive liquor laws. Motoring offences, which greatly outnumber all other offences taken together, constitute a separate category of crimes, and in the nature of things the more serious traffic infringements are often highly aggressive. However, as death on the road is frequently the consequence of a driving offence, it would scarcely be reasonable to study correlations between two such closely interlinked phenomena. It has also to be remembered that violent offences against the person are comparatively rare crimes compared with the bulk of illegal acts, consisting mainly of property offences, omitting, of course, the very large number of motoring offences. Consequently, when making correlations between violent crime and road deaths only a very small part of the total criminal behaviour in society is under scrutiny.

After examination of the criminal statistics of a number of countries, only four classes of violent crime were included for further analysis. Homicide in all its forms was an obvious example, but manslaughter by negligence was deliberately omitted owing to the failure of some countries to distinguish this offence from causing death by dangerous driving. The more serious classes of assault, regarded as felonies or indictable offences and covered by such terms as 'aggravated assault' and 'malicious wounding' could also be included for the United States and Canada, but differences of terminology between one country and another made comparisons impossible. Attempted murder was classed with aggravated assault, but common assault, which could not be estimated and compared in the different countries, had to be excluded. Forcible rape and attempted rape are obvious examples of the more violent kinds of sexual offence, and little difficulty was experienced in finding agreed definitions covering the legal enactments of the states examined. Robbery, armed or unarmed, also appears to be an offence of an identifiable and comparable nature. For the purposes of this study the definitions given in the United States *Uniform Crime Reports* published annually by the Federal Bureau of Investigation seemed the most satisfactory. These reports contain four types of violent crime known to the police in the individual states of the United States: homicide, which includes non-negligent manslaughter, forcible rape, robbery, and aggravated assault. As far as the United States is concerned, the uniformity of these reports allowed direct comparisons between states to be made. However, as already indicated, aggravated assault is a term which is defined in a number of ways by different countries and one could not feel confident that valid comparisons between states could be made for this offence. Even in Australia, the different state laws lead to some uncertainties about the validity of the aggravated assault figures. Consequently, although the four classes of violent crime listed in the *Uniform Crime Reports* were finally chosen for compilation of violent crime indices, aggravated assault had to be omitted from the final scores for the six Australian states and the 27 world states. All these crimes were expressed as the number of offences known to or reported to the police per 100,000 of the total population of each state.

Criminal statistics can be presented at least three different ways:

1. Crimes known or reported to the police.
2. The number of criminal prosecutions.
3. The number of convictions.

Obviously the first method is the most satisfactory basis for the complication of criminal statistics, since by no means all offenders are brought before the courts and prosecuted; and of these only a comparatively small proportion are convicted. Even so, crime reported to the police probably represents only a proportion of the totality of criminal activity in a community. Homicide and aggravated assault probably reach official notice more often than rape and robbery. In Spain, for example, it has been said that only 10 per cent of cases of rape come to the notice of the police. Thus the incidence of officially reported or known crime may bear very little relationship to the real extent of criminal activity. On the whole, the less serious the crime the more commonly will it occur and the greater will be the discrepancy between its true frequency and official recognition of its existence. However, as the *Uniform Crime Reports* of the United States list crimes 'known to the police', every attempt was made to obtain this class of statistical information for as many countries as possible. All the English-speaking countries provided these data, and they were also available for the separate states of Australia and Canada. Scandinavian countries and a number of European countries also provide figures for crimes known to the police in a manner making them more or less comparable with the statistics of the English-speaking countries. Unfortunately, many countries such as Switzerland, West Germany, and France give numbers of convictions only, and, as a result, criminal statistics for only 15 of the 27 countries could be used for this part of the investigation. Some thought was given to the possibility of using conviction rates instead of reported crime rates in all countries, but too many uncontrollable variables enter into the decision to convict or even to prosecute. Variations in police procedure and legal systems have a very marked influence on the final conviction rates, and, even within a country such as Great Britain, police procedures vary greatly between one police force and another. Similar considerations undoubtedly apply to the United States and all other countries examined in this survey. A sudden zeal for the detection of a particular crime can lead to quite remarkable increases in that offence in an area where police vigilance is greatest. In a neighbouring police force the same class of offence might well be overlooked or treated with comparative indulgence, with a consequent fall in its incidence. Kinsey's figures for the variations between states in prosecutions for different classes of sexual offence are good examples of this kind of effect (Kinsey *et al.*, 1948).

In the end it seemed wisest to make use of the smaller number of countries providing data of known offences. In the United States, Australia, and Canada the numbers of reported offences were available but special difficulties were created by the lack of uniformity between states for these data in Australia. Initial information on the selected crimes known to the police for the years 1955, 1960, and 1964 was obtained from the Chief Police Commissioners for each state. However, since 1964 an attempt has been made to provide uniform crime statistics for the Australian states similar to those used in the United States. Unfortunately, the figures given by the Commonwealth Bureau of Census and Statistics for serious assault for the years 1964–7 cannot be compared because of different definitions given to this offence in different states. In Australia, therefore, violent crime was limited to homicide, forcible rape, and robbery, whereas in Canada all four classes of offence could be used. Canada also provided satisfactory figures for juvenile delinquency and, bearing in mind the youth of a large number of offenders and drivers killed on the road, it seemed reasonable to include these delinquency figures in the part of the study devoted to Canadian statistics.

On the basis of Sellin and Wolfgang's application of their measurement scale to USA crime statistics, I decided that this procedure was justifiable for the 48 states in that country. Akman and Normandeau (1967) have carried out a somewhat similar procedure for the Canadian Uniform Crime Reporting System and found a large measure of agreement between their weightings and those of Sellin and Wolfgang. Consequently, I used for Canadian criminal statistics the same weightings as those applied in the USA. There were 26 for homicide, 14·7 for rape, 4·6 for robbery, and 5·0 for aggravated assault. So far nobody has constructed a similar scale for Australia and, although I have used the same weightings for the three violent offences on the basis that attitudes to crime in Australia are probably closely similar to those observed in the USA and Canada, I have also given the individual and total rates for these three offences. As will be seen, the total weighted score for violent crime in Australia correlated far more significantly with road deaths than did the unweighted score. In the 27 world states the variability in criminal statistics and attitudes to crime would not permit the use of the Sellin and Wolfgang scale, and consequently the rates for the three crimes, homicide, rape, and robbery have been presented individually and together without any weighting attached.

However, it has to be said that the small number of violent crimes and uncertainty about the relationship of reported felonies to the true incidence of these offences compel one to conclude that findings based on such figures must be treated with the greatest reserve. Unfortunately, it is difficult to supplement official criminal statistics with information from other sources, and even experienced criminologists encounter great difficulty when attempting to make international comparisons of crime rates. In this study, violent-crime rates have been included not only because they are among the most obvious manifestations of social violence but also because of the known criminal propensities of a fair number of persons involved in repeated accidents. Because of the uncertainties surrounding the reliability of the published figures, high positive correlations between road deaths and violent-crime rates were not anticipated, but it remained to be seen whether such correlations as would be obtained supported the general hypothesis.

Statistical Methods

Once the data had been assembled, calculation of Pearson's r was carried out for the different pairs of variables. Miss J. H. A. Cane, Senior Tutor in Medical Statistics in the University of Queensland, carried out the multiple linear regression analysis of the United States findings which appears at the end of the appropriate section in the next chapter. Because of the completeness of the United States statistics, regression analysis was carried out on this country only. The small number of individual provinces in Canada and states in Australia did not permit this kind of detailed investigation and, as far as the 27 world states were concerned, the statistical data were incomplete for many of the variables.

For Australia, with data available for only six states, Spearman's rank-order technique was used for inter-pair comparisons and Kendall's coefficient of concordance for estimating the degree of association between more than two sets of variables. For the ten Canadian provinces, Pearson's method was used. The results of all these investigations were submitted to the usual tests of significance which were expressed in terms of probability. The significance of the findings in the section devoted to an examination of the drunkenness statistics in English towns and cities was estimated by the conventional Student's t test and checked by the Mann–Whitney U test.

REFERENCES

AKMAN, D. D., and NORMANDEAU, A. 1967. The measurement of crime and delinquency in Canada. *Brit. J. Criminol.* **7**, 129–49

CALLEJA, D. 1965. An index of road danger. *Carrterras*, **102**, 27–32.

CARLQUIST, J. C. A. 1966. Safe or dangerous: an international comparison of road traffic figures. *Traffic Engineering*, August, 31–5.

EFRON, V., and KELLER, M. 1963. Selected statistical tables on the consumption of alcohol 1850–1962 and on alcoholism 1930–1960. Rutgers Center of Alcohol Studies, New Jersey.

KINSEY, A. C., POMEROY, W. B., and MARTIN, C. E. 1948. *Sexual behaviour in the human male.* Philadelphia: Saunders.

NORMAN, L. G. 1962. *Road traffic accidents.* Public Health Paper No. 12. Geneva: WHO.

SELLIN, T., and WOLFGANG, M. E. 1964. *The measurement of delinquency.* New York: Wiley.

SMEED, R. J. 1949. Some statistical aspects of road safety research. *J. roy. stat. Soc.* (A) **112**, 1–23.

—— 1953. The international comparison of accident rates. *Internat. Rd Safety and Traffic Rev.* **1** (i), January.

TAFT, P. 1966. Violence in American labor disputes. *Ann. Amer. Acad. pol. soc. Sci.* **344**, 127–40.

9 · Results

27 WORLD STATES

The statistical data for 27 world states are set out in *Table 1* in Appendix II. Columns A and B show the two different methods of recording road-death rates and column C–F¹ set out the individual and total rates of violent death, the weighted sum of these three forms of death being shown in column F^1. As already mentioned, the ratio of observed to expected road deaths was taken as the best available measure of the true extent of road violence in relation to the numbers of the populations, the vehicles, and the annual totals of miles driven.

Table 1A shows the intercorrelations between the two measures of road deaths and the 14 other variables. Both the road-death rates showed significant positive correlations with the violent-death rates apart from homicide deaths alone. This is in contrast to the significant positive correlations with homicide deaths known to the police (G) in 15 countries only. Why homicide death rates appearing in vital statistics should differ from homicide death rates in criminal statistics in some countries is inexplicable. The fact remains that all measures of violent death and violent crime correlated positively and, in most instances, significantly with the two road-death indices. I had hoped to include serious assault among the violent crimes to be considered, but unfortunately it was quite impossible to make reliable comparisons for this class of offence in the 15 states providing statistics. Rape, robbery, and murder are probably more comparable, but the well-known errors in criminal statistics require that these positive findings should be accepted with caution. However, the similar positive correlations in the USA, where some attempt to achieve uniformity in criminal statistics for the 48 states has been made, give general support to these findings in the 27 world states.

H

That there were no significant correlations between the road-death rates and convictions for drunkenness (K) and drunken driving (L) was hardly surprising. Public attitudes towards these two forms of behaviour vary greatly from country to country and conviction rates may have very little to do with the true incidence of drunken behaviour. This is particularly evident when one compares France with Norway.

Efron and Keller (1963) showed that, of 21 countries listed, France had the highest alcohol consumption per capita of population, over seven times greater than that of Norway. These inequalities of alcohol consumption probably account for the differences in male death rates from cirrhosis of the liver (Column O), where again France has the highest rate and Norway one of the lowest. Nevertheless, compared with France, Norway has far higher conviction rates for public drunkenness and drunken driving. Almost certainly these are due to the contrasting attitudes on the part of public and police in the two countries towards intoxication in public. As Eliot and Hillman wrote (1960), 'arrests are said to be made [in Norway] for public intoxication, *in se*, not merely for disorder when drunk'. In Norway, with a strong evangelical tradition that brings clergy into active participation in the treatment of alcoholism, it is clear that public disapproval of drunkenness leads to high arrest and conviction rates for this kind of behaviour. In 1960 the convictions for 'misdemeanours of drunkenness' amounted to 25,100, giving a rate of 69·8 per 100,000 compared with 56,537 in France, that is 12·5 per 100,000. These figures indicate sufficiently well that statistics of convictions for drunkenness are unreliable indices of excessive drinking and alcoholism in a community, an argument that applies with equal force to the figures for convictions for drunken driving.

However, when one comes to examine male deaths from cirrhosis of the liver a more positive picture is obtained, since highly significant correlations exist between this cause of male mortality and both measures of road deaths. It is noteworthy that neither convictions for drunkenness (K) nor drunken driving (L) correlates significantly with male deaths from cirrhosis of the liver (O), a finding that seems to imply that the high, positive correlations between road deaths from hepatic cirrhosis are due to a third variable which is distinct from alcoholic intemperance. The reliability and validity of deaths from cirrhosis of the liver as guides to the prevalence of alcoholism in the community can certainly be questioned. In fact, there is reason to believe that cirrhosis rates correlate more significantly with the annual consumption of alcohol per head of population – and more particularly the class of alcoholic beverage consumed – than with other indices of excessive drinking. Some of these points relating to alcohol and road-accident rates will be taken up in a later section of this chapter.

The other two measures of social pathology – extra-nuptial births (M) and divorce (N) – show no significant correlations with road-death rates. Undoubtedly the various religious, legal, and social attitudes in the countries studied will be more important determinants of these phenomena than any single aspect of behaviour, such as violence or sociopathy. There is evidence suggesting that divorced persons – at least in the United States – have higher accident rates than the married (Zylman, 1968). However, this finding does not show up in the correlations between road deaths and divorce rates in the 27 countries, and Parry (1968), in his sample of British drivers, found that married men tended to be slightly more aggressive in their driving behaviour and attitudes than single men. The small number of divorced or separated men did not allow for statistical analysis but Parry concluded that marital status may have very little to do with the quality of behaviour on the road.

Full data were not available for all the 27 countries, so a further analysis was made of the 8 English-speaking countries and the 4 Scandinavian states, all of which provided complete statistical information. As these states have certain cultural and social features in common, with correspondingly high standards of development, it seemed likely that the more limited analysis would have greater validity than the examination of the incomplete data of the 27 countries already discussed. The statistical data for these 12 countries are set out in *Table 1* and their correlations are shown in *Table 1B*.

Both measures of road deaths show positive correlations with the various types of violent death but for the most part these are not statistically significant. Similar considerations apply to the violent-crime figures. No doubt the smaller number of states involved is partly responsible for the failure to achieve statistical significance in the majority of the intercorrelations but the general trend is similar to that provided by the larger number of world states. Of some interest is the finding of significant positive correlations between convictions for drunken driving (L) and both road-death indices and convictions for drunkenness (K) with the ratio of observed to expected road deaths. On the other hand neither of the 'non-violent' varieties of social pathology – extra-nuptial births and divorce rates – correlated significantly with road deaths any more than they did in the 27 world states.

The absence of complete information for the 27 countries made further statistical analysis impossible. However, intercorrelations between the unweighted and weighted sums of violent deaths (F and F^1) and the variables in columns J–O were examined. From the results set out in *Table 1A* it could be argued that violence in general, and violent deaths in particular, might well play significant roles in the aetiology of some of the social pathology being considered.

It is possible, of course, that more complete data for all countries would invalidate this assumption, although the eight English-speaking and Scandinavian countries showed fairly similar relationships between violent death and the other variables. It would be going far beyond the data to argue that violence and aggression are the main factors determining these social disturbances, but at least the trend shown by the figures gives adequate support to the main hypothesis: that road-death and injury rates are the result, to a considerable extent, of the expression of aggressive behaviour; and that the countries with the highest road-death rates will, in general, have the highest rates for other forms of violent behaviour. Or, argue the matter differently, those societies with the greatest amount of violence and aggression in their structure will show this by externalizing some of this violence in the form of dangerous and aggressive driving with correspondingly high casualty and accident rates.

The relationship between road deaths and other forms of violent death in the 24 European countries is shown in graphic form in the histogram in *Figure 1*, and the two maps (*Figures 1A* and *1B*) which rather more crudely illustrate the same point. It is evident that some areas of Europe are more aggressive or pacific than others, but consideration of these interesting variations must be deferred until all results have been presented.

United States of America

Of the 51 component states of the United States, the District of Columbia, Alaska, and Hawaii were omitted: the District of Columbia because separate statistical data for this area were not available for 1955; the other two states, because of their geographical separateness and climatic and cultural differences.

The statistical data for the 48 states and the derived intercorrelations are set out in *Tables 2* and *2A*. The three maps illustrate the distribution of road deaths, other violent deaths, and violent crime (*Figures 2, 2A,* and *2B*).

In the United States, statistics of annual vehicle mileage, based on the yearly sales of motor fuels, were available for each state, so the figure of 100 million vehicle-miles per annum was used as the basis for calculating road-death rates. However, the other measures already described were also estimated for each state. A satisfactory degree of correlation between road deaths per 100 million vehicle-miles and the ratio of observed to expected deaths was noted ($r = +0.777$, $t = 8.371$, $p \ll .001$). A correspondingly significant correlation was demonstrated between road deaths per 100 million vehicle-miles and road deaths per 100,000 of the population ($r = +0.673$, $p < .001$). These figures provided a satisfactory check on the validity of the observed to expected death ratio as a measure of the degree of road violence in the communities where the vehicle-miles per annum statistic was not available.

Data for all the states were complete except for the extra-nuptial birth rate. Only 32 of the selected states provide figures for extra-nuptial births, so although these findings were included in the final correlations, the intercorrelations between extra-nuptial birth rates and the other variables could not be used for further analysis. Divorce rates are provided by all 48 states, but the very elevated rate for Nevada was so grossly deviant from all other states that it was necessary to exclude Nevada when carrying out correlations between divorce rates and the other findings. Undoubtedly the local divorce laws seriously inflate the Nevada rates which, consequently, do not truly reflect the degree of marital disturbance in that state alone.

The findings in the United States of America for the most part correspond closely with those obtained in the 27 world states. However, the larger number of states and the greater degree of homogeneity and reliability of the statistical data not only produced more highly significant correlations but also permitted greater confidence in the findings which confirmed and amplified those obtained from other parts of the world. Road deaths correlated positively and highly significantly with the three other forms of violent death, weighted and unweighted, except for death by suicide. A highly significant correlation between road deaths and other accidental deaths (not shown separately in *Table 2A*) was also observed ($r = +0.650$, $p < .001$). The other strongly positive correlation – that between homicide deaths and road deaths – seems to emphasize the relationship of aggression to road deaths since homicide is generally accepted as the most extreme example of violent behaviour in Western society. The positive association between road deaths and violent crime is consistent with the general thesis concerning the relationship of aggressive behaviour to road deaths and, no doubt, the less significant positive correlation with prison admission rates also reflects a similar connection.

Mental hospital admission rates on the other hand showed a significant negative correlation with road-death rates, as did industrial disputes and the estimates of alcoholism. There was little enough reason to anticipate a positive correlation between road deaths and industrial disputes, an aspect of social unrest that correlated positively and significantly with mental hospital admissions alone. On the other hand, the highly significant negative correlation between road deaths and alcoholism was a distinctly unexpected finding, for which there is no simple explanation. If half the road deaths in the United States are caused entirely or partly by excessive drinking while a considerable number of persons killed in this way are alleged to show signs of cirrhosis of the liver (Waller, 1967), one has to conclude that either the basis for estimating alcoholism rates is unreliable or the relationship between alcoholic excess and road deaths is greatly overshadowed by other factors, including that of violence. Certainly the association between excessive drinking and aggressive behaviour is well known and strongly supported by data from the United States and many other countries.

However, whatever effect alcohol might have on normal control of aggressive behaviour this would not be an adequate explanation of the paradoxical finding, in the USA, that estimates of alcoholism correlate significantly but negatively with the road deaths. In fact, if one accepts the current technique for assessing the prevalence of alcoholism in a community as valid, no satisfactory explanation of this finding is available. Consequently, a brief critical discussion of the relevance of hepatic cirrhosis death rates to road deaths and estimates of alcoholism may not be out of place, even though a full exposition of this subject could not be attempted in a monograph of this nature.

Two points need to be kept in mind: the comparative unreliability of cirrhosis death rates; and the evidence that deaths from this disease do not necessarily indicate the extent of alcoholism in a community. So far as the first objection is concerned it is obvious that many persons suffering from cirrhosis of the liver die from other causes, particularly violence. An alcoholic suffering from cirrhosis may be killed in a road accident and, should that occur, his death will be listed as due to the accident and not to cirrhosis, even though the cirrhosis may have been advanced and likely to prove fatal had he survived for a longer period. The percentage of patients suffering from cirrhosis caused by alcoholic excess can only be deduced from death certificates, which specifically mention alcohol as an aetiological factor. For obvious reasons many families would prefer to conceal a deceased relative's alcoholism and may ask the medical practitioner not to mention alcohol as a cause of cirrhosis in the death certificate of a person who has died from the disease. It follows, therefore, that the official record of deaths from cirrhosis may differ greatly from the true prevalence of that disease and may tell us little about the number of sufferers whose cirrhosis has been caused by alcoholism.

The second objection concerns the reliability of cirrhosis death rates as a measure of alcoholism prevalence rates. Schmidt and Bronetto (1962) have shown that the incidence of hepatic cirrhosis in the USA is related to the type and quantity of alcoholic beverage consumed, being higher in states where cheap wine is plentiful. An unpublished study of my own shows that in 37 countries male deaths from cirrhosis of the liver correlate very highly with the quantity of alcohol consumed and that this correlation is even stronger for the quantity of alcohol taken in the form of wine. In countries such as Italy, Spain, and Argentina, where wine is the major alcoholic beverage, cirrhosis rates are comparatively high but alcoholism is said not to be a problem. In France, Switzerland, and Chile where wine-drinking and cirrhosis rates are also high, alcoholism is common. Both groups of countries have high wine intake and high cirrhosis rates, yet one group has a high and the other a low alcoholism prevalence rate. In the USA, where the individual state alcoholism rates are based on the cirrhosis death rates, the correlation between cirrhosis and total alcohol and wine-alcohol consumption are $+0.780$ and $+0.795$ respectively. Road-traffic accidents in contrast show small negative correlations with total and wine-alcohol consumption ($r = -0.186$; $r = -0.161$). In the face of evidence of this kind, one is compelled to question the reliability of the cirrhosis death rate as a guide to the extent of alcoholism. At the same time one may well doubt the value of cirrhosis death rates as indicators of the contribution made by alcohol and alcoholism to road-traffic fatalities.

A third source of error rises from the belief that persons involved in road-traffic accidents where alcohol is a factor are, inevitably, alcoholics. This may be true for a number of drivers, but evidence from Australia strongly suggests that young male drivers involved in road-traffic accidents frequently have high blood-alcohol concentrations, without necessarily showing symptoms and signs of alcoholism. The statistical findings in the USA can scarcely invalidate the numerous investigations that have demonstrated a clear relationship between alcohol consumption and road accidents. However, they certainly should lead one to question the significance of the part assigned to the alcoholic as a cause of road deaths. That a number of proven alcoholics are involved in road accidents is certain. Their total contribution to road deaths may be only marginal when compared with that of the more numerous, occasionally intoxicated, youthful drivers who, through inexperience, both as drinkers and drivers, are potentially greater dangers to themselves and to others. Indeed, one wonders how many chronic alcoholics own or drive motor vehicles and to what extent longer driving experience enables some of them to keep out of trouble even when they have been drinking. There is no immediate answer to these questions, which need to be answered before one accepts the widespread belief that the alcoholic rather than the drinking driver is the real problem so far as alcohol and road accidents are concerned.

Why the USA findings should be diametrically opposed to those observed in the 27 world states cannot be satisfactorily explained. In the USA alcoholism rates refer to both sexes, whereas in the 27 countries male cirrhosis deaths have been taken as indicators of alcohol consumption and alcoholism. Neither set of figures tells us anything about the relative drinking habits of men and women, the quantity and type of alcohol consumed, or the nutritional state of the inhabitants in the various states and countries. Without these data it would be unwise to draw too many conclusions from cirrhosis death rates alone, and for the time, at least, one can do little more than record the findings. Ultimately, a paradox of this kind can only be resolved by specific research and, so far, research of this nature has not been performed.

The significant positive correlations between road deaths and divorce and extra-nuptial birth rates are at variance with the findings in the 27 world states. Once again, one might explain this contrasting finding by reference to the greater cultural homogeneity of the United States and the quality of the statistical data made available each year. Needless to say there are no grounds for assuming a direct causal relationship between these two social variables and road deaths. Rather does one have to consider whether the type of individual who kills or is killed on the road has some quality which will render him more liable to unstable and irregular interpersonal relationships. Such a conclusion may well be going far beyond what is justified by the evidence and for the time being consideration of such explanations must be postponed.

Statistical Analysis of USA Results

I am indebted to Miss J. H. A. Cane, Tutor in Medical Statistics in the University of Queensland, for carrying out the multiple linear regression analysis of the United States results and providing the following discussion of methods and results:

For the United States of America, information on 12 factors was available for 48 states. However, the divorce rates for the State of Nevada, which were so markedly deviant from all others, would have seriously affected the validity of the results of statistical analysis had this state been included. Consequently, for the multiple linear regression analysis, Nevada was omitted, leaving 47 states for further examination.

After examining the intercorrelations between the 12 variables, the question was posed as to whether the observed variation in one variable (hereafter called the dependent variable) could be partially explained in terms of a reduced number of the remaining 11 variables. It will be appreciated that the figures in columns C–F are functions of the weighted sum of violent deaths in column B. Consequently, the factors examined in the multiple regression analysis were those set out in columns A, B, and H–L. The extra-nuptial birth rate (M) was omitted, since data were available for only 32 states.

Taking first as the dependent variable the factor 'weighted sum of violent death' (*Table 2*, column B), and as the independent variables the factors listed in the table below, a multiple linear regression was carried out.

As a preliminary investigation, the multiple regression was performed without application of any statistical criteria for inclusion or exclusion of variables. The regression coefficients and the corresponding values of F used for testing their significance were as indicated in the table. The amount of variation in the dependent variable that could be explained by this set of independent variables was 75·7 per cent. The mean square error was 1874.

No.	Table factor	Regression coefficient	F value (1, 39)	Significance level
G	Weighted sum violent crime	0·110	42·3	$p < ·001$
A	Road death	1·196	3·74	NS
H	Prison admission	8·156	4·78	$p < ·05$
L	Alcoholism	−1·733	4·46	$p < ·05$
I	Mental hospital admission	3·621	1·31	NS
K	Industrial unrest	0·566	0·75	NS
J	Divorce	−0·043	0·003	NS

Constant term $= 18·065$

The main analysis was then carried out, this being a stepwise multiple regression. In this, at the first stage, the variable which had the largest regression sum of squares associated with it was selected. At each subsequent stage, the next variable to be included was the one which, together with the previously selected variable, made the largest reduction in the residual sum of squares. An end-point was reached when the largest reduction in residual sum of squares produced by the introduction of any of the remaining variables was not significant.

The results of the analysis were as follows:

At the first stage, 'weighted violent crime' was included. The percentage of the total variation explained by this factor was 55·1 per cent.

At the next stage, 'road-death rate' was included, with the corresponding proportion of total variation being 66·3 per cent.

Then 'prison admission' was included. The proportion of total variation explained by these three variables was 72·5 per cent. No other single variable made a significant reduction in the residual sum of squares. Hence, the final regression equation contained three independent variables. It was as follows:

$$Y = 0.102X_1 + 1.756X_2 + 10.286X_3 - 31.376$$

where   Y = weighted sum of accidental, suicidal, and homicidal deaths
   X_1 = weighted sum of violent crime
   X_2 = road-death rate
   X_3 = prison admission rate.

The *F* tests for the inclusion of the three variables in succession were 40·08 ($p < ·001$), 10·74 ($p < ·01$), 9·59 ($p < ·01$) (degrees of freedom; $n_1 = 1, n_2 = 43$). The *F* values were significant at the levels indicated in parenthesis. The residual mean sum of squares was 1921.

This analysis shows that the variation in the factor 'violent death' could largely be explained in terms of the factors violent crime, road deaths, and prison admissions. Given these three factors, no other factors made any significant contribution to the variation in violent-death rates. To be specific, 55 per cent of variation could be explained by the variation in violent-crime rates. The latter factor combined with road-death rates explained 68 per cent of the variation, and both of these combined with prison admission rates explained 72·5 per cent. Correlations of violent-death rates with each of these three factors were positive.

Prison admission, of course, must be looked on as a factor determined to some extent by the amount of violent crime. Consequently, one would be inclined to pay more attention to the link between road death and violent crime than the connection between prison admissions and the two death rates.

The next step was to carry out a further linear regression analysis with road-death rates as the dependent variable. Here it was found that 36·7 per cent of the variation in road deaths would be accounted for by the variation in the weighted sum of violent death alone. This factor and the factor of alcoholism accounted for 47·1 per cent of the variation in road deaths, but no other factor made any significant contribution. The regression occasion was:

$$Y = 0.07699X_1 - 0.41700X_2 + 59.19$$

where   Y = road death rates
      X_1 = the weighted sum of violent deaths
      X_2 = alcoholism rates.

The situation here is complicated by the negative correlations of road deaths with the estimates of alcoholism in the individual states of the United States. For reasons set out elsewhere, the alcoholism figures were regarded as unreliable and, although they undoubtedly contributed to the mathematical variation in the road-death factor, it could hardly be said that such a finding has much meaning in the real-life situation where excessive drinking and road deaths go hand in hand. Unfortunately, as already shown, alcoholism cannot be equated with drunken driving and public drunkenness. In the absence of data for these phenomena in the individual states of the United States, one has to conclude that the introduction of alcoholism into the linear regression analysis could well be misleading.

A third analysis was carried out, omitting alcoholism rates from the calculations. It was found that 33·8 per cent of the variation in road deaths could be explained by variations in the weighted sum of violent death alone. No other factor made any significant contribution. The regression equation was:

$$Y = 0.09843X + 40.78$$

where   Y = road deaths
      X = the weighted sum of violent death.

This analysis goes some way to confirming the original hypothesis, while at the same time showing that, despite the strong influence of violent behaviour on road-death rates, violence alone is not the entire problem. Such a conclusion is in keeping with everyday observation and common sense. However, bearing in mind the numerous factors contributing to road casualties, this significant role of violence is a disturbing finding. If such behaviour derives from some quality inherent in mankind our chances of reducing the road toll by exhortation and safety campaigns are comparatively slight. Human nature alone is the problem where violence is concerned, and that is unlikely to alter in the immediate future.

Although violent crime was positively associated with road deaths in the correlation tables, this factor seems not to make any significant contribution to the variance in these accidental-death rates. On the other hand, violent deaths – which do not include road deaths – are strongly influenced by violent crime. It appears that violent death – whatever form it takes – is the central theme in this analysis, a finding which is supported by the significant correlations between road deaths and the many other forms of accidental fatalities in the United States. The lack of contribution of the less 'violent' varieties of social pathology is not surprising in the light of these observations, but it should not be assumed that the United States findings have a general applicability elsewhere. Unfortunately, a lack of reliable statistics for some of the factors precluded an extensive analysis of the findings in the 27 world states; while small numbers limited the significance of the results in Australia and Canada. All one can note at this stage is the similar trend of the correlations, while making a tentative assumption that violence plays as important a role in road-casualty rates in these areas as it appears to do in the United States of America.

AUSTRALIA

The statistical data for 17 variables for Australia are set out in *Table 3*. Columns A–C represent the three estimates of road-casualty rates and columns D–E[1] show the weighted and un-weighted deaths from violence, excluding those due to road accidents. Columns F–I[1] give the rates for the three types of violent crime, given individually and combined, with a final weighted rate for all three in I[1]. As already mentioned, I felt that the relative cultural similarities between the USA, Canada, and Australia might permit the use of the Sellin–Wolfgang Scale, bearing in mind the very similar weightings given to a number of offences by the Canadian investigators (Akman and Normandeau, 1967).

The histogram (*Figure 3*) compares the five more 'violent' forms of social pathology for the six states. The fourteen columns (D–O) were correlated with the three measures of road deaths and injuries using Spearman's rank-order technique, the results of which are shown in *Table 3A*. It has to be remembered that with only six states it would have been unrealistic to expect many correlations of significance. However, the majority of the findings were very much in line with the statistically significant findings obtained from the 27 world states and the United States of America.

All three measures of road casualties correlated positively with other forms of violent death (D–F), some types of violent crime, drunkenness, and drunken driving. The road-death and injury rates (A) in particular show the highest correlations with violent death and homicide but show negative figures for rape and robbery and non-significant positive correlations with the other measures of social pathology set out in the last four columns. The road-death and injury rate also shows a strong positive correlation with the weighted sum of violent crime as do the other two measures of social violence, but it is obvious that the heavy weighting for homicide (26) markedly influences the total weighted score resulting in much the same values for correlations in column I[1] as those seen in column F. Consequently, not too much should be made of the total weighted score for violent crime, although the significant values of *rho* when two of the measures of road violence are correlated with this variable, have to be considered in conjunction with similar significant positive findings noted in the 27 world states and the USA. Kendall's coefficient of concordance was used to test the degree of association between the three indices of road violence with the four 'violent' and the four 'non-violent' varieties of social disturbance. The highly significant associations between road deaths and other social violence contrasted strongly with the non-significant figures for the four other variables, a finding that tends to support the belief that the aggressive qualities of social behaviour are more relevant to road deaths and injuries than are non-violent kinds of deviance.

Once again one finds negative or non-significant positive correlations between the three measures of road deaths and injuries and male deaths from cirrhosis of the liver. The reasons for these findings have already been discussed in the previous section of this chapter. However, some additional consideration will be given to the problem on pages 117–20. In the meantime, one should note the significant positive correlation between convictions for drunken driving and road-death and injury rates, a finding that again emphasizes the, probably, more important role of excessive drinking as distinct from alcoholism as a contribution to traffic accidents.

CANADA

The Canadian data for sixteen variables are set out in *Table 4* and the product–moment correlations between the three measures of road deaths (A–C) and the other thirteen variables in *Figure 4*. In striking contrast to the findings obtained elsewhere, practically all these correlations were negative while the great majority were not statistically significant. There seemed to be no immediate explanation for these unexpected findings, but, bearing in mind the warning given in the Canadian yearbook that road-accident statistics in the various provinces are difficult to compare on account of terrain and climate, I decided to examine and contrast the ten southern Canadian provinces with the states in the USA immediately adjacent to the border between the two countries. I assumed that these states would have geographic and climatic qualities relatively similar to those in the southern parts of the Canadian provinces where the majority of the Canadian population lives. When one correlates the road-death rates per 100 million vehicle-miles for the states of Washington, North Dakota, Minnesota, Wisconsin, Michigan, Pennsylvania, New York, Vermont, and Maine, and the province of Manitoba with the rates for the other forms of violent death, instead of the expected significant positive findings, one obtains a negative result (Spearman rho -0.105). Such a finding is in keeping with a similar negative observation in Canada and strongly suggests that the influence of violence as a contributor to road deaths was being overshadowed by other factors.

Accordingly, figures for annual snowfalls in the capital cities in the ten Canadian provinces were obtained (column X, *Table 4B*) and these were correlated with the road-death rates per 100 million vehicle-miles. A highly significant correlation ($r = +0.8379$) was obtained. Furthermore, compared with the eastern provinces, the central and western provinces had considerably more motor vehicles per head of population (column Y, *Table 4B*). As the number of motor vehicles is an integral part of annual vehicle-mileage calculations, it is obvious that this disparity in the number of vehicles in the provinces would lead to higher death rates per 100 million vehicle-miles in provinces with fewer motor vehicles and smaller death rates in those provinces more highly motorized. It will be recalled that the road-death rates in countries with few motor vehicles are low when calculated on the basis of population but high when estimated on the number of motor vehicles. In highly mechanized countries the converse effect is seen.

The total variance contributed to road deaths per 100 million vehicle-miles by the dependent variables, annual snowfall, vehicles per head of population, and the weighted sum of violent death (G) was 72·91 per cent. Of this sum, 46·07 per cent was accounted for by snowfall, 24·09 per cent by the effect of different numbers of motor vehicles, and only 2·75 per cent by the violent-death rate. To allow for this influence of snowfall and non-uniform motor vehicle numbers, new values for road-death rates were calculated from the following formula: $Y_c = \bar{x} + b_1(z_1 - \bar{z}_1) + b_2(z_2 - \bar{z}_2)$ where $\bar{x} =$ the mean road-death rates per 100 million vehicle-miles, z_1 the snowfall, and z_2 the ratio of motor vehicles to the population in each province. b_1 and b_2 were obtained from the regression equation

$$Y_c = x + b_1z_1 + b_2z_2$$

from which values for b_2 and b_2 were +0·5225 and −0·1186 respectively. It was necessary, on account of the statistical effect of small numbers of motor vehicles, to reverse the positive sign before the formula $b_2(z_2 - \bar{z}_2)$. The correlations between the corrected values for road deaths per 100 million vehicle-miles (A') and the other variables were then calculated and are seen in part 2 of *Figure 4A*.

One now finds very strong positive values for the correlations between road deaths and homicide, suicide, total violent death, violent crime, divorce, and extra-nuptial births, and positive but statistically non-significant figures with convictions for drunkenness, drunken driving, juvenile delinquency, and male deaths from cirrhosis of the liver.

Clearly, these findings must be treated with caution before one concludes that aggressive behaviour – after making due allowance for climate and motor vehicle numbers – is a major contribution to road deaths in Canada. The influence of snowfall can be further shown by calculating the number of deaths per hundred accidents in each province and correlating these with the snowfall figures. A significant positive correlation ($r = +0.6672; p < .05$) between these two variables strongly suggests that snowfall alone was a major factor to be taken into account when analysing road-death rates in Canada. The apparent effect of snowfall was to enhance the risk of a fatal outcome to an accident in provinces with high snowfall rates compared with accidents occurring in the central and more western provinces, where the climatic circumstances were, from the point of view of road traffic, less hazardous. That aggressive behaviour is significant is shown by the strongly positive intercorrelations between those variables that appear to measure violence. Other forms of unnatural death, violent crime, and, to a lesser extent, drunkenness and drunken driving, were all positively and in many cases significantly associated with one another. If one takes into account the similar findings in the USA and elsewhere one can probably conclude with some certainty that aggression on the road contributes significantly to Canadian road casualties and that if this factor was diminished the road-death rates would be lower, irrespective of the climatic and other variables contributing to road accidents.

ALCOHOL AND ROAD ACCIDENTS

The review of the relationship of alcohol and alcoholism to road accidents indicated clearly enough the important role of liquor in this respect. Consequently, one might have expected to discover significant correlations between the various social manifestations of alcohol misuse and road-casualty rates. The main difficulty, of course, lies in the lack of reliable and comparable figures for these social variables with the inevitable failure to derive intercorrelations of a meaningful kind. It was all too evident that conviction rates for drunkenness and drunken driving in the various countries bore very little relationship to the true incidence of these problems, a fact which was exemplified by the findings in Norway and France. That French statistics of drunken driving are wholly misleading was noted by Luke (1967), when he observed that although only 2 per cent of road accidents in France are *officially* ascribed to alcohol, 38 per cent of drivers in a sample of road-traffic accidents had blood-alcohol concentrations greater than 100 milligrams per 100 millilitres of blood.

Some of the difficulties inherent in relating road accidents to alcoholism have already been discussed in earlier pages, although attempts were made to overcome these by examining as many indices of alcohol use and misuse as possible. Convictions for drunkenness and for drunken driving, alcoholism rates when available, male deaths from cirrhosis of the liver, and actual alcohol consumption per capita of population at risk were all examined. Despite some suggestive findings, it was rarely possible to place much reliance on the statistical data, which could do little more than provide occasional numerical support for the more precise clinical and epidemiological studies; and in some instances the statistical information was downright contradictory of all that is known about drink and driving.

I

As far as the 27 world states were concerned, data were incomplete, but even so those countries supplying information on convictions for offences of drunkenness failed to show significant correlations between these offences and road-death rates. The anomalous situation provided by the contrasting findings from France and Norway in this respect has already been discussed. Figures for convictions for drunken driving are equally unreliable as guides to the true incidence of driving or being in charge of a vehicle while under the influence of liquor. For example, it is certainly improbable that in Scotland there are over three times as many drunken drivers on the roads as in England and Wales. All one can conclude from the figures is that the Scots appear to be very much more efficient than the English at detecting and convicting the drunken driver.

The eight English-speaking and four Scandinavian countries showed very much higher correlations between road deaths and offences of drunkenness; by omitting Norway, still higher figures for these correlations were obtained ($r = +0.723$ and $+0.775$ for road deaths correlated with drunkenness and drunken driving, respectively). On the other hand, lower figures were obtained for the correlation between road deaths and cirrhosis deaths when compared with the 26 world states publishing data for this cause of mortality. As already stated, cirrhosis of the liver is not a reliable basis for calculating alcoholism, but so far a more satisfactory method for assessing this disorder has yet to be devised.

The evidence quoted earlier certainly shows that cirrhosis death rates are significantly related to the annual quantity of alcohol consumed and that alcohol taken largely in the form of wine seems to have a more lethal effect in this respect than do other forms of alcoholic beverage. However, the wine-growing countries are reputed to have differing degrees of prevalence of alcoholism, and clearly cirrhosis death rates alone cannot be taken as a useful guide, either to alcoholism or to drunken driving. *Table 1C*, based on data supplied by Efron and Keller (1963), shows a small significant positive correlation between road deaths and alcohol consumption, whereas a very much higher correlation exists between this last variable and deaths from cirrhosis of the liver. Once again these figures suggest that cirrhosis of the liver might well be related to the quality and quantity of alcohol consumed, without necessarily reflecting the extent of alcoholism in the community. The epidemiological data egarding alcoholism and road accidents are neither supported nor refuted by these findings, and the absence of correlation between alcohol consumption and conviction for drunken driving certainly seems to be in keeping with this conclusion.

In the United States, which appears to have the highest incidence of road accidents caused by excessive alcohol, there is, paradoxically, a highly significant negative correlation between road deaths and deaths from cirrhosis of the liver and rates for alcoholism, which are largely derived from the cirrhosis mortality figures. Furthermore, alcohol consumption figures in each state in 1962 (Efron and Keller, 1963) fail to correlate significantly with either road accidents or cirrhosis death rates ($r = -0.190$ and $+0.037$ respectively). Such findings, which conflict wholly with those obtained in the 27 countries, throw serious doubt upon the value of any of the alcohol and alcoholism statistics.

The situation is further aggravated by the Australian findings. Whereas the six states showed a high correlation between convictions for drunken driving and road deaths and injuries, only small, insignificant correlations could be obtained between road mortality, cirrhosis deaths, and convictions for drunkenness. Furthermore, in contrast to all findings obtained elsewhere, cirrhosis deaths bore no relationship to the quantity of alcohol consumed in each state ($r_s = +0.134$). The Report of the Royal Commission into the Sale, Supply, Disposal, and Consumption of Liquor in the State of Victoria (1964) provided figures for road accidents due to alcoholic intoxication in each state. For the years 1955, 1960, and 1963 these could be expressed as a percentage of total road accidents, as shown in the following table:

NSW	Vic.	Qld	SA	WA	Tas.
6·57	2·66	6·60	1·66	2·10	4·23

These figures bore no relationship to cirrhosis deaths (Spearman's $r = -0.028$) but they did show positive correlations with the three road-death and injury rates (Spearman's $r = +0.517$, $+0.486$, $+0.772$).

Once again, the findings suggest that, although deaths from cirrhosis of the liver are not related to road-casualty rates, there is plenty of evidence pointing to the role of alcohol and alcoholism as primary causes of traffic accidents.

In Canada on the other hand, in contrast to the USA, road-death rates correlated positively but not significantly ($r = +0.5172$) with male cirrhosis deaths, and positive but non-significant findings were obtained when road-death rates were correlated with convictions for drunkenness and drunken driving. Bearing in mind the small number of provinces available, it is evident that in these respects Canada more closely resembles the 27 world states than it does the USA.

Faced by these contradictory results, one would be rash indeed to draw more than the most tentative conclusions from a statistical analysis of intercorrelations between rates for cirrhosis deaths, convictions for drunken driving and drunkenness, annual consumption of alcoholic beverages, and road deaths. In all probability, alcoholism as such, which might be predictable from cirrhosis death rates, plays only a small part in the overall drink/driving problem. Gross intemperance of an episodic kind might well be of far greater importance, and if this was the case one would not expect cirrhosis deaths necessarily to correlate with road-death rates. Cirrhosis deaths appear to be too crude and uncertain a measure of excessive drinking in many countries, where other aetiological factors besides alcohol may play a more significant role. On the other hand, the evidence on the contribution of drinking to road accidents can hardly be refuted by the vagaries of statistical analysis. I certainly hoped that such an analysis would have given additional support to this epidemiological data, but it may well be that the measures I have used as indicators of excessive drinking are unsuitable for this purpose.

One further attempt was made to relate statistics of drunkenness and drunken driving to road-death rates, and this was based on figures provided by the individual police forces in England and Wales. Annual convictions for offences of drunkenness are given as absolute figures and as rates per 10,000 of the population, while driving under the influence of liquor or drugs or being in charge of a vehicle while under such influence are listed according to the number of prosecutions or convictions for these offences per 100,000 of the population. The rates for convictions for drunkenness vary from 4 to 120 per 10,000 while prosecution rates for motoring offences involving drink and drugs vary from 8 to 100 per 100,000. Because of the disparity between prosecution and conviction figures it was felt that the former rates for these motoring offences would reflect more accurately the true incidence of this class of behaviour in the individual police districts.

Because of the smallness of county areas, it was decided to concentrate on the more discrete urban centres having separate police forces. In all probability, road deaths and drunkenness offences in the county areas away from the main cities and towns would involve persons in transit on the main trunk roads as well as the local population, resulting in only small variation in rates between county areas. In contrast, it was felt that the indices of alcoholic excess and dangerous driving in the more compact urban areas would more probably reflect the behaviour of the local population. The City of London was omitted, because the very small size of its resident population gives quite deviant figures for the offences of drunkenness and drunken driving. Death rates were calculated for the respective urban areas, and convictions for drunkenness were those recorded for the years 1954–64. The results for 69 urban areas are set out in *Table 5*.

The Pearson correlation coefficient for convictions for offences of drunkenness and road deaths showed a small but significant reading ($r = +0.283$, $t = 2.414$, $df = 67$, $p < .02$). An additional study was carried out on 23 urban areas with high conviction rates for drunkenness (>25 per 10,000), which were compared with 28 urban areas with low conviction rates (<15 per 10,000). These results are set out in *Table 5A*. The comparison between these two sets of data showed a low significant positive finding ($t = 2.215$, $df = 49$, $p < .05$).

It will be noted that certain areas deviate markedly from the expected findings. As far as the towns with high conviction rates are concerned, Tynemouth, Kingston-upon-Hull, Grimsby, and South Shields have very much lower death rates than might have been expected from the figures for drunkenness convictions. The fact that these are all seaports might have something to do with this disparity. In contrast Halifax, Bolton, Leicester, and Huddersfield show low conviction rates for drunkenness but unexpectedly high road-death rates. Probably these deviations reflect local police and court attitudes to drunkenness rather than a genuine difference in the incidence of excessive drinking. In fact, two of the towns with high convictions for drunkenness, Tynemouth and South Shields, come from the same urban complex as Newcastle and Gateshead, both areas where conviction rates and road-death rates are high. It is possible, therefore, that the high conviction rates in Tynemouth and South Shields to some extent reflect policy for the area as a whole, without necessarily implying that these two towns have alcohol problems as great as those existing in Newcastle and Gateshead. I am well acquainted with this area of England, and it is instructive to compare the high conviction rates for the whole Tyneside conurbation with the comparatively low rates, and, for that matter, low road-death rate, in the neighbouring city of Sunderland. Somewhat similar considerations apply to the deviant findings for Halifax and Huddersfield, adjacent areas with low conviction rates for drunkenness but high road-death rates. The neighbouring cities of Leeds and Bradford, on the other hand, have high road-death rates and high conviction rates. It is improbable that the citizens of Huddersfield and Halifax are so very much more sober than those in Bradford and Leeds and, again, one might question whether the differences reflect nothing more than contrasting police and court attitudes.

The problem of police and public attitudes to the various motoring offences has been commented on by Elliott and Street (1968), who contrast the rates of prosecutions for a number of traffic infringements in Liverpool, Manchester, Newcastle, and Stoke-on-Trent. They write: 'It will be seen that to drive or be in charge while unfit is much more likely to result in prosecution in Manchester than in the other three cities. . . . Stoke makes up for a complacent attitude to drunken driving by cracking down on careless drivers.'

In the face of these possible causes of deviations from the expected figures, one could hardly expect differences of major statistical significance. However, if the four deviant urban areas with high drunkenness conviction rates but markedly lower death rates and the four towns with low conviction rates and unexpectedly high road-death rates are removed from these tables, a very different picture emerges, as the difference between the high and low conviction areas becomes far more significant ($t = 5 \cdot 164$, $df = 41$, $p < \cdot 001$).

A further study was carried out on prosecutions for driving or being in charge of a motor vehicle while under the influence of drink or drugs, for the years 1961–5. Pearson correlations between prosecutions for drunken driving and road-death rates in 72 urban areas produced a very low positive figure ($r = +0 \cdot 158$, $t = 1 \cdot 337$, $df = 68$, *NS*). These findings are set out in *Table 5B*.

When 20 areas with high prosecution rates are compared with 22 areas with low prosecution rates, again no significant difference exists between the average road-death rates (*Table 5C*). However, it will be seen from this table that once again a number of cities and towns stand out as markedly deviant from the others in the groups. One can surmise that some overall policy governs the low prosecution rates in the geographically related areas of Dudley, Wolverhampton, and Walsall, and possibly a policy of high prosecution for drunken driving is common to the two Devon cities of Exeter and Plymouth. It may well be that towns and cities with high or low conviction rates, showing grossly 'inappropriate' road-death rates, have other causes for road accidents which far outweigh excessive liquor as an aetiological agent. In fact, although there is a significant correlation between rates of prosecution for impaired driving and convictions for drunkenness ($r = +0.54$, $df = 70$, $t = 5.365$, $p \ll .001$), it is evident that many other variables influence the relationship between these two classes of offence and road-death rates. That such a relation exists is certainly supported by the figures presented, and a further check was provided by contrasting 22 areas with high road-death rates (<12 per 100,000) with 19 areas with low death rates (<8 per 100,000) in respect of their rates for convictions for drunkenness. A statistically significant difference exists between these two groups ($t = 2.67$, $df = 39$, $p < .02$).

The multiplicity and complexity of causes are among the main difficulties in all road-accident research. The finding of low correlations between drunken behaviour and road deaths might have been anticipated from a knowledge of the social and clinical aspects of alcoholism and drinking behaviour. Such low correlations, in fact, emphasize by contrast the more striking associations between aggressive behaviour and road-casualty rates. The more violent a society is seen to be, the less likely would alcohol be to assume a role of importance in the production of death and injuries on the roads. Furthermore, only a small part of the population can be classed as alcoholics or problem drinkers. If it is correct to argue that this section of the public is a more serious hazard on the road, one is still required to find reasons for the high accident and casualty rates for the far larger number of persons who are involved in road-traffic accidents without necessarily showing signs of intoxication. Drunkenness and drunken-driving convictions are more frequently secured on alcoholics than on the average social drinker. In that case, the small correlations between drunkenness and road deaths are all that could be expected, even though such considerations do not in any way explain the wholly inconsistent findings in the United States of America.

REFERENCES

AKMAN, D. D., and NORMANDEAU, A. 1967. The measurement of crime and delinquency in Canada. *Brit. J. Criminol.* **7,** 129–49.

EFRON, V., and KELLER, M. 1963. Selected statistical tables on the consumption of alcohol 1850–1962 and on alcoholism 1930–1960. Rutgers Center of Alcohol Studies, New Jersey.

ELIOT, T. D., and HILLMAN, A. 1960. *Norway's families.* Philadelphia: University of Pennsylvania Press.

ELLIOTT, D. W., and STREET, H. 1968. *Road accidents.* Harmondsworth: Penguin Books.

LUKE, C. M. 1967. Alcohol and road traffic accidents. *N.Z. med. J.* **66,** 847–52.

PARRY, M. H. 1968. *Aggression on the road.* London: Tavistock.

SCHMIDT, W., and BRONETTO, J. 1962. Death from liver cirrhosis and specific alcoholic beverage consumption: an ecological study. *Amer. J. pub. Hlth* **52,** 1473–82.

WALLER, J. A. 1967. Identification of problem drinking among drunken drivers. *J. Amer. med. Assoc.* **200,** 114–20.

ZYLMAN, R. 1968. Accidents, alcohol and single cause explanations. *Quart. J. Stud. Alc.* Suppt 4, p. 212.

10 · Causes, speculations, and criticisms

When a road is once built, it is a strange thing how it collects traffic.

R. L. STEVENSON

Evil deeds are done for the mere desire of occupation.

A. MARCELLINUS, *Historia*, Bk 301

'Intra-specific aggression . . . is found in the vast majority of verte-brates and in many invertebrates. There cannot be any doubt about the important functions it achieves in the interest of the survival of the species' Konrad Lorenz (1964).

The results of this study and the statistical analysis of the data in general terms support the initial hypothesis: that road violence is one aspect of social violence, and that the higher the incidence of such intrasocial aggression becomes, the higher will be the rates for death and injuries on the roads. Needless to say, it is not proposed that the level of aggression in society is the sole explanation of traffic accidents, since numerous other factors, some of which have been discussed, make important contributions to their causation. Among such variables will be included the effects of alcohol, the health of drivers and pedestrians, the mechanical efficiency of vehicles, and the nature of the environment. That all these and many other aspects have to be considered in the context of road safety is not disputed. However, of the purely human variables examined, there can be little doubt that the conspicuous aggressive behaviour of a fair proportion of drivers has the most serious consequences for their own safety and that of the public as a whole. The recognition of this fact is embodied in many an aphorism concerning behaviour on the highway. I was once advised that all vehicle drivers should be suspect as homicidal lunatics, whereas all pedestrians, until the contrary had been proved, were to be regarded as potential suicides. It was salutary to reflect, should this advice be heeded, that in the eyes of others we were all potential sufferers from these disturbances of behaviour. That 'a man in a passion rides a mad horse' may well be true, but there can be little doubt about the risks run by the motorist who drives when in a towering rage. It would be difficult to find a surer road to catastrophe.

In a recent monograph, Parry (1968) examined the effects of aggression and anxiety on accident liability in England. Younger motorists were shown to be the most aggressive and to suffer the most accidents, but, leaving aside the author's cautious conclusions, the work provides some fascinating examples of violent behaviour on the roads. Parry was particularly struck by the disparity between the sweet reasonableness and intelligence of some of the subjects interviewed and their known or admitted aggressive behaviour on the road. One such individual, after detailing his numerous prejudices and dislikes ('I don't like blokes in sports cars either . . . when I see one of them about I give him a warning look and if he tries messing about I hoot him like hell'), went on to admit that he had deliberately attempted to drive another car off the road. Another man described with relish how he had driven his car into the rear of another, whose owner refused to move after stopping in a stream with traffic – an episode which almost ended in blows. Many other similar examples could be quoted, but few of the subjects appreciated the effects of their behaviour on the safety of themselves or others. Only one driver acknowledged that his behaviour deteriorated when he was angry: 'Well, I admit my driving must be a bit worse when I'm in a bad mood . . . I suppose you could say I was less considerate . . . but this is only when I am chasing another driver.' Not all these aggressive drivers were male, for one female quoted seemed to believe that she should prosecute the sex-war on the highway. However, as has been shown in many other studies, the young male driver is peculiarly at risk, a finding largely confirmed by Parry's research.

The current investigations have shown that, of the varieties of violent behaviour examined, violent death and crime accounted for most of the variance in road-death rates in the USA. Surprisingly, suicide, which is considered to be the 'cause' of a number of fatal car smashes, seems not to correlate so significantly with the overall scores of highway fatalities as did some of the other measures of violence. Those other potent causes of road accidents – alcoholism and excessive drinking – when measured by the prevalence of drunkenness, drunken driving, and deaths from hepatic cirrhosis, produced a number of conflicting results when correlated with road leaths, a finding which may be due more to the inadequacy of the statistical data than to any lack of effect of alcohol on driving competence. The 'non-violent' varieties of social disturbance, which correlated well enough with violent death and crime, made little contribution to the indices of road deaths and injuries. Consequently, one is compelled to look more closely at those aspects of human behaviour which are manifested as outbursts of rage ending in physical assault and sometimes death. Why, one might ask, should normally reasonable and considerate human beings behave in this fashion once they get behind the wheel of a car? What are the springs and sources of this combative attitude which is so much better controlled when the subject is going about his affairs on his own two feet? It would certainly be beyond the scope of this study to examine the numerous theories accounting for human aggression, but some recent work on the topic may well prove highly relevant to our inquiry.

There appear to be two main theories about human aggressive behaviour: that it is an innate drive capable of being released by a wide variety of signals and situations; or that it is a learned pattern of behaviour in response to frustration or counter-aggression. Without becoming too involved in an interminable debate between these two conflicting possibilities, it is permissible to argue in favour of a middle course which takes evidence from both sides. Much will depend on the circumstances in which aggressive acts occur, and it would be naïve to equate the small child's fights with his siblings for possession or priority with the complex activities of a criminal gang of thieves. In the first example it is difficult to feel that what a more moralistic but now unfashionable world referred to as 'original sin' was not fully in control. Or, to put things differently, that the child was displaying an innate tendency to grab and retain what he wanted without having been taught the elements of such behaviour. In contrast, the criminal gang show numerous varieties of learned behaviour patterns which essentially are moulded by the social and cultural qualities of the environment. Such a gang could hardly exist unless there was a law-abiding, property-owning society on which it could practise its depredations. That the small child in the first example might later become a member of such a gang is no reason for arguing that the determinants of childish aggression are necessarily the sole or even the main driving forces behind later crimes. If motorized aggression is an essential part of the total violence in society, then one will have to consider not only this violence but also the situations which seem most productive of displays of aggressive behaviour.

In a recent publication, Storr (1968) supports the belief that human aggression is an innate drive which is as essential for human survival as other drives. 'It is probable', he writes, 'that when no outside stimulus for aggression exists, men actually seek such stimuli out in much the same way as they do when sexually deprived.' Intra-specific aggression appears to be a feature of many animal societies, and Storr quotes Wynne-Edwards as saying that a society is 'an organisation capable of providing conventional competition'; and, as Washburn has noted, 'throughout most of human history, society has depended on young adult males to fight and to maintain the social order with violence'. Storr, more specifically, points out that 'the entry of our houses by an unauthorized person is resented . . . the presence of a stranger in the garden is generally regarded as a threat, or at least a circumstance requiring investigation.' This observation may be of more importance when it comes to trying to understand highway aggression. In general, aggressive behaviour is more characteristic of boys than of girls owing to different social expectations. Adolescent aggression may in part be a manifestation of the child's struggle to overcome his dependence upon his parents.

At this stage, it is instructive to compare the behaviour of the motorist when in his car with that same motorist as a pedestrian, or when participating in social activities which, in the nature of things, do not permit the isolation of the participants in powered boxes on wheels. Frustration, it is said, is the breeding ground of aggression; and, whatever else one may say about the public highway, frustration abounds. However, it would be too simple to explain the ubiquitous displays of aggression on the road by arguing that such actions are the natural response to the abysmal stupidity and criminal careless-ness of our fellow-mortals in their cars. After all, anyone who, late for an appointment, tries to walk briskly along a crowded city street, heavy with slow-moving shop-gazers, will not improve his speed of progress if he angrily pushes aside his fellow-citizens, swears at them, or threatens them with physical assault. Yet this is precisely what a number of drivers in their vehicles do when pressed for time. No doubt the isolation imposed by the design of the automobile confers a certain immunity from retaliatory action, but it is unlikely that most fist-shaking motorists give a thought to possible consequences should they encounter the victims of their vituperation in less avoidable circumstances. Mercifully, such confrontations are rare, and when they do occur most of us have the grace to apologize, while secretly bolstering our self-esteem by the belief that our behaviour was fully justified by the folly or negligence of the other person. Yet isolation alone cannot be the whole explanation of these unbridled displays of anger on the road. Such anger may be aroused by the irritating behaviour of other drivers who seem joined in a conspiracy to impede our progress. Overweening impatience is in part a common cause of dangerous driving behaviour, yet a moment's reflection should convince us that however hard we drive in crowded city streets the amount of time saved will be infinitesimal in proportion to the emotional energy expended and the danger caused.

Some years ago a contest was arranged between two cars to be driven across a city area. One driver had to observe all signs, traffic lights, and speed regulations. The other was allowed to ignore all three if he could do so without endangering the lives of other road-users. The law-breaking motorist arrived at his destination just – and only just – ahead of his law-abiding antagonist. It follows, therefore, that our reactions and behaviour on the roads are not determined by rational appreciation of the circumstances. Instead, we appear to be at the mercy of emotional forces which compel us to act as we do, often in total defiance of our best interests and knowledge of our real needs. If this is correct, it becomes essential to inquire into the peculiar circumstances of car-driving that distinguish it from other forms of transport or, for that matter, progress on foot. The owner–driver seems more often to be the offender than the transport driver working for a firm or public corporation. In my experience, the long-distance lorry-driver in England is a professional who appreciates the various hazards, while often showing great consideration towards other traffic. Omnibus drivers may not always show such consideration, but allowances must be made for their need to keep to a time-schedule. Even so, their accident record is good considering the distances driven each year in congested city streets by the average employee of a municipal transport organization. Needless to say, the drivers of locomotives do not challenge each other to races or attempt to 'get ahead' of slower trains; captains of ships do their best to avoid ramming other vessels; and pilots of aircraft would quickly lose their licences or lives if they attempted to touch down ahead of competitors on the runway.

Naturally, considerations of safety loom large as determinants of the behaviour of these individuals. The fact remains that they are required to obey rules which for the most part are most strictly observed. Only a minority own the conveyances under their command and, of course, train-drivers, ships' captains, and air pilots are selected for their tasks only after long periods of training and experience. In contrast, the private car-owner, although bound by a large and ever-growing number of traffic regulations, often seems hell-bent on doing his best to avoid obeying them, an attitude to law which will be justified by appeals to the vocal support provided by his fellow-citizens. There appears to be some quality in car-ownership which compels irrational behaviour and emotional reactions. And here we may find that the patient observations of the ethologists will give us some explanatory clues.

Lorenz (1964) said, 'if we put together into the same container two sticklebacks, lizards, robins, rats, monkeys or boys who have not had any previous experience of each other, they will fight'. Later at the same Symposium, he went on to remark, 'there cannot be any doubt . . . that intra-specific aggression is in man just as much of a spontaneous instinctive drive as in most other higher vertebrates'. This theme was elaborated in a later work (1966), when Lorenz wrote,

> I believe . . . that present day civilized man suffers from insufficient discharge of his aggressive drives. It is more than probable that the evil effects of the human aggressive drive . . . simply derive from the fact that in pre-historic times intra-specific selection bred into man a measure of aggressive drives for which in the social order of today he finds no adequate outlet.

Such instinctive forces, it would seem, are particularly required for the gaining and holding of territory, and Ardrey's views on how this concept can be applied to understand human behaviour have been outlined in two stimulating books (1961, 1967). The degree of intra-specific enmity, he argues, varies inversely with the amount of external threat and danger. In times of war, internal political and social differences disappear in the face of the threat to the homeland. Absence of war leads to too much security, with consequent boredom. The outcome will be crime, drug addiction, and violence in order to achieve self-discovery. The doctrine is a depressing one, in that it implies that our efforts to bring about abolition of war between nations can only result in increased destructiveness and violence within the community. Ardrey wrote (1967),

> we may agree, for example, that our societies must provide greater security for the individual; yet if all we succeed in producing is ... increased anonymity and ever increasing boredom we should not wonder if ingenious man turns to such amusements as drugs, house-breaking, vandalism, mayhem, riots or, at the most harmless, strange haircuts, costumes, standards of cleanliness and sexual experiments.

Fortunately, the existence of aggressive behaviour is not a total disaster. Without it friendship, affection, and morality could scarcely develop, a consequence which is emphasized by the close psychological affinities between love and hate. For, as Lorenz (1966) has shown, the bonds between pairs or groups of certain animals appear to be the counterpart of aggressive behaviour directed towards other members of the species. In the animal kingdom, intra-specific agression occurs most commonly in defence of territory. The invader is invariably driven off, because fighting on its own stamping-ground confers on the defending animal greater energy for attack than would be available if it were on neutral soil. There is no reason to believe that acquisitive, property-owning man is immune from this tendency. In defending his home and family from an intruder, he may summon up qualities of courage and attack that may afterwards surprise him. Rational appreciation of the dangers to be overcome may be in abeyance, while emotional instinctive drives take over the control of his behaviour with far greater efficiency and effect. Is it possible that the average car-owner acts in similar fashion when he finds his vehicle threatened or its progress unjustifiably impeded?

The strong emotional attachment of a man to his motor-car is a common enough phenomenon, and it is not stretching the evidence too far to suggest that many drivers look on their vehicles as pieces of movable real-estate which share with house property the same capacity to arouse anger and aggressive behaviour in their defence. Let it be remembered that many of the aggressive acts of drivers cannot be explained in rational terms. The motorist's determination to surpass other drivers, his manifest rejection of laws and regulations designed to diminish the ill-effects of his egotism, his feeling that he has some inalienable right to unimpeded progress on the highway regardless of the rights and needs of others, all these attitudes and reactions become understandable if one accepts that an owner, once he is behind the wheel of his car, ceases to be a wholly reasonable being. That an Englishman's home is his castle is an adage sanctioned by law. It may also be a reason for our negative attitudes to police officers engaged on traffic control. The police have little or no right of entry into our homes – apart from the right to search for prohibited drugs – but are empowered to stop and search an automobile if they have reason to believe that the driver is breaking the law.[1] Hence arises a conflict between police and public which is less commonly aroused when the more traditional crimes are being investigated. Traffic offences in England and Wales in 1967 constituted 78·1 per cent of convictions for all indictable and non-indictable offences tried before the courts. It is not difficult to deduce that infringement of traffic regulations can hardly be avoided, and that the majority of motorists have scant respect for most of the current enactments regulating highway usage. The design of the automobile to some extent fosters the feeling that house and car are part of each other, an illusion enhanced by making the garage an integral part of the house. Enclosed in his vehicle, the man, his wife, and his children can and do behave towards each other exactly as if they were in the privacy of their home regardless of the fact that they have moved out into the public sector of life. Such behaviour contrasts strongly with the decorum that generally prevails when families are intermingling on the pavements. In the car the presence of household goods or the towing of a caravan increases the illusion of mobile domesticity. Some owners even decorate the interior of their vehicles with curtains and flowers as if to perpetuate the feeling of domestic security; and more expensive cars are equipped with air-conditioning and cocktail cabinets. The presence of the family is also liable to increase the emotional heat should some altercation or accident occur. In such circumstances the sanctity of the home has been attacked and, understandably, counter-attack becomes the order of the day. We do not expect other persons to invade our houses and gardens, for we assume that their boundaries will remain inviolate. If we transfer such expectations to our cars, we will certainly encounter some sharp disappointments with, in most instances,

---

[1] Desmond Morris (1968) has shown how recognition of the 'territorial' aspects of the motor vehicle could be used, in conjunction with appeasement gestures, to mollify the attitudes of police officers who were about to reprimand the driver for minor traffic offences.

emotional reactions resembling those aroused when what we regard as inalienable human rights have been infringed.

Motor manufacturers, of course, have been quick to seize on pride of ownership as a basis for advertising and selling their goods. As Western society develops, with more persons owning cars compared with the number of freeholders of house property, one can contemplate with some alarm the likely trend of aggression which, no longer of service in defence of the individual's home, now comes into action in furtherance of the driver's sense of property rights. There can be little doubt that, as car-ownership has become more general, the incidence of serious accidents has correspondingly risen. It is improbable that this rise could be accounted for solely in terms of the number of vehicles and the congestion of the roads. Indeed, in many countries, road-death rates were higher in the 1930s than in the 1950s when far more vehicles were on the highway. Let it be recalled again that the young men in Western society have the highest casualty rates on the road. Young men have the strongest aggressive drives, but in general they do not own real-estate. On the other hand, a good many own cars of various vintages to which a quite irrational degree of attachment is often shown. Macfarland and Moore (1960) have commented on the symbolic value of the automobile to adolescent and young adult males. The car is no longer a means of transport; it has become a symbol of power and prestige, a part of one's territory to be defended by aggressive displays whenever its integrity is threatened or breached; it can even become a double bed.

These speculations, of course, rest on the unproven assumption that the ethological concept of territorial behaviour applies equally to man and to other animals. Such a theory at least makes sense of some apparently wholly irrational behaviour on the roads, but admittedly it is difficult to test its truth. Furthermore, it would be unwise to assume that such an explanation excludes other psychological theories partly accounting for the prevalence of traffic accidents. These will require additional consideration, but beforehand it will be worth inquiring into the possibility of critical investigations to support or refute the ethological exposition outlined in the previous pages.

Ardrey stressed the role of external enmity as a generator of internal concord. If this view is correct, one might anticipate a decline in violent crime, death by suicide and homicide, and road

K

casualties during full-scale international wars. In fact, this is precisely what occurred during the Second World War, as the graphs in Appendix II show (*Figures 2C, 3A, 3B, 4A, 5*). In Australia in the years 1939 to 1945, road deaths dropped sharply, and there was an accompanying decline in the suicide and homicide rates. New Zealand showed a similar fall in road deaths, but changes in the suicide and homicide rates were not particularly striking. In Great Britain, road-death rates rose sharply during the first 18 months of the war, only to decline until well after the end of hostilities. This initial rise was largely due to blackout conditions that greatly increased the hazards of the roads at night, particularly for pedestrians who contributed predominantly to the increase of road deaths during this part of the war (Ministry of Transport, 1941). Suicide rates fell between 1939 and 1945, to rise again to around 10 to 12 per 100,000 thereafter. Canadian figures are similar to those for New Zealand, but the most striking changes occurred in the United States. Admittedly, homicide and suicide rates were falling steadily well before the entry of the United States into the war in late 1941. They continued to fall during the war, and increased again in 1945. The violent-crime rates were also falling before 1941, but rose sharply after 1944. The rates for violent crime for the years 1931 to 1956 are not comparable with those from 1957 onwards. Road deaths per 100,000 showed the expected drop during the war, but were unaffected by the Korean War between 1950 and 1953. Many explanations can be found for these findings. A considerable number of the young men who would normally swell the road-death and crime statistics were engaged in the armed forces on aggressive activities of a socially approved nature. Concentration on production for the armed forces meant fewer motor vehicles, tyres, and fuel for the civilian population. However, the number of military vehicles on the roads presumably increased as private civilian transport declined. Shortage of fuel leading to fewer vehicle-miles travelled could certainly account for the falls in road deaths in Great Britain, Australia, and New Zealand but this would hardly explain the similar changes in the United States and Canada. Suicide is predominantly an act of older persons who would not be absent on overseas service. The falls in suicide rates seen during large-scale international wars could be due to removal of that proportion of younger men who might otherwise have taken their lives in their homelands. It is doubtful whether such an explanation is adequate to account for the phenomenon, since, even in countries not directly involved in the two world wars, suicide rates were also lowered (see Dublin, 1963). The effect of war on mental health, which is improved by the closer bond of comradeship and greater sense of purpose despite the stresses and strains of war, will almost certainly influence the rates of suicide resulting from severe psychiatric disorder. Nevertheless when suicide, homicide, violent crime, and road-death rates are taken in conjunction, it is remarkable that these fall during wartime only to rise sharply once hostilities have ended. Such a finding is quite in keeping with the ethological concepts of territory and intra-specific aggression, even though one could hardly claim that these alone are sufficient causes of the observed changes.

If the transfer to the automobile of some of the drives normally devoted to acquisition and protection of property is a partial explanation of aggressive behaviour on the road, one might expect that car-owners who otherwise have little in the way of possessions, land, or property would, other things being equal, have higher accident rates. Such a hypothesis could be tested by an adequately controlled survey, bearing in mind that age rather than any other variable may have most to do with the ownership of property. Even so, young men, who do not normally own houses or land, have the highest road-death rates. Socio-economic class has been shown to influence road-accident and casualty rates and, once again, members of the lower social groups are less likely to own their own homes. An attempt was made to estimate the extent of house-ownership in the United States in the hope that this might show some significant negative correlation with road-death rates. Unfortunately, property-ownership is too vague a concept to be used in this connection, but a significant correlation was obtained between the percentage of persons living in *rented*, as opposed to owner-occupied, properties in the 48 states of the United States of America and the road-death rates, provided Rhode Island and New York were omitted ($r = +0.403$, $df = 44$, $p < .01$). For reasons unknown, to me, these two states have markedly deviant numbers of persons in tenanted properties, but elsewhere the trend was very much in keeping with the underlying hypothesis. A further test in the United States showed that the proportion of tenant-farmers compared with owner-farmers in the 48 states correlated significantly with road-death rates ($r = +0.396$, $df = 46$, $p < .01$). Such findings, of course, are open to more than one interpretation, since a significant correlation does not necessarily imply a causal connection, but some support comes from statistics for Australia for the years 1960 to 1964. Here it was found that the road-death and injury rates per 100 million vehicle-miles correlated negatively with the number of rural holdings per thousand of the population and the number of persons living on farm properties; positively with the number of new motor vehicles purchased per 10,000 persons, the ratio of vehicles to population, and the revenue obtained from motor-vehicle taxation; and negatively with the ratio of expenditure on new homes to motor-vehicle tax revenue. These last two items showed the most consistent correlation with the three indices of road deaths but, because of the small number of states, few of the findings were statistically significant. Nevertheless, the trend was suggestive without giving more than tentative support to the ethological hypothesis.

The other main theory of human aggression, which centres on the response to frustration, may not be wholly opposed to the ethological theory. Lorenz (1964) has pointed out that intra-specific fighting over territory rarely leads to serious death or injury of the participants unless overcrowding in artificial circumstances occurs. The resulting combats can then become lethal. As far as the human species is concerned, Iskrant and Joliet (1968) have quoted studies showing that high homicide rates are associated with densely populated parts of cities in the United States. This, of course, may merely reflect racial and socio-economic factors which are more responsible for these differences than the housing situation. It would be difficult to assess the effects of road congestion on accident and casualty rates, but clearly there is no simple relationship between these variables. Countries such as the Netherlands and Great Britain, with high traffic densities, have fairly moderate road-death rates, whereas in countries such as Australia, Finland, and the United States, with low traffic densities, road-death rates are high. It is impossible to make deductions from the traffic-density rates for whole countries because the figures fail to differentiate between urban and rural areas. Even so, there is no evidence from Great Britain that the largest and, presumably, the most congested towns and cities have the highest road-death and casualty figures. In Australia, where many country roads are bad and the distances travelled are great, the effects of these variables in conjunction with fatigue have to be taken into account as contributory causes of road accidents in country areas. On such roads single-vehicle accidents are fairly common and, once again, the effects of fatigue, alcohol, and speeds unsuitable for poorly constructed roads are probably all important factors. Frustration on the road can occur in the country as well as in the town, and anyone in Great Britain who has travelled by car in the southwest part of the country at the height of the summer holiday season will willingly testify to this statement. It is improbable that frustration is entirely, or even predominantly, a response to overcrowding on the roads, for everyday experience should convince most motorists that maximum irritation can be engendered by driving behind a slow or erratic driver on twisty but otherwise empty country roads.

Further support for the belief that aggressive impulses are partly responsible for road casualties comes from the United States, where accidents occurring in the years 1959 to 1961 have been analysed by Iskrant and Joliet (1968). Prior to settlement of the United States by Europeans, fighting in defence, or for the acquisition, of territory was endemic among the Indian tribes. This inter-tribal aggression ultimately had to cease, and among the possible consequences are the high rates among American Indians for accidental deaths in general and for motor-vehicle and firearm accidents in particular. I have calculated the percentage of American Indians in each state and compared those twelve with the highest proportions in the population with the ten containing the lowest proportions. There were no significant differences between these two groups for the rates of suicide and homicide. On the other hand, deaths as a result of shooting accidents and motor-vehicle accidents were more frequent in the states with the higher percentage of American Indians in the population ($t = 2.889, df = 20, p < .01$; $t = 2.434, df = 20, p < .05$). States with high Negro populations had significantly higher homicide rates but lower suicide rates ($t = 12.123, df = 20, p < .001$; $t = 2.258, df = 20, p < .02$), but there were no significant differences between states with high and low Negro populations for fatal shooting accidents.

Accidental death from gun-fire is to say the least a somewhat equivocal verdict, and, whereas in the United States there is a significant correlation between road deaths per 100 million vehicle-miles and all other forms of accidental death ($r = +0.543, p < .001$), the correlation is very much higher for accidental deaths from fire-arms ($r = +0.779, p < .001$). In a country where all adults have a constitutional right to own firearms in defence of hearth and home, it may well be that this prerogative for aggression sometimes spills out onto the highway with the disastrous consequence of 52,000 deaths in 1967.

It would be erroneous to insist that territorial aggression is the sole cause of angry displays on the road. From the points of view of the moralist and the theologian ordinary human selfishness no doubt plays a part, as two clerical writers have pointed out (Waterson, 1961; Tymms, 1968). Furthermore, if as Lorenz has suggested, the human race has a need to engage in aggressive behaviour, one could have anticipated that the mass production of fast, potentially lethal motor vehicles would rapidly lead to their being used for displays of violence. A number of authors have remarked on the disparity between an individual's attitudes and manners in a motor vehicle with the same characteristics in other circumstances. Whether the man behind the wheel is acting as he normally does, or in a wholly unpredictable fashion, will depend largely on his personality qualities. Tillman and Hobbs (1949) believe that 'a man drives as he lives', but this conclusion may have resulted from an examination of a particular group of drivers with notable sociopathic traits. Parry (1968), on the other hand, seemed to feel that a man drove as he would *like* to live, a supposition which is more appropriate for the average motorist who has fewer opportunities for aggressive behaviour at home or at work. Undoubtedly the abnormal sociopathic or paranoid personalities make notable contributions to road-accident statistics, but the average driver will not show these traits to any great extent. Consequently, the 'territorial' explanation of road behaviour may have greater applicability to the average, psychologically normal driver compared with the aggressive sociopath whose angry feelings are unleashed in a wide variety of situations.

The relationship between criminal behaviour, convictions for drunkenness, alcoholism, and road accidents would not contradict the hypothesis that aggressive behaviour in an automobile is a response to a feeling for territorial rights. However, alcoholism and crime are more likely to be complications of unfortunate or undesirable qualities of character conducing to aggressive behaviour that will occur more readily after liquor has been consumed. Alcohol probably releases suicidal and paranoid tendencies as well, for both these behavioural attributes are often observed in alcoholics. If this is the case, it would be reasonable to presume that the drunken driver would become more dangerous in proportion to the degree of hostile or suicidal ideation present at the time.

A good deal has been written about the sexual symbolism of the automobile and some manufacturers appear to make use of this theme in their advertisements. Indeed, at times it is not easy to be certain whether the girl in the picture will be thrown in for good measure if only one will buy the car. Other advertisements hint that virile displays of mastery over a powerful vehicle will have the most gratifying effect upon the (male) driver's girl friend. Nevertheless, there can be no certainty over the symbolism of the automobile. Whether its shape is interpreted as a bullet or a phallus will depend more on the observer's state of mind than on any testable objective fact. Furthermore, the gender of the sex symbol to be applied is also in doubt; I recall an article portraying the American male eternally polishing and massaging the flanks of his car, an erotic activity denied to him by his cold and unsympathetic wife.

Perhaps rather closer to this thesis is the problem of rape, an offence which in Australia, at least, seems to require the use of a motor vehicle for its successful accomplishment. Here sex, violence, the automobile and, frequently enough, alcohol, all act in concert by leading to pack rapes of solitary girls by gangs of youths in a car, or assaults by solitary males carried out when the girl has been removed from any sources of help. In a recent study (Wilson, 1968) of 248 instances of rape, a motor vehicle was used as an adjunct to the offence in 71 per cent of cases.

Ardrey (1961) made the point that in the animal kingdom the female is attracted to the male, not always by his sexual allure, but more by his possession of a piece of real-estate/territory. The automobile may well serve the human being in similar fashion: possession and control first, sex afterwards. The aggressive significance of the automobile has been stressed more often than its sexual aspects, a fact emphasized by Packard (1964) when he quoted a number of authors who believe that many people liked to drive high-powered fast cars to let off aggressive impulses. Certainly motor manufacturers appear to have a predisposition to naming their products after the swiftest and/or most ferocious animals or birds. Hawks, Falcons, Panthers, Jaguars, and Gazelles make their annual contribution to road accidents. Javelins, Arrows, Rebels, and Valiants epitomize the more human aspects of aggression; and nobody, to my knowledge, has suggested that you should put a terrier in your tank. The status significance of automobiles seems to have more to do with territorial behaviour in the social order than with sexuality (see Packard, 1962), another fact which is again stressed by advertisers wishing to promote the snob appeal of their wares. Here one strikes against some of the less attractive aspects of mankind – social climbing, sex superiority, and racism. All can be regarded as partial consequences of territorial behaviour, while all are evoked too frequently by the complexities and frustrations of road traffic. Depending upon one's particular tastes, persons on the highway who irritate, impede, or threaten are women, Jews, wogs, psychopaths, or individuals who in the driver's opinion have little right to be on the road and even less to own a car. These stereotypes are invoked and vilified when aggressive feelings are aroused, and it is noteworthy that membership of an 'out-group' is often ascribed to the sources of our annoyance. One is reminded of Howler monkeys hurling abuse at their neighbours when engaged in protecting their territorial boundaries.

It is, of course, difficult to place too much reliance upon the subjective interpretations of a person's behaviour when choosing a car, and whether a convertible is really an idealized mistress while the sedan represents respectable marriage is a matter for conjecture, the truth of which would be difficult to establish since we often respond to psychological probing in accordance with the expectations of the investigator. Sex and aggression are sufficiently closely interlinked to make too much separation impracticable. Nevertheless it would be difficult to indict sex alone as a significant contributor to reckless driving and automobile accidents.

In summary, it has been argued that strong aggressive impulses underlie a good deal of dangerous and inconsiderate behaviour on the roads. However, before this opinion is accepted too readily, some critical examination of data is clearly required. In the following paragraphs I have attempted to assess the quality of the observations and the inferences drawn from them.

Some attention has already been given in an earlier chapter to the validity of the statistical data. One can only reiterate that official figures for the different classes of violent death are not wholly accurate while, at the same time, taking note of the observed significant intercorrelations. It is probably justifiable to assume that the more accurate and homogeneous statistical information from the USA to some extent makes up for the less reliable data from the other 26 countries. The fact that the findings in the USA and the 26 world states were broadly in agreement seems to indicate that, whatever statistical shortcomings there might be, within these limits they are reliable enough to provide support for my general thesis. On the other hand criminal statistics are notoriously unsatisfactory guides to the true prevalence of crime in a society. The fact that I have limited this part of the study to four serious offences involving violence at least makes it more likely that the official figures will be closer to the truth than would be the case if I had included all types of crime. For obvious reasons a large number of motoring offences, minor assaults, and petty thieving occur undetected and unreported. Even so, homicide can be concealed and, no doubt, some instances of rape, robbery, and serious assault may not come to the notice of the police. I would not, therefore, wish to make too much of the positive correlations between violent crime and road-death rates, but once again one can justifiably point to the United States findings and note that they support similar findings elsewhere.

The selection of countries and the years chosen for the collection of statistics might have led to results that would not be repeated should other countries at different time periods be chosen. However, as already pointed out, my choice was largely decided by the availability of statistical data and relatively stable conditions within the various communities. Possibly the figures for England and Wales, Scotland, and Northern Ireland should have been presented under one heading, that of the United Kingdom, but a reduction by two of the number of world states does not appear seriously to affect the findings. The greater values for intercorrelations in the USA are partly due to the larger number of states and may, of course, reflect social conditions in that country, which cannot be strictly applied to others. Certainly the less positive findings in Canada and Australia would support such a criticism but, as already shown, the 10 Canadian provinces are probably not comparable so far as road-death rates are concerned, owing to major differences in terrain and climate. In Australia the greater homogeneity of the population and similarity of terrain and climate in the five mainland states almost certainly tend to minimize differences, whereas in the USA, with far greater variety and 48 states, one might anticipate that some of the difficulties noted in Canada would cancel each other out.

If one accepts that the statistical data are sufficiently reliable to permit conclusions to be drawn from them, one is still faced by the problem of assessing the validity of these conclusions. Indubitably it would be desirable to carry out longitudinal studies comparing violent-death rates over periods of 30–40 years in as many countries as possible. One might then discover that the findings based on the years 1955, 1960, and 1964 are not truly representative of trends developing over a number of decades. Certainly it could be argued that rising road-death rates are strongly related to increasing numbers of motor vehicles, but this cannot be the whole explanation, since in a number of countries road-death rates were higher or, at least, as high in the early parts of the 1930s than they were in the 1950s when far more vehicles were on the road. In Great Britain, New Zealand, and the USA, as *Figures 5, 3B, 2C* show, road deaths were higher in the 1930s, and in Switzerland the road-death rate in 1930–4 (17·6 per 100,000) was only a little lower than it was in 1950–4 (20·3 per 100,000). In the meantime the number of motor vehicles on the roads had increased by more than threefold. Similar findings can be discovered in a number of other European countries. On the other hand, Canada and Australia both show steadily rising death rates over a period of 35 years. Possibly the geographical size of these countries may have something to do with the road-death rates that contrast markedly with those found in some of the smaller and more crowded European states.

Inevitably, as car-ownership has come within the reach of more and more members of the public greater numbers of young persons and emotionally disturbed individuals – including heavy drinkers, alcoholics, and aggressive psychopaths – have obtained possession of instruments ideally suited for the expression of inner violent feelings. Such an observation does not explain *why* some members of society drive dangerously or aggressively; it only points to the means whereby this can be accomplished more frequently and at less cost.

Are societies becoming more violent and showing this violence in a number of ways, or is it possible that greater exposure to violence on the roads has led to an overall blunting of feelings with, consequently, a greater readiness to express aggression in other ways? If this was true, one might expect that countries showing low levels of social violence would become more violent as car-ownership has increased. Fortunately, such a disturbing conclusion is not adequately supported by the evidence. Countries like Great Britain, the Republic of Ireland, Norway, and the Netherlands – generally regarded as having stable and socially pacific populations – seem not to be showing more social violence over a period of two decades during which the use of the motor vehicle has increased enormously.

Another factor of obvious importance is the role of alcohol. The figures provided by the Produktschap voor Gedistilleerde Dranken (1969) show that in all the 27 countries studied there have been increases in the per capita annual consumption of alcoholic beverages between the years 1950 and 1966. The rise has been least in France and Portugal and greatest in Austria and East and West Germany, with most countries showing a 50 per cent increase during the 17-year period. At the same time in all these countries there have been very large increases in the numbers of motor vehicles on the roads. Small significant correlations can be found between the two measures of road deaths in the 27 states and the quantity of alcohol consumed by each adult in these states in 1960 ($r = +0.407$, $p < .05$, $r = +0.455$, $p < .05$). There can be no doubt that increasing use of the motor vehicle has resulted in greater numbers of drunken drivers and more accidents caused by excessive drinking. However, excessive alcohol is well known to have a strong capacity for unleashing aggressive behaviour. Consequently, although alcohol is a factor in rising road-death rates – partly due to its effect on judgement, perception, and reaction time – the role of aggression as a major contributor to road accidents is not thereby diminished.

Possibly some hidden variable, more basic to these phenomena, is the real 'cause' of all the forms of violent behaviour in society. It is customary to look at the effect of war and revolution, social unrest, the decline of organized religion, and changes in the parental role and then claim that these are the 'causes' of current social problems. Unfortunately, these are difficult variables to measure in statistical terms. Although the various classes of violent and non-violent social pathology tend to intercorrelate positively and significantly – and all at one time or another have been 'explained' in terms of declining moral standards, increased affluence, and general unrest – it has to be remembered that for the most part road deaths correlated only with violent and not with non-violent behaviour. The statistical analysis of the USA data shows this in a more convincing manner than do the simple intercorrelations provided by all other countries, and so, whatever hidden cause might be responsible, one is still faced by the apparent relationship of road-death rates to other forms of social violence.

The territorial-defence theory of aggression on the roads may not be the sole reason for this class of behaviour but, at present, it seems to account for most of the facts, including the markedly irrational nature of so much dangerous and aggressive driving. Nevertheless, more intensive studies might well lead to a better understanding of the origins of this violence, which may then need to be stated in other terms. That some individuals appear to be more pugnacious and have less control of their angry feelings than others is all too well known. Whether this fact is to be explained in terms of neurophysiology, social and cultural influences, or the effects of upbringing is not known, but it is pertinent to note that outward manifestations of violence are more commonly seen in, and condoned by, those in the lower socio-economic classes – that is, those with the least reason to be satisfied with their position in the hierarchy of territorial ownership.

In summary, it seems justifiable to argue that aggressive drive, possibly representing innate feelings for territorial rights, underlies a good deal of dangerous and inconsiderate behaviour on the roads. At first sight it might appear that such behaviour is but an example of the aggressiveness of the young let loose on the highway in 'control' of powerful instruments well suited to expressing these drives. This may well be the case with a small group of sociopaths who, drunk or sober, frustrated or bored, behave violently and selfishly with small provocation. As an explanation of the aggressive behaviour of the large number of apparently normal motorists it is scarcely adequate. The majority of men and women show reasonable consideration towards other persons in most social situations. In our homes the cultural customs require restraint and courtesy towards visitors, while the visitor who obeys the rules refrains from asserting himself or interfering with his host's prerogatives. Should he fail to act in this way he will rapidly become a most unwelcome guest. However, on the highway we act very differently, looking on the majority of road-users as rivals for precedence or impeders of our rightful progress. We resent the rules that curb what we feel to be our natural right of place and ownership. Aggression in defence of territory makes sense of much of this unusual and dangerous behaviour, for the strength of the drive is more than enough to overcome rational restraint. As an explanatory hypothesis accounting for aggressive behaviour on the road, it covers a number of facts, which otherwise remain inexplicable. Some epidemiological and ecological findings could be interpreted as supporting this theory, but certainly this requires verification by more exact investigations designed to discover the extent and form of territorial aggression in man. In the meantime

t is appropriate to take note of this as a possible cause of road
accidents, so that we may decide what should be done to minimize
their occurrence.

REFERENCES

ARDREY, R. 1961. *African genesis.* London: Collins.
—— 1967. *The territorial imperative.* London: Collins.
DUBLIN, L. I. 1963. *Suicide.* New York: Ronald Press.
ISKRANT, A. P., and JOLIET, P. V. 1968. *Accidents and homicide.*
   Cambridge, Mass.: Harvard University Press.
LORENZ, K. 1964. In Carthy, J. D., and Ebling, F. J. (eds): *The
   natural history of aggression.* London: Academic Press.
—— 1966. *On aggression.* London: Methuen.
MACFARLAND, R. A., and MOORE, R. C. 1960. *Youth and the
   automobile.* Golden Anniversary White House Conference on
   Children and Youth Inc.
MORRIS, D. 1968. *The naked ape.* London: Corgi Books.
PACKARD, V. 1962. *The status seekers.* Harmondsworth: Penguin
   Books.
—— 1964. *The hidden persuaders.* Harmondsworth: Penguin Books.
PARRY, M. H. 1968. *Aggression on the road.* London: Tavistock.
PRODUKTSCHAP VOOR GEDISTILLEERDE DRANKEN 1969. How
   many alcoholic beverages are being consumed throughout the
   world? Schiedam–Nederland.
STORR, A. 1968. *Human aggression.* Harmondsworth: Penguin
   Books.
TILLMAN, W. A., and HOBBS, G. E. 1949. The accident prone auto-
   mobile driver. *Amer. J. Psychiat.* **106,** 321–31.
TYMMS, W. W. 1968. The seven deadly sins of the road. *St Peter's
   Church Parish Magazine.* Stockton on Tees.
WATERSON, J. H. L. 1961. Religion and road safety. *Theology* **64,**
   228–33, 271–4.
WILSON, P. 1968. Rape in Australia. Personal communication.

11 · Accidents: prevention or cure?

There are few ways in which a man may be more innocently employed than in getting money.
SAMUEL JOHNSON

Violence, as we have seen, can produce only the effects of violence . . . where violence is used for a long period, a habit of violence is formed, and it becomes exceedingly difficult for the perpetrators of violence to reverse their policy.
ALDOUS HUXLEY, *Ends and Means*

Well, some people talk of morality, and some of religion, but give me a little, snug property.
MARIA EDGEWORTH

To avoid casualties we must prevent accidents. So far we appear to have been singularly ineffective in escaping either; and the reasons for our incapacity are multifariously stated according to the preconceptions and preoccupations of the individual writers. This monograph is concerned with violence on the road and elsewhere. Consequently, the lessening of violence in society or its diversion into less destructive channels of expression appears to be the obvious way of reducing the road-casualty and accident rates. Such a policy may appear Utopian, and clearly is but one contribution to lower road-accident rates. It should not be presumed that I am unaware of the numerous other factors that could promote road safety. Hence it might be as well to discuss some of these briefly before proceeding to the closer examination of the more urgent problem of human aggression.

Physicians in general, and surgeons in particular, have devoted a good deal of thought to the repair of road-accident victims. Indeed, one particular reason why traffic deaths are not higher is the competence of surgical treatment of injuries which in the past would have proved fatal. That a number of those saved go on to lead lives crippled by physical and mental damage is an aspect of this medical expertise which is not our immediate concern. Patching up the victims of accidents, although essential, is a second-best procedure, but probably all that can be offered in the absence of planned public health measures designed to avoid the deaths and injuries which occupy ever-increasing amounts of surgical time and beds. Attempts at prevention have in some countries led to legislation making obligatory the wearing of crash helmets by motor-cyclists and the fitting of seat belts in all motor vehicles. The evidence that both these devices save lives is overwhelming, but it is difficult to convince some drivers that in their own interests they should make use of them. Specious excuses are offered; single instances of seat-belt injuries are quoted as reasons for rejection of their use; and, as a result, safety devices of this kind are not yet standard pieces of equipment on the majority of motor vehicles. Most motoring correspondents include in their reviews of new cars some comments on their safety. With monotonous regularity they note the absence of seat belts, a criticism that seems to exercise little influence on governments or manufacturers. Morgan (1967) recently investigated the use of seat belts in the United States. One-third of all car-owners had vehicles with belts, but of this group practically one-quarter never used them and only one-third used them all the time. The higher the educational level of the motorist the more likely was he to use belts. Families who had saved money, who were protected by medical insurance schemes, and who had been vaccinated against poliomyelitis used belts more often, as did persons in the higher-income groups. These families not only appeared to be more safety-conscious but had also a more rational appreciation of the value of public-health measures. Age, interestingly, was not a factor differentiating the user from the non-user.

One obvious answer to this situation lies in the hands of the insurance companies. Lower premiums for those owning cars with seat belts, and lower benefits for those without them or those involved in accidents when not wearing seat belts already available, should rapidly lead to their more widespread use. There may be technical objections to such measures, for they are certainly not universal features of car-insurance policies. Similar considerations apply to the motor-cyclist who refuses to wear a crash helmet. In the United States there is a rising accident toll of young motor-cyclists (see Dillehurst *et al.*, 1966, and the American Medical Association's

Committee on Medical Aspects of Road Safety, 1968). One can safely assume that a considerable proportion of those killed received serious head injuries which could have been prevented had safety helmets been worn.

Medical writers have given some attention to the prevention of accidents caused by sudden physical illnesses affecting drivers. Regular medical check-ups, particularly of older motorists, would, it is held, reduce the frequency of such accidents. In fact, as was shown earlier, fatal accidents caused by sudden loss of consciousness of the driver are remarkably uncommon. In all countries studied the epileptic is already prohibited from driving unless his attacks are particularly well controlled, so leaving the patient suffering from cardiovascular disease as the one most liable to sudden illness from coronary thrombosis or cerebral haemorrhage. The recommendation that regular medical examination should be a condition for holding a driving licence rests on the unfounded assumption that current techniques are sufficient to detect the patients most at risk. Few things are more notoriously unpredictable than a sudden change for the worse in a person's health. If that is the case, there would be little point in subjecting all motorists to regular clinical testing, which in any case could end by being perfunctory or open to abuse. Repeated, thorough examination of healthy subjects is a frustrating and boring task because the clinical examination is devised largely to confirm or refute the diagnosis made from the patient's history. If the patient claims that his health is satisfactory, any minor anomalies found on routine investigation will not necessarily point to significant pathology. Finally, the medical examination for fitness to drive would almost certainly fail to detect the alcoholic, the drug-dependent, and the aggressive psychopath; and, let it be remembered, it is the healthier section of the population, the young adult males, who provide the highest accident figures.

We have yet to devise techniques that can permit us with any certitude to predict a man's behaviour when he gets into his car. Psychiatrists are busy enough with the unending problems of frank mental illness without having their time taken up by the detection of suspected sociopaths. It is, in any case, for society to make up its mind about who should or should not drive and, since trial, conviction, and disposal of social misfits by psychiatrists are mercifully still a long way off, the onus for detecting these problem drivers cannot be placed on the shoulders of the medical profession. In the meantime it looks as if the individual with traits constituting a real menace to the motoring and pedestrian public will continue to drive unimpeded by the results of medical and psychological tests.

Turning to the engineering side of accident prevention, it is fairly obvious that roads and vehicles can be made safer. Ergonomists have provided some useful contributions to our understanding of the layout of vehicle controls, driver visibility, and the design of roads and road 'furniture'. Anyone who has driven in a number of different countries will appreciate the clarity and legibility of the directions and signs on the major roads of Britain and the USA. However, in Australia far too many signs are placed in the wrong position, at the wrong height, or phrased in such a way that the motorist can only with difficulty grasp their meaning. Poor road surfaces, camber, and width are other features too well known to require detailed comment. Night-driving in indifferent weather, headlight dazzle, the chaotic perceptions induced by variable street lighting, neon signs, and the glare of over-bright brake lights and traffic indicators, are all fruitful sources of inappropriate responses resulting from the confusion and irritability of the driver. Even so, bad roads, inadequate street lighting, and conflicting signs are no excuse for indifferent driving. Many motorists claim that poor conditions 'caused' their accidents, without seeming to be aware of their duty to drive within the limits set by the environment. Inexperience and poor car design can, on occasion, explain a sudden disaster such as skidding or overturning due to excessive speed. However, driving under hazardous conditions should result in greater caution. The driver who notes the poor road, the shoddy surface, and the limitations in visibility, yet fails to take the appropriate defensive measures, has only himself to blame if he comes to grief.

Regular mechanical inspection of vehicles has been proposed as one way of reducing road-accident rates. Such inspections were introduced in Great Britain in 1960 without apparently causing any significant drop in accident rates in the ensuing years. This may be partly due to the infrequency with which accidents are caused by sudden mechanical failure of the vehicle. Such accidents undoubtedly do occur, but they seem not to be major causes of road fatalities. Unfortunately the Ministry of Transport Annual Road Accident Reports do not analyse accidents by cause but one Report (1963) noted that 'the results of the vehicle-testing scheme cannot be evaluated in precise terms'.

L

Buxbaum and Colton (1966) in the United States found a significant difference between traffic-death rates for men aged 45 to 54 in states which insisted on one or two vehicle inspections each year compared with states where mechanical inspection was not compulsory. United States figures have been commented upon in the *Lancet* (Editorial column, 1967), where it was pointed out that when adjustments had been made for a number of variables – including the age of car and driver – the reduction in accidents and casualties in the states making regular inspections fell by 5–10 per cent. It was estimated that a national annual inspection would cost the United States motorist between \$210,000,000 and \$280,000,000 each year. A 5 per cent fall in accident rates would save about \$325,000,000. It is of course very difficult to measure human death and injury in purely financial terms and presumably the saving would not be confined solely to the cost of human trauma. From the point of view of those involved in accident prevention any measure that will reduce annually increasing death and injury rates will be welcomed, but it could be argued that compulsory annual vehicle inspections make only a marginal contribution towards lowered accident rates. Needless to say, nobody would question the need for regular servicing and maintenance of motor vehicles and quite obviously many car-owners ensure that such work is regularly carried out. Unfortunately the young, sociopathic driver may not only own an older, less road-worthy vehicle but he is less likely to have either the inclination or the money to maintain it properly. Once again one is faced by the problem of how far government should go in penalizing the law-abiding, responsible motorist in order to prevent the irresponsible law-breaker from killing himself or others on the roads.

On one other point medical opinion has been reasonably unanimous – the role of alcohol in the causation of road accidents. The overwhelming evidence showing the relationship between the excessive consumption of liquor and the incidence of traffic accidents, often of a particular, readily identifiable kind, should point the way to methods of control. Some countries, such as Sweden and East Germany, make it an offence to drive whenever *any* alcohol, no matter how little, has been taken. Other countries have set limits to the amount the motorist can drink while still presumed to remain reasonably competent to drive. However, whenever restrictions have been imposed their inception has been bitterly resisted and regularly flouted. Here one seems to be touching on the territorial concepts of car-driving and ownership. In the privacy of our homes we can drink to our heart's content. It is fairly obvious that many drivers feel that they can do likewise in the privacy of their cars, with consequent resentment towards law and police when the 'liberty of the individual' is infringed. It is a curious fact that lawyers whom one might suppose capable of seeing the truth and value of curbing the drinking motorist spend a good deal of time and ingenuity trying to protect his 'rights' or secure his acquittal, often in the face of incontrovertible evidence that their clients were 'drunk as lords'. Fortunately, government is not entirely in the hands of lawyers, and some countries have been resolute enough to insist on sobriety when driving. In Great Britain the introduction of the breathalyser in October 1967, led to a fall in accident rates, particularly during the dangerous hours of darkness, so that, by May 1968, 866 fewer people had been killed on the roads compared with the same period in 1966 to 1967 (Australian Broadcasting Commission, 15 September, 1968). It remains to be seen whether this trend will persist, but at least it has been in the predicted direction even if some inconvenience has been caused to the social customs of the country.

Compared with alcohol, drugs and drug addiction seem to play only a minor part in the road-accident problem. Admittedly, not all writers share this opinion (see Braunstein *et al.*, 1968), but I have seen only a few patients who have been involved in serious car accidents as a result of excessive consumption of drugs. Much, of course, depends on the level of drug-taking in society, the type of drug taken, and its effect on the driver's ability. Long-distance transport drivers who use amphetamines to stay awake are particularly at risk, owing to the psychotomimetic effect of this group of drugs. Sedative drugs appear more often in Western society to be consumed to excess by female patients, leaving alcohol as the chosen anodyne for the male. None of my drug-dependent female patients have to my knowledge driven a car while affected by barbiturates, perhaps for the simple reason that the majority of these patients are lying up at home in a state of semi-intoxication quite incapable of dressing properly, let alone of driving a car. In the United States of America the more widespread use of narcotic and psychedelic drugs may well pose special problems if these are consumed by motorists. Driving under the influence of cannabis has been reported. No doubt, any restrictions placed on the use of alcohol apply with equal force to other drugs capable of impairing a man's control of his car. That the risk of such impairment may be slight at present in most countries is a good reason for resisting attempts to permit the more wide-spread use of potentially dangerous drugs. The argument that smokers of cannibis do not drive fast cars dangerously is not exactly true. That the incidence of such driving at present, compared with drunken driving, is very small merely reflects the successful control of the use of cannabis. There is certainly no reason to believe that sobriety and responsibility would always be the principal character-istics of some marihuana-users, should this drug be made widely available.

So far we have been discussing those aspects of prevention which stand on the periphery of the central theme of this book. Aggression appears to be an essential ingredient of human behaviour. If that is so, it would be wise to recognize the fact, while learning to control its more deplorable consequences. I make no pretension to providing a solution but the main thesis of this book should enable us to examine clues that might prove to be more reliable guides to road-safety programmes than the assumptions that have guided them in the past. Even so, it would be fallacious to assume that any single proposal will cover the numerous varieties of aggressive behaviour on the road. What applies to the normal motorist may well be ineffective in controlling the acts of the alcoholic and the antisocial psychopath. Prevention of aggressive behaviour resulting in accidents is clearly preferable to curing their consequences; but prevention raises formidable problems of regulation and the rights of the citizen which cannot be overlooked when it comes to framing practical proposals to reduce road-traffic casualties.

However, one thing is certain: whether or not aggressive behaviour is a learned or innate human attribute, there can be no doubt that driving a car is a learned skill which can be taught well or badly. Long before a child is old enough to hold a driver's licence, he or she will have been watching the behaviour of parents and older relatives in their cars, behaviour which will largely determine his own attitudes when his turn arrives to become a car-owner and driver. The comments of Iskrant and Joliet (1968) are highly relevant to this theme. They wrote,

it seems likely that the example set by parents in the motor vehicle strongly influences the child's attitudes, especially in later life when he himself drives. 'Cop-watching', unpleasant remarks about other drivers and boasts about speed and the breaking of traffic regulations probably profoundly affect attitudes of children, attitudes difficult to change when driving age is reached. The problem is magnified if a child's peers, who in turn are influenced by their parents' attitudes, exert similar influences upon them.

In short, if the child's parents drive badly, dangerously, and aggressively so, all other things being equal, will the child when he grows up. The lesson to be learned is clear; we, as parents, are as much responsible for the quality of our children's behaviour on the roads as we are for their ability to become law-abiding citizens in all other respects. If we neglect this duty or set bad examples, we are partly responsible for the accidents which might kill or permanently maim our children. None of us are perfect as parents and very few of us would be able to swear in good faith that when our children are with us in our cars we always wear our seat belts, that we never exceed the speed limit, and that we are always calm and considerate towards other road-users. We expect our children to behave courteously towards others. Should they act otherwise we will check such behaviour with reprimand or punishment. However, if on the road we hurl abuse at other motorists or drive at excessive speeds – sometimes admittedly at our children's behest – we can hardly expect our adolescents to be all sweetness and light on the road if our own behaviour is so lacking in these qualities.

That poor teaching may be one reason for bad driving is borne out by the effect of compelling offenders against traffic regulations to attend lectures and demonstrations on driving techniques. It is said that some of those who have had repeated accidents or have regularly violated traffic rules profit from this experience in that their subsequent driving record improves. Lack of experience, of course, is one reason for the high accident rates in youth since it appears to take some years to become a moderately safe driver. This must be regarded as a contributory factor in the sharp fall in road deaths after the age of 25.

Perhaps of greater importance than the learning of technical skills is the perfection of the art of defensive driving. Many motorists proceed on the assumption that nothing will occur to impede their too rapid progress. Consequently, where a right-of-way rule exists they drive aggressively with complete disregard for the possibility of the emergence from a side-road of a vehicle which has, and takes, precedence over their own car. Sudden braking, swerving, or collision are the inevitable outcome of such encounters. Intelligent anticipation of events can be taught, but the driver described by Quenault (1967) as dissociated may act as he does for inherent psychological reasons or because of poor training. Use of the rear mirror, correct or well-timed signals, and preparation for avoidance of the child who runs onto the road in pursuit of a ball, are all aspects of defensive driving which are the very antithesis of the aggressive, thrusting behaviour of the motorist determined to 'get ahead' of everyone else on the road. Gissane (1967) estimated that 10 per cent of accidents in Great Britain could be eliminated by training or re-training of drivers. Such an observation raises questions of testing, re-testing, and the issue of provisional licences to those who have passed an initial examination. An accident-free law-abiding record for one year following the initial permit would then be the basis for issuing a full licence to drive. A dossier of accidents and violations should result in further inquiry, a period of instruction, or provisional licensing.

Such methods will make little difference to the behaviour of the young aggressive psychopath who may unleash his dangerous qualities as a result of excessive drinking. Under present regulations it is impossible to detect this individual before he has been involved in serious accidents or been before the courts for major traffic offences. A full social and psychiatric report at this stage would almost certainly enable the courts to assess his qualities with ensuing withdrawal of his right to drive. Unfortunately, withdrawal of licence, as Willett has shown, may be wholly ineffective in preventing such an individual from driving. The sociopathic personality, by definition, is one who has scant regard for normal conventions and regulations while possessing a marked incapacity to profit from the lessons of experience. Punishment or the threat of punishment is in consequence a futile exercise, except as a mark of retribution. Such an individual will, given the chance, continue to drive while unlicensed and now no longer covered by third-party insurance. Should he have a serious accident, his victim will not be able to recover damages, leaving only one possible disposal for the courts – imprisonment. Perhaps it would be wise to consider the concept of punishment as an inappropriate method for controlling traffic offenders. If traffic accidents and casualties constitute a public-health problem of epidemic proportions, the public-health measures of isolation and prevention seem to be the logical answers. A psychiatrically ill man regarded as dangerous to himself or others can be compulsorily detained until such time as his symptoms have remitted. Applying such a principle to the psychopathic road offender should lead to his detention for re-education and training with, at the same time, impounding of his vehicle should he be its owner. Not until he has given proof of competence and safety as a driver will the car be restored; and even then a provisional licence, exchangeable after one year's safe driving for a full licence, should be the rule. To mitigate the rigours of such a policy, it might be desirable to have a points or warning system which would make it clear to the offender beforehand that should he not mend his ways he would lose his licence, his car, and, for the time, his liberty.

The problem of legal attitudes to road offenders has not yet been satisfactorily solved. At present, minor infringements are dealt with by fines and major ones by loss of licence, fines, and/or imprisonment. Punishment is, in fact, the basic philosophy guiding the courts, despite the obdurate opinion of the average motorist that traffic offences are different from ordinary crime. There is no reason to believe that the law is always right or the general public wrong in this respect. Undoubtedly, some traffic offences are shocking examples of negligence and callous disregard for the rights of others. The great majority, however, are nothing of the sort. If, by some machinery, it was possible to provide instant investigation and justice for traffic offences, then there might be some point in equally brisk punishment. Unfortunately, between the commission of an offence and its consideration by the court lies often enough a period of weeks or even months. In the meantime the alleged offender has continued to drive, a privilege which will make his subsequent conviction and punishment appear unjust or irrelevant. Many motorists caught up in the toils of the law will feel resentment but little guilt. Almost certainly they will receive more sympathy than condemnation from their acquaintances. A better method for *not* improving a driver's competence or respect for the law could hardly be devised. If it has little enough effect on the otherwise law-abiding citizen, one can hardly be surprised that the aggressive psychopath pursues his lawless way wholly unrepentant.

If the ethological concept of territorial aggression is a useful explanatory hypothesis of road violence, it should be possible to consider its use as a method of control. Punishment in the ordinary sense is of little value in preventing transgression of traffic law. The average motorist will, in most instances, rationalize his actions in order to justify the feeling that he was within his human and territorial rights when he committed the offence for which he has been prosecuted. If, in fact, the car and the use of the car are looked on as similar to ownership and use of private property, it follows that denying the owner this privilege – or right – might have a salutary effect. The threat of loss of licence seems to be one of the main reasons why road accidents and road-death rates have fallen in Great Britain and Queensland since the recent introduction of tougher laws on drinking and driving, even though such threats will have little influence on the behaviour of the alcoholic or the psychopath. The alcoholic, in particular, provides problems of an order quite different from those presented by the social drinker who on occasion drinks excessively; a fact which seems to point to the need for a rather different type of management for the alcoholic. As sociopathic persons disregard court orders prohibiting them from driving, loss of vehicle might be the only effective method of preventing them from staying on the roads. Such impounding of a vehicle should occur as soon as possible after an offence has been committed, since this would have the most immediate impact on the owner's feelings for territorial rights, while at the same time denying him the use of a vehicle pending a court hearing. Few actions have such potentialities for arousing public sympathy and resentment as the eviction of tenants from their homes. The emotions aroused are as bitter and violent as any encountered in ordinary civilian life, as many a government bent on compulsory purchase of land has learned. Indeed, confiscation of land and property is always looked on as the height of injustice, doubtless because of the householder's intense feeling for the right to occupy his house without interference from government or law. The sudden loss of the motor vehicle for a limited period of time – depending on the seriousness of the offence – would no doubt arouse strong feelings of resentment and injustice but at least it would ensure that the offender could not drive unlicensed and uninsured during the period of deprivation. That such a procedure would be strongly resisted by the public is not necessarily a reason for keeping it off the statute book. To be effective it would need to be carried out at the time of the offence. The sudden loss of means of transport – if only for a few hours – would certainly impose inconvenience and some financial loss on the offender. These hours could profitably be spent at a traffic or re-education centre where certain elementary lessons on road behaviour could be learned and reinforced. Unfortunately, the institution of such traffic courts to deal immediately with offending motorists poses formidable administrative problems if injustice and arbitrary actions by traffic police are to be minimized. Almost certainly, such courts would be set up in close proximity to police stations, unless an entirely new kind of traffic law enforcement organization were established independent of the traditional police forces. If one is looking on traffic accidents and infringements of traffic law as public-health rather than legal problems, one might compare a traffic court designed to deal with all aspects of these events with a casualty department of a hospital providing a 24-hour service for medical emergencies. Perhaps if the ordinary police were excluded from road-traffic duties, while their preventive and remedial roles became the function of the traffic courts and their servants, less resentment would be aroused by their activities. Such a policy might sound Utopian in the extreme, but in the long run could be more humane and rewarding than the repeated imposition of heavy fines and punishments which neither reform the offender nor protect the public.

It will be objected that, however desirable it is to reduce law-breaking, our main concern is with the prevention of accidents, injuries, and deaths. In that a large number of accidents result from disregard of the traffic regulations, one might anticipate that curbing the offender would lead to improved road-accident figures. It may be too soon to argue that the introduction of the breathalyser and the points system of penalties is responsible for the decline in the accident and casualty rates in those countries applying these techniques. Both are penal measures aimed at the traffic offender but are at the same time designed to reduce the hazards of road usage, even though it is not always easy to grasp the rationale of some regulations. Nevertheless, punishing the offender will not prevent a large number of infringements and accidents for reasons already given.

If, as Storr (1968) believes, men seek out opportunities for aggression in as compulsive a manner as they search for sexual gratification, it might be as well to accept this basic fact of human nature and learn to live with it. The average young man is taught to control his aggressive feelings in most social situations, even though he is expected on occasion to stand up for his rights by exhibiting pugnacity. The fast sports car is the ideal instrument for displays of aggressive behaviour in civilian life. If some of this energy could be diverted into less harmful channels one might begin to see a decline in the mortality rate of young motorists. Pure substitution in the shape of competitive sports or other classes of socialized aggression seem not to be very effective, partly, perhaps, because of the small number of citizens engaging in these activities. Some aggressive feelings are released by spectators of 'sporting' activities, as Harrington has recently shown (1968). Pointless destruction of property, however boorish and irritating this might be, seems to be a well-recognized feature of Western life. That a lot of it occurs in conjunction with attendance at sporting fixtures is an interesting aspect of the aggressive feelings released by the prospect of becoming a supporter and spectator of football and other matches. It is probably appropriate that our age, so preoccupied with the prevention of global war, should through the mass media of communication appear to glorify violent spectacles. We deplore the gladiatorial shows of ancient Rome as barbarous and cruel. Yet compared with the sadistic realism of a film like *From Russia With Love*, the circuses of Rome were the efforts of amateurs. There has been much debate concerning the effects of television and literary violence on the minds of the young (see Tanenbaum and Greenberg, 1968). In the absence of wars, public executions, and other opportunities for extreme violence, this concentration on aggressive behaviour in books, films, and television might serve as a useful safety-valve for the violent emotions and aggressive drives of the otherwise peaceful citizen. In *The Toys of Peace*, 'Saki' wrote about the efforts of parents to protect their children from the fascinations of war. They were unsuccessful, because the municipal and civilian substitutes for toy soldiers and cannons were rapidly grouped into defensive and attacking configurations whereby military was converted into civil strife.

However, aggressive substitutes may have little appeal to the youth whose life centres on his car or motor-cycle. Outside many American towns and cities what are termed 'drag-strips' have been established, where persons so inclined can, for a small fee, drive their vehicles as fast and aggressively as they like with small risk to themselves and others. The popularity of motor race meetings among the young suggests that the satisfactions to be obtained from drag-strips or other opportunities for fast and daring driving might serve a useful function by channelling aggressive behaviour associated with car-ownership away from the roads.

When one looks at the rates for road deaths in the various countries included in this study it is difficult to understand why some countries have high and others low rates. National characteristics, and the use of alcohol, no doubt play a part, but possibly the history and culture of some states are more significant. Switzerland, for example, has a particularly high road-death rate, and Storr has commented on the bitterness of Swiss politics which contrasts starkly with the country's record of international peace. One could surmise that had the Swiss Cantons been unified in a struggle against their neighbours for territorial integrity, inner concord would be more assured at the expense of external warfare. In contrast, the Spanish nation has low rates for road and other violent deaths. The history of Spain, to say the least, has hardly been a placid experience. Death and the Spaniard seem inseparable images, yet despite this, life in Spain, as judged by violent-death rates and social pathology, seems remarkably free from the ills which plague other European nations. It might be argued that the Civil War of the 1930s drained enough aggression from the nation to ensure comparative harmony for decades. Another source of vicarious violence is the Corrida, but considering the violence of Mexico it is doubtful whether civil war or bullfighting can alone explain the pacific qualities of Spanish life. Death and violence pervade Spanish art, but possibly because of this exteriorization of aggression violence is less commonly seen in Spanish civil life. An organized society dominated by Church and State may also play a part, in that some of the natural aggression of the inhabitants can be directed against rulers who are by no means universally accepted. Dictatorship alone, of course, is hardly a satisfactory explanation, as the record of neighbouring Portugal shows. Here one finds considerably greater than expected road-death rates, in conjunction with higher than average homicide rates.

In contrast to Spain, Catholic Austria suffers high rates for road deaths and death by violence. The disintegration of the Austrian Empire, the country's subjugation by Hitler's Germany, and the necessity of living quietly in reduced circumstances between the rival forces of East and West Europe may have led to a good deal of aggression, no longer available for territorial defence and aggrandizement, being directed internally. Both Northern Ireland and the Republic of Ireland have a remarkably low rate for road accidents in spite of the popular reputation for pugnacity and liquor consumption enjoyed by the average Irishman. How far the rivalry between

Ulster and the Republic, which periodically erupts into open violence, is responsible for the comparative lack of violent social pathology in each state is an open question. Certainly recent events in Ulster demonstrate an astonishing degree of violent antipathy between rival religious factions but to what extent this behaviour will be correlated with an increase or decrease in other forms of aggression remains to be seen.

Nonetheless, as externally directed aggression is accompanied by a lowering of the observed rates of hostile behaviour within a nation, one can certainly argue that a good war is one of the quickest ways to reduce road-death rates. It is of course a quite unjustifiable price to pay for social cohesion, but whether our attempts to preserve international peace can only be bought at the expense of violent action within society is one of those disturbing possibilities that may make nonsense of well-intentioned road-safety campaigns.

If anger has to be expressed on the highway, let it be limited to verbal abuse and fist-shaking. The Howler monkey appears to manage his territorial affairs on this basis and perhaps this is the place to consider 'appeasement gestures' as observed in the animal kingdom. Intra-specific aggression, contrary to popular belief, rarely proceeds to outright slaughter. The weaker or more timid animal either flees back to its own territorial area or makes a gesture of submission which effectively prevents further aggression by the victor. That soft answers do not always turn away wrath is more likely to be a feature of human than of non-human aggression but a greater use of placatory gestures on the road would be a small price to pay if they led to fewer displays of anger. Certainly one is aware of some individuals who drive aggressively without ever acknowledging by wave of hand or other friendly actions the minor courtesies shown to them by their fellow-motorists. When such acknowledgements are bestowed, the recipient feels rewarded for his patience; he has even secured 'merit' as a consequence. Official road crossings are a source of irritation to motorists and pedestrian alike. The man on the pavement feels outraged because the traffic refuses to allow him to pass, while the motorist curses what he regards as the deliberate slowness of those crossing the road. In such circumstances the pedestrian who nods or waves his thanks does a lot to mollify the savage feelings aroused as a result of his lawful presence on the highway. All this, of course, may simply be a matter of tolerance and good manners. But considerate behaviour implies the need to

control one's own aggressive drives, a fact which society acknow-
ledges when it develops customs and conventions capable of limiting
or binding aggressive feelings. One can question whether the wave
of a hand, a smile, a nod of thanks, or a hand-shake are appeasement
gestures designed to avert aggression. Their use, however, does a lot
to smooth the ways of social interaction, and no man in a vehicle
need feel that his virility has been diminished if he makes more use
of them.

In the previous chapter it was suggested that owning house and
land was enough to satisfy the territorial needs of the average
citizen without his having to include his car in the area to be defended. Unfortunately, the young males in the community who are
so greatly at risk as traffic casualties are least likely to own land;
with a consequent transfer of the full weight of territorial aggression
onto their vehicles. It would be unrealistic to give everyone 'ten
acres and a cow', but it would be interesting to ascertain the amount
of property owned by those involved in serious accidents compared
with a control group drawn from the general population. In the
meantime, advertising the automobile as a status symbol or as an
instrument of aggression should be discouraged. It is a means of
transport designed to carry its owners and passengers safely and
with reasonable expedition to their destinations. It should not at the
same time be an instrument for self-aggrandizement with a built-in
assurance that it will move at speeds far greater than the roads can
safely accommodate.

The irrational nature of much overtaking on the roads has rarely
been examined. Without doubt, many motorists – not all of whom
are young and male – look on all other drivers as challengers of their
supremacy on the road. Such attitudes are usually manifested by
compulsive overtaking irrespective of need and by harassing tactics
such as driving as close as possible to the vehicle ahead. Other
drivers seem to be equally disturbed should anyone attempt to over-
take them. In such circumstances the response is often immediate
acceleration to frustrate the efforts of the overtaking vehicle. Should
this puerile manœuvre result in a fatal accident, the law might well
consider whether the driver whose behaviour has caused the disaster
should be charged as an accessory to murder or manslaughter. So
far he appears to escape unscathed.

However, irrespective of legal action, some of this behaviour is
probably aggravated by sales campaigns which present vehicles as

instruments designed to ensure priority, power, and prestige for their owners. The simple transport function of the vehicle has been replaced by the image of the status-symbol, the piece of real-estate whose value must not on any account be diminished or its position ahead of all other vehicles challenged.

Territorial aggression in animals is said to be increased by over-crowding, when intra-specific fighting can end fatally. How far congestion in large cities can be held responsible for the aggressive behaviour of their inhabitants is uncertain. The actual site of a road accident – rural or urban – tells us nothing about the domicile of the victims. Indeed, there is plenty of evidence showing a higher death rate for car occupants in rural compared with urban areas (see Iskrant and Joliet, 1968), but this should not be taken to mean that those involved in accidents on country roads necessarily live in the vicinity of the crash. The most overcrowded areas of cities usually house members of the lowest socio-economic groups. Consequently it would be difficult to separate overcrowding from race, class, income, and a number of other factors, any one of which could be as important as population density as a contributory cause of accidents. It was interesting to note in Iskrant and Joliet's study that, whereas farmers and farm managers had the lowest rates of *injuries* caused by vehicles on the highway, the farm labourers had the highest rates. Both groups, one presumes, live in the country, the significant difference being that the former group have reasonably well-satisfied territorial needs, whereas the latter group are comparatively deprived in this respect. At this stage, speculation should not be pushed further, since a good deal more needs to be known about domicile and occupation of those killed and injured in road accidents.

The problem of alcohol and drunken driving has been considered so often that it would be difficult to say anything constructive that has not been said before. However, if alcoholics and problem drinkers are the main offenders it becomes all the more essential that these persons should be detected, treated, and debarred from driving until the courts or other agencies are satisfied that their disorders have been controlled. The universally unsatisfactory responses to treatment of alcoholism indicate that withdrawal of licence and/or impounding of motor vehicle will be more effective measures for limiting the accident rate than reliance upon medical techniques. Elliott and Street (1968) discuss public attitudes to the offence of drunken driving but, beyond noting the ambivalent feelings of the public on this matter, have little to offer in the way of preventive measures. Whatever is done, some hardships will undoubtedly follow, but I have yet to be convinced that perfect justice is meted out by courts in any branch of law, least of all those dealing with motoring offences. If that is the case, one has to accept some injustice for the good of society as a whole. Control of alcohol intake when driving is an obvious target for those concerned with road safety; and if the results justify the methods of supervision the majority of citizens should not grieve over some limitations on current social practices. In the meantime we must hopefully wait for the perfect antidote to alcohol intoxication or more effective methods of treatment for alcholics. Until that day dawns, common sense dictates legal penalties for drunken drivers despite the inevitable inconvenience caused by loss of licence and/or vehicle.

The young men who drink and drive constitute a rather different problem. Inexperience and poor tolerance of liquor both add their share to disasters caused by the drunken youth at the wheel, a finding which might point to a partial solution. Undoubtedly, young men in our society will continue to drink – sometimes very heavily – at a time when their capacity to 'hold their liquor' is not well developed. If this is correct, one might make it an absolute offence for motorists aged less than 25 years to take any alcohol whatsoever before driving, while leaving the older members of the community a permissible level of blood alcohol currently regarded as consistent with safe management of a car. A youth who broke the law would automatically lose his licence and car for a statutory period of time. If there is evidence that his drinking already points to some excess or loss of control, compulsory treatment might conceivably be more effective than it is at present with older persons. Most of the alcoholics I have treated had become heavy drinkers by the time they reached the age of 20. An energetic programme of treatment at that age might be far more effective in preventing subsequent alcoholism and drunken driving.

In this sceptical age it is considered unfashionable and unscientific to introduce concepts of morality and sin into what is supposed to be a detached and scientific appraisal of a social problem. That I am far from being impartial and dispassionate should be apparent enough to the reader; and in any case much depends on what is implied by words like morality and sin. If sin is to be equated with the ruthless exhibition of inborn, instinctive drives, then the un-fettered expression of the territorial and status drives can be so re-garded. Nobody would dispute that aggression and status rivalry perform valuable functions within society. However, to obtain the best results for society and mankind it is essential to recognize the nature of the forces which give vigour to our behaviour lest their hidden but unbridled expression results in disaster. Ignorance of their existence in certain situations may be far more damaging than their controlled expression. The Reverend W. W. Tymms (1968), in an engaging review of the part played by the Seven Deadly Sins in our daily road behaviour, is perhaps a little indiscriminate in indicting them all. The Reverend J. H. L. Waterson (1961) believed that a moral problem was involved in the rising rate of road accidents. He felt that when driving a car one reverts to a more primitive level of personality; or, putting things differently, certain latent but ever-present forces became more apparent. Certainly Mr Waterson was well aware of the use of the car as a means of displaying ruthless aggression. Indeed as diagnosticians the moralist and the theologian seem to be saying in their own terminology very much the same as the psychologist. It is doubtful whether at this stage either expert can offer more than a tentative solution to the problems of road accidents.

This, of course, does not alter the fact that, however we explain the origins of undesirable behaviour, we should make some attempt at control of our own aggressive feelings. Anger, anxiety, and depres-sion are all part of the human lot. If we drive while strongly affected by these emotions it might be as well to take note of their presence in the hope that this will lead to moderation of our driving behaviour. Self-awareness is always desirable if it leads to greater understanding and control of the vagaries of our feelings. For, as many a moralist – and psychologist – has pointed out, ignorance of the inner springs of action can be quite as disastrous as our more calculated malignities. Nevertheless, it is too much to hope for that degree of introspection which would permit the average human driver to avoid unnecessary hazards brought about by his own state of mind. One can merely point to the emotional cause and traumatic effect in the hope that the lesson will be well learned before it is too late.

This monograph opened with a quotation from the Scriptures. For obvious reasons the Testaments – Old and New – say little about the road behaviour of the numerous personages described, but that

Jehu has been singled out for special comment may not be entirely coincidental. For, after the summary dispatch of Jezebel following her defenestration, Jehu went on to a career of slaughter and extermination which, even by the standards of the time, was remarkable. Violent behaviour was Jehu's principal characteristic, a finding which strikes a singularly modern note when taken in conjunction with the personality traits of a large number of persons today who are responsible for dangerous and drunken driving. Needless to say, although justified by reference to the will of the Lord, most of Jehu's destructive acts were largely determined by his own drives for territorial aggrandizement. One instance does not confirm a theory. It may, however, demonstrate that ancient wisdom can point at some aspect of human behaviour which, painfully and at great cost, we are slowly beginning to recognize.

REFERENCES

AMERICAN MEDICAL ASSOCIATION (Committee on Medical Aspects of Automotive Safety). 1968. Medical aspects of motorcycle safety. *J. Amer. med. Assoc.* **205,** 290–1.

BRAUNSTEIN, P. W., WEINBERG, S. B., and CORTIVO, L. D. 1968. The drunk and drugged driver versus the law. *J. Trauma* **8,** 83–90.

BUXBAUM, R. C., and COLTON, T. 1966. The relationship of motor-vehicle inspection to accident mortality. *J. Amer. med. Assoc.* **197,** 31–42.

DILLEHURST, R. C., MALTBY, G. L., and DRAKE, E. H. 1966. The increasing problem of motor-cycle safety. *J. Amer. med. Assoc.* **196,** 1045–7.

ELLIOTT, D. W., and STREET, H. 1968. *Road accidents.* Harmondsworth: Penguin Books.

GISSANE, V. 1967. Research evidence on the nature and causes of road accidents with particular reference to car occupants. *N.Z. med. J.* **66,** 427–31.

HARRINGTON, J. A. 1968. *Soccer hooliganism.* Bristol: John Wright.

ISKRANT, A. P., and JOLIET, P. V. 1968. *Accidents and homicide.* Cambridge, Mass.: Harvard University Press.

LANCET. 1967. Economics of road safety. Editorial in Part ii, p. 709.

MORGAN, J. N. 1967. Who uses seat belts? *Behav. Sci.* **12,** 463–5.

M

QUENAULT, S. W. 1967. *Driver behaviour: safe and unsafe drivers.* Road Research Laboratory, Ministry of Transport Report LR 70.

STORR, A. 1968. *Human aggression.* London: Methuen.

TANENBAUM, P. H., and GREENBERG, B. S. 1968. Mass communications. *Ann. Rev. Psychol.* 351–86.

TYMMS, W. V. 1968. The seven deadly sins of the road. *St Peter's Church Parish Magazine.* Stockton on Tees.

WATERSON, J. H. L. 1961. Religion and road safety. *Theology,* **64,** 228–33, 271–4.

WILLETT, T. C. 1964. *Criminal on the road.* London: Tavistock.

Appendix I · References to sources of statistical data

GENERAL DATA

The following books, annuals, and other official publications were used for the compilation of vital and mortality statistics:

Yearbooks of Statistics for the following countries

Australia
Austria
Belgium
Canada
Czechoslovakia
Denmark
Finland
France
German Democratic
    Republic

Federal Republic of
    Germany
Great Britain
Republic of Ireland
N. Ireland (Ulster)
Italy
Luxembourg
Netherlands
New Zealand
Norway

Poland
Portugal
Spain
Sweden
Switzerland
Yugoslavia
United States of
    America

State Yearbooks for the individual states of Australia

New South Wales
Victoria
Queensland

South Australia
Western Australia
Tasmania

USA

World Almanack and Book of Facts, Newspaper Enterprise Association Inc., New York.
Mortality Statistics, Dept of Health Education and Welfare, Public Health Services, Washington.
Patients in Mental Institutions. US Dept of Health, Education and Welfare.

UNO and WHO

United Nations Demographic Year Book. New York.
Statistical Yearbook of the United Nations. New York.
World Health Statistics Annual. Geneva: WHO.

Whitaker's Almanack. London.
Statesman's Yearbook. London.
Europa Yearbook. London.

Great Britain

Great Britain: Vital Statistics. Annual Report of the Registrar
General.

ROAD TRAFFIC AND ACCIDENT STATISTICS

Great Britain. *Road Traffic Accidents*. Ministry of Transport.
Scotland. *Road Traffic Accidents*. Scottish Development Dept.
Northern Ireland. *Road Traffic Accidents*. Ministry of Development.
Canada. *Road Accident and Transport Statistics*. Canadian Motor
Transport Statistics.
Australia. *Road Traffic Accidents Involving Casualties*. Canberra
Commonwealth Bureau of Census and Statistics.
Road Accident Statistics in Great Britain. London: Royal Society for
the Prevention of Accidents.
Accident Facts. Chicago: US National Safety Council.
Road Traffic Accidents in Europe. New York: UNO.
Road Research Laboratories Annual Reports. Ministry of Transport.
HMSO.
Research in Road Safety. RRL Min. of Transport. HMSO, 1963.
Annual Bulletin of Transport Statistics for Europe. New York: UNO.
International Road Federation, *Statistical Data*, 1965. Washington
DC.
Basic Road Statistics 1956–65. London: British Road Federation.
New Zealand, *Motor Accident Statistics*. Transport Dept of New
Zealand.

CRIMINAL STATISTICS AND STATISTICS RELATING TO
DRUNKENNESS AND ALCOHOL CONSUMPTION

Annual Criminal Statistics for the following countries were examined
for the years 1955, 1960, and 1964.

England and Wales, Scotland, and Northern Ireland.
Republic of Ireland.
Canada. Statistics of Criminal and Other Offences. Canadian Police
Dept.

USA. Uniform Crime Reports of the USA. Washington: FBI.

Australia. Annual Chief Commissioners of Police Reports for the States of NSW, Victoria, Queensland, SA, WA, and Tasmania.

Federal Republic of Germany, Netherlands, Belgium, France, Italy, Switzerland, Austria, Norway, Sweden, and Denmark.

New Zealand. Police Dept.

International Crime Statistics. Paris: Interpol.

Offences of Drunkenness in England and Wales. Home Office. HMSO.

Return of Offences relating to Motor Vehicles. Home Office. HMSO.

Annual Reports on Drink Offences. London: Christian Economic and Social Research Foundation.

Statistics of Alcohol Use and Alcoholism in Canada, 1871–1956. R. E. Popham and W. Schmidt. Toronto, 1958.

USA. Selected Statistical Tables on the Consumption of Alcohol 1850–1962, and on Alcoholism 1930–1960. V. Efron and M. Keller (1963). J. Studies on Alcohol Inc., New Brunswick, NJ.

Appendix II · Statistical Data

Table 1 Twenty-seven world states, 1955, 1960, and 1964
Statistical data

	A	B	C	D	E	F	F¹	G	H	I	J	K	L	M	N	O
Canada	21·90	1·08	32·25	1·43	8·12	42·80	105·43	1·22	3·07	39·40	43·69	63·46	117·5	4·7	4·1	7·7
United States of America	23·42	1·05	31·16	4·77	10·45	46·38	200·17	4·85	9·17	50·53	64·55	119·49	169·8	5·5	23·0	15·4
England and Wales	13·42	0·77	24·82	0·64	11·73	37·19	91·95	0·56	0·99	4·27	5·82	13·79	14·1	5·8	6·1	3·0
Scotland	13·12	0·87	34·66	0·79	7·88	43·33	89·28	0·77	0·98	12·46	14·21	17·00	47·4	4·7	4·0	5·3
Northern Ireland	12·85	0·81	22·57	0·59	4·68	27·84	57·87	0·49	0·35	1·54	2·38	11·21	38·0	2·6	0·8	3·1
Republic of Ireland	10·89	0·79	24·77	0·37	2·44	27·58	44·92	0·24	0·49	1·88	2·61	12·09	30·4	1·9	—	3·4
Australia	25·28	1·29	28·52	1·55	11·82	41·89	119·77	2·56	2·56	5·80	10·92	134·03	147·0	5·1	10·8	6·2
New Zealand	17·92	0·91	32·51	1·38	9·12	43·01	107·48	1·35	4·26	5·33	10·94	18·39	34·2	6·6	6·3	3·0
Denmark	17·16	0·99	32·74	0·50	21·92	55·16	139·95	0·63	5·02	6·24	11·89	37·29	93·1	7·8	14·4	6·5
Finland	17·03	1·30	35·21	2·57	20·10	57·88	188·51	2·33	2·51	6·00	10·84	151·84	99·9	4·2	8·8	3·8
Norway	8·99	0·57	34·49	0·40	7·05	41·94	75·17	0·34	2·04	2·80	5·18	82·75	58·0	3·7	6·4	3·8
Sweden	15·64	0·90	28·79	0·70	18·34	47·83	125·92	1·07	6·57	6·41	14·07	73·48	89·7	11·4	12·0	7·9
Austria	31·15	1·88	45·53	1·04	23·05	69·62	171·54	—	—	—	—	—	—	12·9	11·9	35·1
Belgium	25·81	1·55	37·05	0·71	14·05	51·81	115·86	—	—	—	—	—	60·5	2·1	5·3	11·8
Czechoslovakia	15·33	1·06	35·63	1·12	20·63	57·83	153·44	—	—	—	—	—	—	4·9	11·2	11·5
France	26·34	1·37	42·23	1·07	15·56	58·86	136·98	—	—	—	—	12·03	28·2	6·1	6·6	45·6

Country	A	B	C	D	E	F	F¹	G	H	I	J	K	L	M	N	O
German Democratic Republic	11·14	0·78	36·10	1·10	17·93	55·13	141·80	2·24	1·68	4·08	8·00	—	—	11·2	14·1	—
Federal Republic of Germany	26·65	1·64	33·15	1·26	19·99	54·40	151·78	2·35	1·58	13·57	27·50	—	129·7	6·2	8·9	28·2
Greece	6·80	0·83	24·58	1·58	3·52	29·68	80·94	—	—	—	—	—	—	1·3	0·39	21·0
Italy	17·38	1·13	22·11	1·38	6·01	29·50	83·92	1·82	3·96	36·85	42·63	—	—	2·6	—	28·0
Luxembourg	32·34	1·79	32·35	1·49	9·33	43·17	111·29	—	—	—	—	16·31	50·4	3·1	4·3	29·4
Netherlands	16·93	1·03	21·37	0·48	6·60	28·45	62·10	—	—	—	—	7·13	46·4	1·4	5·3	4·7
Poland	8·20	0·84	29·82	1·20	7·40	38·43	92·79	—	—	—	—	—	—	4·4	5·5	5·9
Portugal	15·16	1·73	31·82	1·17	9·16	41·54	101·04	—	—	—	—	—	—	9·8	0·9	34·7
Spain	7·91	0·78	23·31	0·67	5·22	29·20	63·03	—	—	—	—	—	—	2·8	—	19·4
Switzerland	23·87	1·55	59·03	0·83	19·09	78·95	162·64	—	—	—	—	—	117·6	3·8	8·7	23·7
Yugoslavia	5·47	0·89	25·99	1·65	12·19	39·85	121·31	—	—	—	—	—	—	8·3	11·3	9·8

A   Road deaths/100,000 population
B   Ratio of observed to expected road deaths (O/E)
C   Accidental deaths/100,000 population
D   Homicide deaths/100,000 population
E   Suicide deaths/100,000 population
F   Total violent deaths/100,000 population (unweighted)
F¹ Total violent deaths/100,000 population (weighted)
G   Homicide deaths known to the police/100,000 population
H   Forcible rape known to the police/100,000 population
I   Robbery known to the police/100,000 population
J   Total violent crime known to the police/100,000 population
K   Convictions for drunkenness/10,000 population
L   Convictions for drunken driving/100,000 population
M   Extra-nuptial births as percentage of all live births
N   Divorce rates/10,000 population
O   Male deaths from cirrhosis of the liver/100,000 males

Table 1A Twenty-seven world states, 1955, 1960, and 1964
Product-moment correlations

	B	C	D	E	F	F¹	G	H	I	J	K	L	M	N	O
A	+0·837 $p < ·001$	+0·509 $p < ·01$	+0·217	+0·464 $p < ·02$	+0·541 $p < ·01$	+0·516 $p < ·01$	+0·656 $p < ·01$	+0·706 $p < ·01$	+0·512 $p < ·05$	+0·612 $p < ·02$	+0·142	+0·411	+0·131	+0·190	+0·492 $p < ·01$
B		+0·518 $p < ·01$	+0·143	+0·455 $p < ·02$	+0·549 $p < ·01$	+0·485 $p < ·02$	+0·536 $p < ·05$	+0·629 $p < ·02$	+0·299	+0·406	+0·148	+0·337	+0·212	−0·029	+0·695 $p < ·001$
N =	27	27	27	27	27	27	15	15	15	15	15	18	27	24	26

	J	K	L	M	N	O
F	+0·067	+0·429	+0·422	+0·481 $p < ·02$	+0·446 $p < ·05$	+0·3552
F¹	+0·459	+0·669 $p < ·01$	+0·694 $p < ·002$	+0·490 $p < ·01$	+0·635 $p < ·001$	+0·335
N =	15	15	18	27	24	26

A Road deaths/100,000 population
B Ratio of observed to expected road deaths (O/E)
C Accidental deaths/100,000 population
D Homicide deaths/100,000 population
E Suicide deaths/100,000 population
F Total violent deaths/100,000 population (unweighted)
F¹ Total violent deaths/100,000 population (weighted)
G Homicide deaths known to the police/100,000 population
H Forcible rape known to the police/100,000 population
I Robbery known to the police/100,000 population
J Total violent crime known to the police/100,000 population
K Convictions for drunkenness/10,000 population
L Convictions for drunken driving/100,000 population
M Extra-nuptial births as percentage of all live births
N Divorce rates/10,000 population

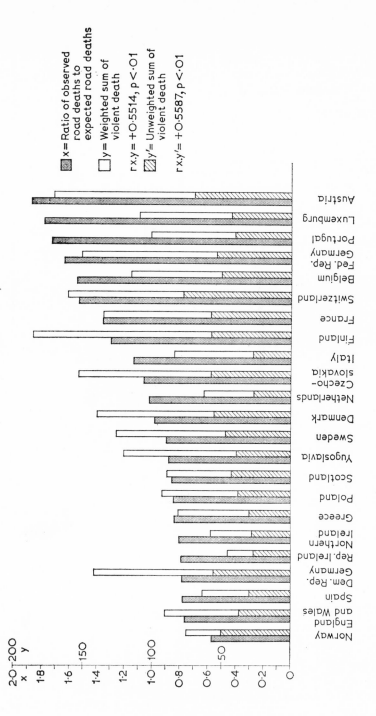

FIGURE 1 Europe, 1955, 1960, and 1964
Road deaths and violent deaths

x = Ratio of observed road deaths to expected road deaths

y = Weighted sum of violent death

r x.y = +0·5514, p < ·01

y' = Unweighted sum of violent death

r x.y' = +0·5587, p < ·01

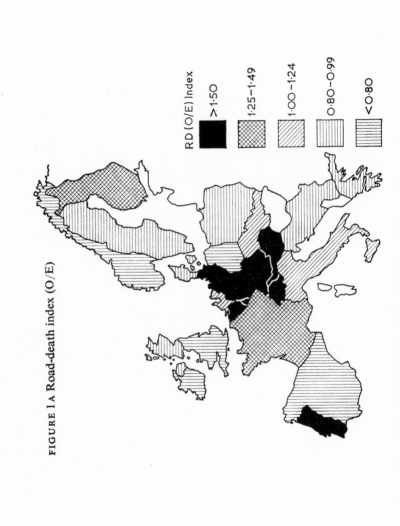

FIGURE 1A Road-death index (O/E)

RD (O/E) Index

> 1·50

1·25 - 1·49

1·00 - 1·24

0·80 - 0·99

< 0·80

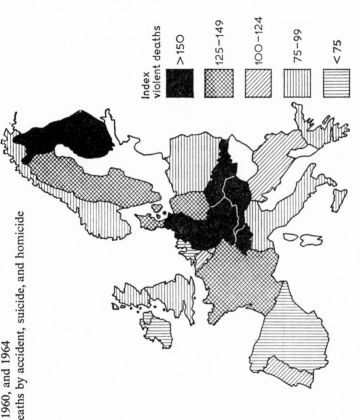

FIGURE 1 B Europe, 1955, 1960, and 1964
Weighted sum of deaths by accident, suicide, and homicide

Index
violent deaths

>150

125–149

100–124

75–99

<75

Table 1B Eight English-speaking and four Scandinavian states, 1955, 1960, and 1964
Product–moment correlations

	B	C	D	E	F	F¹	G	H	I	J	K	L	M	N	O
A	+0·818 $p < ·01$	+0·186	+0·655 $p < ·05$	+0·296	+0·378	+0·639 $p < ·05$	+0·760 $p < ·01$	+0·589	+0·607 $p < ·05$	+0·652 $p < ·05$	+0·564	+0·828 $p < ·001$	+0·255	+0·525	+0·624 $p < ·05$
B		+0·264	+0·553	+0·495	+0·537	+0·686 $p < ·05$	+0·628 $p < ·05$	+0·291	+0·308	+0·349	+0·677 $p < ·05$	+0·709 $p < ·01$	+0·123	+0·342	+0·331
N =	12	12	12	12	12	12	12	12	12	12	12	12	12	11	12

A Road deaths/100,000 population
B Ratio of observed to expected road deaths (O/E)
C Accidental deaths/100,000 population
D Homicide deaths/100,000 population
E Suicide deaths/100,000 population
F Total violent deaths/100,000 population (unweighted)
F¹ Total violent deaths/100,000 population (weighted)
G Homicide deaths known to the police/100,000 population

H Forcible rape known to the police/100,000 population
I Robbery known to the police/100,000 population
J Total violent crime known to the police/100,000 population
K Convictions for drunkenness/10,000 population
L Convictions for drunken driving/100,000 population
M Extra-nuptial births as percentage of all live births
N Divorce rates/10,000 population
O Male deaths from cirrhosis of the liver/100,000 males

Table 1C Seventeen world states, approximately 1960
　　　　Road deaths, cirrhosis deaths, and consumption of alcohol
　　　　(figures from Efron and Keller, 1963)

State	Road-death index (O/E)	Cirrhosis deaths /10,000 pop.	Annual alcohol consumption per capita (litres of pure alcohol)
	A	B	C
France 1955	1·37	45·6	25·72
Italy 1960	1·13	28·0	13·26
Switzerland 1950–5	1·55	23·7	10·85
Australia 1960–1	1·29	6·2	9·66
New Zealand 1960	0·91	3·0	9·03
W. Germany 1960	1·64	28·2	8·84
Belgium 1960	1·55	11·8	8·48
USA 1962	1·05	15·4	7·99
Canada 1961	1·08	7·7	7·23
Poland 1959	0·84	5·9	5·58
Denmark 1959	0·99	6·5	5·57
Sweden 1959	0·90	7·9	4·98
E. Germany 1960	0·78	—	4·60
Rep. Ireland 1959	0·79	3·4	4·15
Norway 1960	0·57	3·8	3·45
Finland 1960	1·30	3·8	3·33
Netherlands 1958	1·03	4·7	3·19

Column A correlated with column B; $r = +0.584$; df 14, $p < .02$
　,,　　A　　,,　　,,　　,,　　C; $r = +0.492$; df 15, $p < .05$
　,,　　B　　,,　　,,　　,,　　C; $r = +0.879$; df 14, $p < .001$

Table 2 USA, 1955, 1960, and 1964
Statistical data

State	A	B	C	D	E	F	G	H	I	J	K	L	M
Maine	4·4	128·01	92·35	14·11	12·65	1·46	215·2	4·42	8·88	22·3	18	42	3·57
NH	4·6	114·19	83·44	14·46	13·48	0·98	139·0	1·36	12·63	19·7	5	36	—
Vt	6·4	110·40	74·58	15·72	15·20	0·52	125·3	5·74	16·75	13·7	8	41	—
Mass	3·6	104·75	72·40	9·52	8·07	1·45	370·2	1·73	15·93	11·7	28	57	3·31
RI	2·6	100·46	70·90	8·92	7·42	1·50	304·1	1·76	14·82	11·3	18	59	3·31
Conn	3·1	113·51	87·70	11·60	9·86	1·74	371·2	2·80	15·44	11·7	31	48	—
N. York	5·0	158·92	131·35	12·43	8·84	3·59	891·3	3·01	10·88	4·3	19	55	—
NJ	3·3	126·33	101·49	10·88	7·82	2·61	732·0	3·55	12·34	8·3	22	48	4·81
Penn	4·4	144·77	114·00	12·33	9·52	2·81	735·6	1·88	8·58	12·7	27	43	5·34
Ohio	5·3	163·41	135·28	14·15	10·72	3·43	634·3	3·77	9·82	24·3	21	43	5·39
Ind'a	5·8	167·55	134·20	15·06	11·86	3·20	633·0	2·84	6·91	29·0	25	38	4·79
Ill	5·5	165·86	143·95	13·19	9·17	4·02	1577·2	2·53	10·67	21·0	13	50	7·25
Mich	5·9	163·11	135·86	13·68	10·13	3·55	1335·7	4·61	9·18	22·0	19	43	4·93
Wisc	6·3	109·95	80·77	12·27	10·62	1·35	253·9	3·35	12·25	11·3	21	50	3·46
Minn	5·0	113·00	77·86	11·10	9·71	1·39	339·6	1·85	7·94	13·0	13	33	3·83
Iowa	5·7	116·97	83·12	12·92	11·65	1·27	205·1	2·94	9·63	17·3	15	28	3·11
Mo	5·9	300·87	263·81	19·92	11·71	8·21	1271·3	4·01	7·63	27·3	31	23	6·76
N. Dak	6·0	93·37	56·61	9·14	8·37	0·77	178·6	2·06	12·00	9·7	4	35	3·30
S. Dak	7·3	136·23	99·42	12·17	10·00	2·17	255·5	4·97	10·00	12·7	2	25	3·85
Nebr	5·1	128·53	92·04	12·22	10·40	1·82	336·6	5·01	9·13	16·0	6	30	—
Kan	5·8	160·49	125·97	14·56	11·64	2·92	620·0	4·45	6·95	23·7	15	24	3·59
Del	5·3	184·66	156·51	14·85	10·58	4·27	549·2	4·21	15·72	14·3	14	40	9·60
Md	4·7	230·49	202·23	16·70	10·69	6·01	1300·3	13·49	14·66	18·3	15	40	—
Va	5·6	283·51	252·77	12·40	11·62	7·80	1411·1	4·48	11·05	19·3	5	23	8·67
W. Va	6·5	93·10	55·50	5·59	4·14	1·45	495·5	2·64	8·69	19·3	19	31	6·91

	A	B	C	D	E	F	G	H	I	J	K	L	M
Kent	7·6	255·39	216·94	16·79	10·12	6·67	1008·5	5·27	12·61	24·7	27	32	5·73
Tenn	6·8	273·90	241·71	16·95	9·17	7·78	832·6	3·31	9·65	26·3	31	29	9·83
Ala	7·5	367·09	331·92	19·66	8·26	11·40	1370·4	8·21	7·38	39·7	37	18	11·44
Miss	7·9	328·70	287·77	16·61	6·64	9·97	847·4	3·62	10·14	24·0	10	29	14·91
Arks	6·8	267·15	225·67	15·44	8·10	7·34	882·9	5·05	9·19	30·7	12	29	—
La	8·2	291·83	253·76	16·22	7·74	8·48	1215·3	4·95	9·09	13·4	21	39	10·23
Oakla	6·0	211·80	174·97	14·60	9·43	5·17	782·8	6·52	10·37	50·7	5	21	—
Texas	5·7	275·88	242·45	16·97	9·16	7·81	1158·7	5·14	7·86	37·7	8	28	6·01
Mont	7·2	205·48	152·36	16·66	12·94	3·72	496·2	5·93	12·05	29·3	27	50	—
Idaho	6·8	171·01	127·57	15·84	13·10	2·74	376·2	3·79	8·11	38·7	57	19	—
Wyo'g	6·8	233·32	182·16	21·63	17·54	4·09	601·8	7·60	8·15	39·3	10	23	3·09
Col	6·1	207·64	170·63	18·64	14·47	4·17	951·3	6·54	15·65	31·7	11	41	—
N. Mex	7·9	186·34	149·95	13·11	8·89	4·22	873·2	4·71	11·10	30·0	20	30	—
Ariz	7·7	251·08	216·71	17·95	11·76	6·39	1459·3	5·44	11·48	49·7	22	30	—
Utah	6·4	128·04	94·86	11·21	9·06	2·15	471·2	2·58	4·96	27·0	30	20	1·87
Nev	9·4	388·65	326·60	32·15	23·47	8·68	1385·2	7·13	8·32	295·6	20	66	4·23
Wash	4·8	170·26	133·82	16·89	14·07	2·82	469·1	3·44	10·28	34·0	17	28	4·18
Oreg	5·8	167·77	129·95	16·62	13·92	2·70	595·3	4·53	7·98	33·3	25	25	4·40
Calif	5·6	206·57	178·32	20·25	16·05	4·20	1512·3	3·18	10·28	32·0	14	64	—

A Road deaths/100 million vehicle-miles
B Weighted sum of deaths by accident, suicide, and homicide
C Weighted sum of deaths by suicide and homicide
D Suicide and homicide deaths/100,000 population
E Suicide deaths/100,000 population
F Homicide deaths/100,000 population
G Weighted sum of violent crime
H Prison admissions/10,000 population
I Mental hospital first admissions/10,000 population
J Divorce rates/10,000 population
K Industrial disputes: man-days lost as percentage of estimated working-time $\times 100$
L Estimated numbers of alcoholics/1000 population aged 20 years and over
M Extra-nuptial births/100 live births

Table 2A USA, 1955, 1960, and 1964
Product-moment correlations

N =	48 B	48 C	48 D	48 E	48 F	48 G	48 H	48 I	47 J	48 K	48 L	32 M
A	+0·650 $p < ·001$	+0·614 $p < ·001$	+0·552 $p < ·001$	+0·157	+0·600 $p < ·001$	+0·440 $p < ·002$	+0·361 $p < ·02$	−0·330 $p < ·05$	+0·341 $p < ·02$	−0·352 $p < ·02$	−0·547 $p < ·001$	+0·446 $p < ·02$
B		+0·978 $p < ·001$	+0·778 $p < ·001$	+0·174	+0·974 $p < ·001$	+0·752 $p < ·001$	+0·522 $p < ·001$	−0·211	+0·431 $p < ·01$	−0·251	−0·421 $p < ·01$	+0·691 $p < ·001$
C			+0·755 $p < ·001$	+0·143	+0·963 $p < ·001$	+0·773 $p < ·001$	+0·512 $p < ·001$	−0·228	+0·437 $p < ·01$	−0·232	−0·390 $p < ·02$	+0·729 $p < ·001$
D				+0·699 $p < ·001$	+0·647 $p < ·001$	+0·543 $p < ·001$	+0·546 $p < ·001$	−0·164	+0·600 $p < ·01$	−0·002	−0·277	+0·257
E					−0·039	+0·052	+0·292 $p < ·05$	−0·023	+0·398 $p < ·01$	+0·223	+0·015	−0·086
F						+0·776 $p < ·001$	+0·464 $p < ·001$	−0·195	+0·347 $p < ·02$	−0·290 $p < ·05$	−0·394 $p < ·01$	+0·809 $p < ·01$
G							+0·273	−0·214	−0·341 $p < ·02$	−0·038	−0·122	+0·586 $p < ·001$
H								+0·078	+0·373 $p < ·02$	−0·184	−0·278	+0·260
I									−0·333 $p < ·05$	+0·451 $p < ·002$	+0·536 $p < ·001$	+0·129
J										+0·238	−0·427 $p < ·01$	+0·089
K											+0·029	+0·027

A Road deaths/100 million vehicle-miles
B Weighted sum of violent death/100,000 persons
C Weighted sum of suicide and homicide deaths/100,000 persons
D Unweighted sum of suicide and homicide deaths/100,000 persons
E Suicide deaths/100,000 persons
F Homicide deaths/100,000 persons
G Weighted sum of violent crime
H Prison admissions/100,000 persons
I Mental hospital admissions/100,000 persons
J Divorces/10,000 persons
K Industrial disputes as percentage of man-hours per annum × 10
L Estimates of alcoholics aged 20 or over/1000 persons
M Extra-nuptial births as percentage of live births

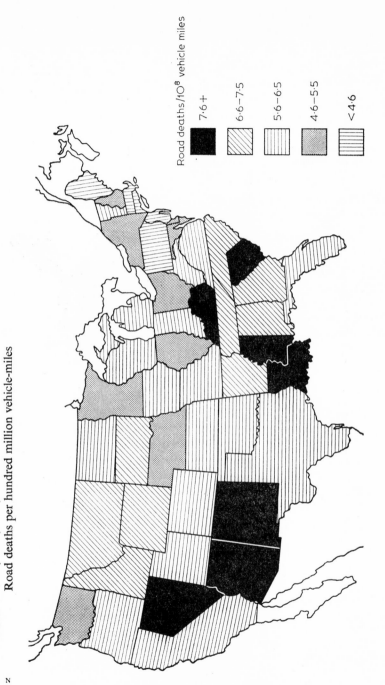

FIGURE 2 USA, 1955, 1960, and 1964
Road deaths per hundred million vehicle-miles

Road deaths/10^8 vehicle miles

7·6+

6·6–7·5

5·6–6·5

4·6–5·5

<4·6

FIGURE 2A USA, 1955, 1960, and 1964
Weighted sum of deaths by accident, suicide, and homicide

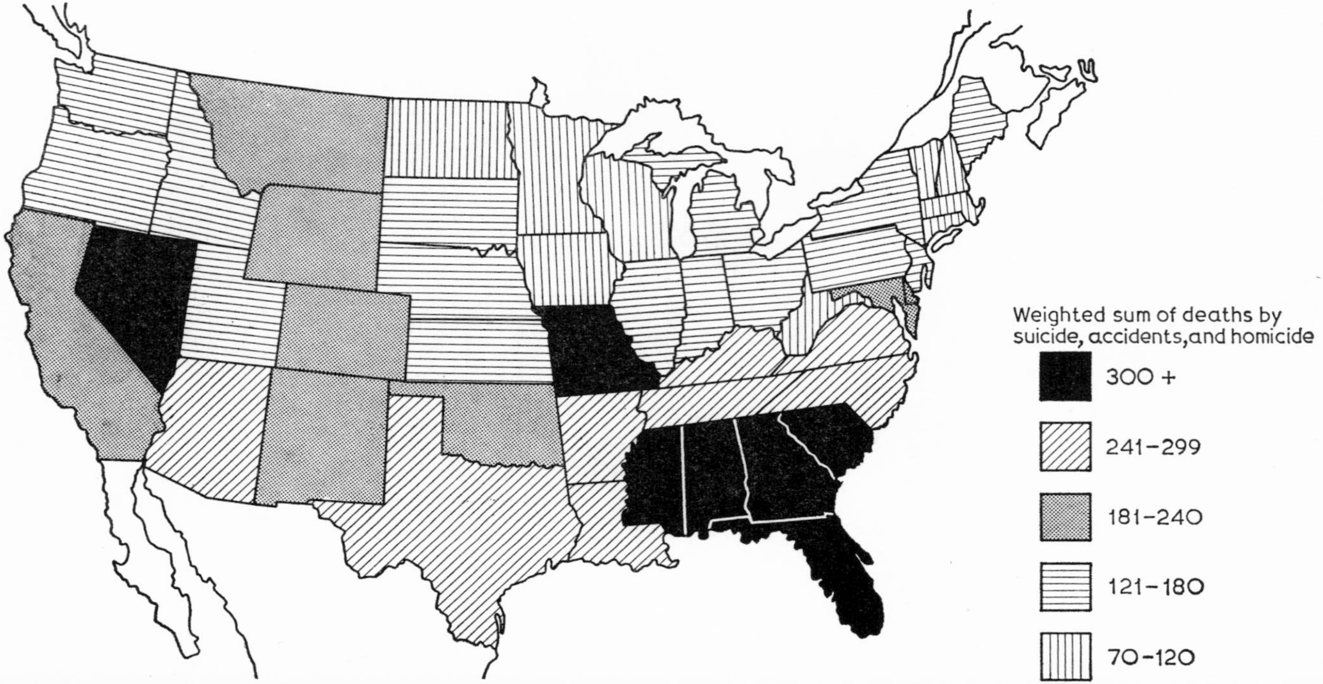

Weighted sum of deaths by
suicide, accidents, and homicide

300 +
241–299
181–240
121–180
70–120

FIGURE 2B USA, 1955, 1960, and 1964
Weighted sum of violent crime

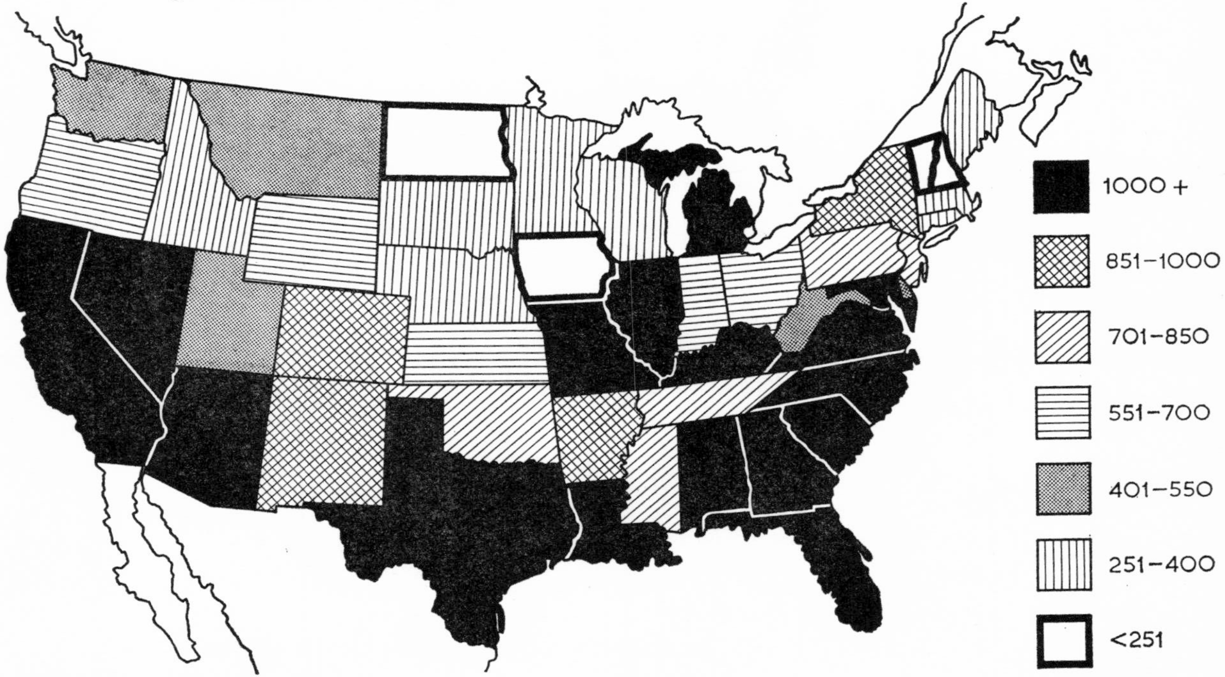

■	1000 +
▨	851–1000
▨	701–850
▥	551–700
▦	401–550
▤	251–400
☐	<251

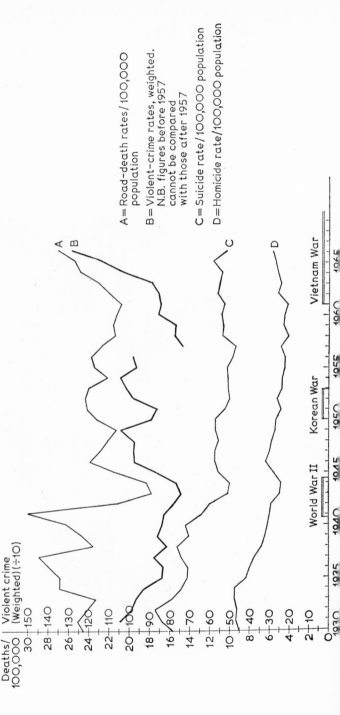

FIGURE 2C USA, 1930–1966
Road deaths, suicide, homicide, and violent crime

A = Road-death rates/100,000 population

B = Violent-crime rates, weighted. N.B. figures before 1957 cannot be compared with those after 1957

C = Suicide rate/100,000 population

D = Homicide rate/100,000 population

Table 3 Australia (six states), 1960–1964
Statistical data

	A	B	C	D	E	E¹	F	G	H	I	I¹	J	K	L	M	N	O
New South Wales	254·1	1·41	11·32	15·87	40·27	126·5	4·56	2·88	5·17	12·61	203·58	165	135	5·72	8·08	5·4	6·38
Victoria	227·5	1·31	10·11	11·53	31·73	96·3	1·75	4·07	9·42	15·24	165·93	78	40	4·45	5·80	6·4	7·23
Queensland	261·3	1·23	11·02	18·08	43·68	138·3	5·08	1·26	3·90	10·24	178·81	181	92	7·15	6·03	9·8	5·20
South Australia	244·8	1·00	7·82	15·83	39·53	121·1	1·72	2·58	4·15	8·45	103·96	63	56	4·85	7·85	2·1	5·94
Western Australia	238·1	1·20	8·70	15·21	39·41	119·1	2·22	1·04	2·22	5·48	117·51	66	32	6·43	7·19	2·4	4·48
Tasmania	157·4	1·01	8·44	10·06	37·06	98·7	1·61	2·34	5·41	9·36	93·91	14	50	5·35	7·09	1·4	5·95

A Road deaths and injuries/100 million vehicle-miles
B Ratio of observed to expected deaths O/E
C Road deaths/100 million vehicle-miles
D Suicide and homicide deaths/100,000 population
E Accidental, suicide, and homicide deaths/100,000 population (unweighted)
E¹ Accidental, suicide, and homicide deaths/100,000 population (weighted)
F Homicide deaths known to the police/100,000 population
G Offences of forcible rape known to the police/100,000 population
H Offences of robbery known to the police/100,000 population

I Total violent crimes known to the police/100,000 population (unweighted)
I¹ Total violent crimes known to police/100,000 population (weighted)
J Convictions for drunkenness/10,000 population
K Convictions for drunken driving/100,000 population
L Extra-nuptial births as a percentage of live births
M Divorce rates/10,000 population
N Industrial disputes; man-days lost as percentage of total man-work days
O Male deaths from cirrhosis of the liver/100,000 males

Table 3A Australia (six states)

Spearman rank-order (rho) correlations

	D	E	E¹	F	G	H	I	I¹	J	K	L	M	N	O
A	+1·00 $p < ·001$	+0·943 $p < ·01$	+0·943 $p < ·01$	+0·829 $p < ·05$	−0·143	−0·314	+0·086	+0·771	+0·772	+0·829 $p < ·05$	+0·600	+0·315	+0·600	−0·314
B	+0·314	+0·143	+0·143	+0·657	+0·486	+0·486	+0·771	+0·886 $p < ·05$	+0·772	+0·315	+0·143	+0·143	+0·795	+0·486
C	+0·543	+0·429	+0·429	+0·829 $p < ·05$	+0·200	+0·257	+0·657	+0·943 $p < ·01$	+0·886 $p < ·01$	+0·486	+0·429	+0·028	+0·429	+0·248

Kendall Rank Correlations

Columns A E I J K: W = 0·643, $p < ·005$
,, B E I J K: W = 0·611, $p < ·005$
,, C E I J K: W = 0·643, $p < ·005$

,, A E¹ I¹ J K: W = 0·762, $p < ·001$
,, B E¹ I¹ J K: W = 0·680, $p < ·001$
,, C E¹ I¹ J K: W = 0·730, $p < ·001$

,, A L M N O: W = 0·230, NS
,, B L M N O: W = 0·209, NS
,, C L M N O: W = 0·223, NS

A Road deaths and injuries/100 million vehicle-miles
B Ratio of observed to expected deaths
C Road deaths/100 million vehicle-miles
D Suicide and homicide deaths/100,000 population
E Accidental, suicide, and homicide deaths/100,000 population (unweighted)
E¹ Accidental, suicide, and homicide deaths/100,000 population (weighted)
F Homicide deaths known to the police/100,000 population
G Offences of forcible rape known to the police/100,000 population
H Offences of robbery known to the police/100,000 population
I Total violent crimes known to the police/100,000 population (unweighted)
I¹ Total violent crimes known to the police/100,000 population (weighted)
J Convictions for drunkenness/10,000 population
K Convictions for drunken driving/100,000 population
L Extra-nuptial births as a percentage of live births
M Divorce rates/10,000 population
N Industrial disputes; man-days lost as percentage of total man-work days

FIGURE 3 Australia (six states) 1956-1964

Road deaths and injuries, violent death, violent crime,
convictions for drunkenness, and convictions for drunken
driving

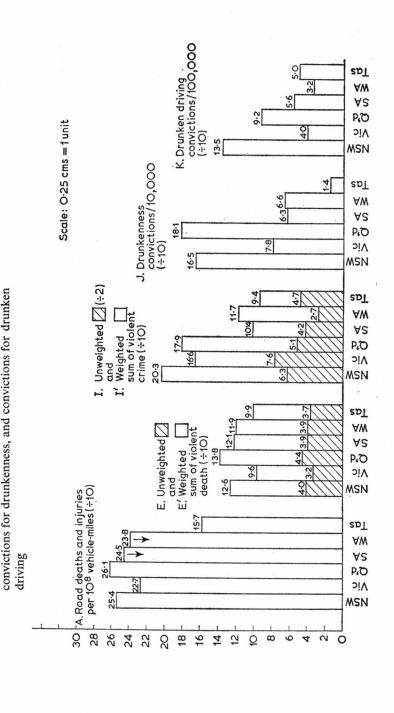

Scale: 0·25 cms = 1 unit

A. Road deaths and injuries
per 10⁸ vehicle-miles (÷10)

E. Unweighted ▨ (÷2)
and
E'. Weighted ☐ sum of violent
death (÷10)

I. Unweighted ▨ (÷2)
and
I'. Weighted ☐ sum of violent
crime (÷10)

J. Drunkenness
convictions/10,000
(÷10)

K. Drunken driving
convictions/100,000
(÷10)

FIGURE 3A Australia, 1930–1967
Road deaths, suicides, and homicides

Road deaths/100,000 population
x——x Suicides and homicides/100,000 population

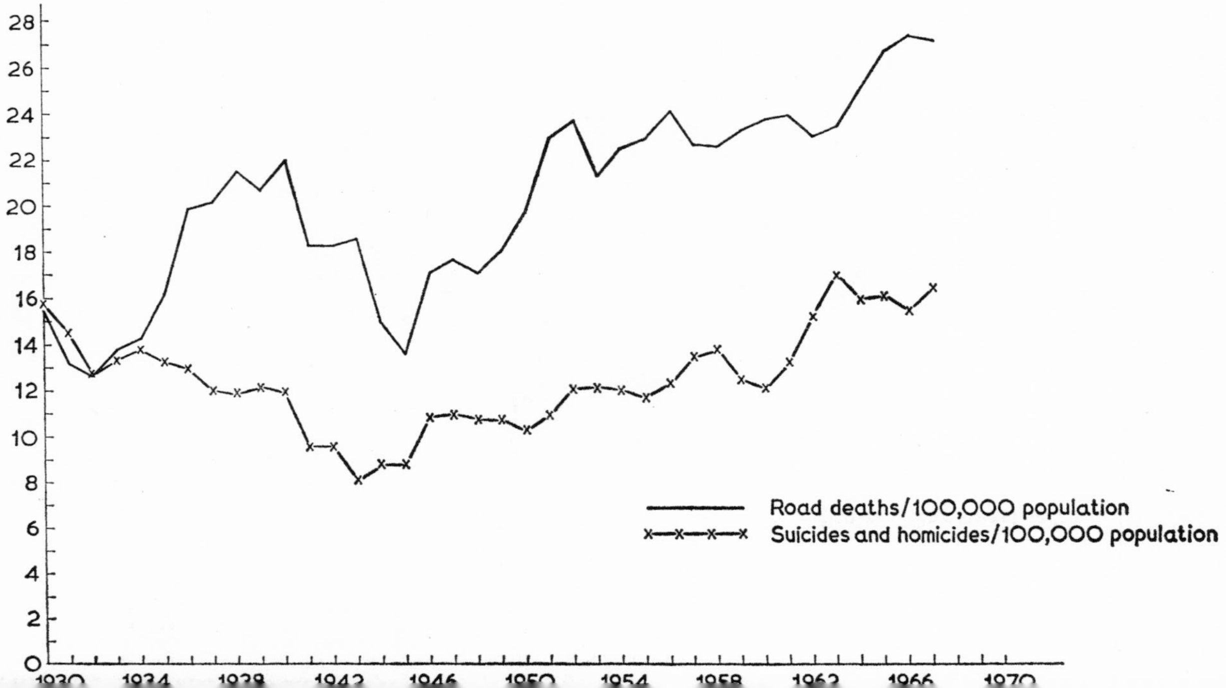

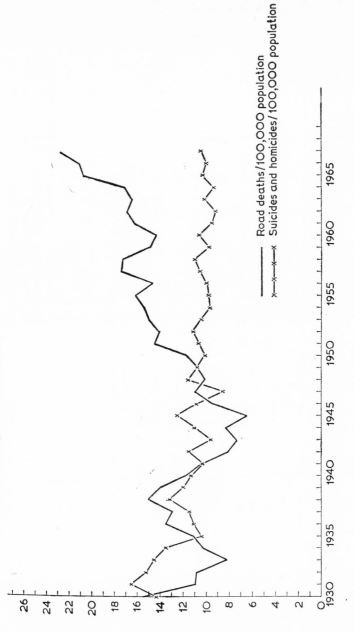

FIGURE 3B New Zealand, 1930–1965
Road death, suicide, and homicide rates

———— Road deaths/100,000 population
×—×—× Suicides and homicides/100,000 population

Table 4 Canada (ten provinces), 1955, 1960, and 1964
Statistical data

	A	B	C	D	E	F	G	G¹	H	H¹	I	J	K	L	M	N
Newfoundland	13·47	13·52	0·87	39·02	7·76	0·44	47·22	83·8	167·28	857	252	103	0·13	4·5	204	2·31
Prince Edward Island	12·23	21·35	1·10	50·18	8·73	1·26	60·47	120·8	124·26	622	966	314	0·62	4·7	105	3·84
Nova Scotia	13·16	22·68	1·18	41·35	6·22	1·19	48·76	99·0	309·94	1586	918	130	3·55	7·2	261	5·27
New Brunswick	15·16	28·93	1·56	39·21	5·13	0·85	45·19	83·4	222·67	1129	1072	113	3·31	4·9	177	4·79
Quebec	11·40	24·65	1·37	33·87	5·12	1·01	40·00	82·1	137·09	712	216	90	1·03	3·9	127	9·12
Ontario	8·05	21·06	1·01	41·69	8·42	1·22	51·33	109·6	301·54	1539	825	188	5·01	3·9	354	9·54
Manitoba	7·36	16·76	0·82	43·17	10·09	1·33	54·59	121·1	197·54	1048	904	124	4·12	6·8	275	7·47
Saskatchewan	7·69	18·66	0·86	42·31	9·21	1·53	53·05	121·7	338·69	1748	474	130	2·93	6·2	85	6·05
Alberta	8·52	23·44	1·08	44·76	9·75	1·65	56·16	129·6	365·05	1902	908	162	7·42	6·8	240	5·66
British Columbia	8·55	20·11	0·94	36·45	11·85	1·92	50·22	137·3	493·07	2546	1591	247	10·28	7·9	377	8·92

A Road deaths per 10^8 vehicle-miles
B Road deaths/100,000 persons
C Ratio of observed to expected road deaths
D Accidental deaths/100,000 persons
E Suicide deaths/100,000 persons
F Homicide deaths/100,000 persons
G Total sum of accident, suicide and homicide deaths
G¹ Total sum of accident, suicide and homicide deaths (weighted)
H Offences of violence known to the police/100,000 persons

H¹ Offences of violence known to the police/100,000 persons
    (weighted)
I   Convictions for drunkenness per 10,000 persons
J   Convictions for drunken driving/100,000 persons
K   Divorce rates/10,000 persons
L   Extra-nuptial births as a percentage of live births
M Juvenile delinquency; prosecutions/100,000 persons aged less than
    20 years
N   Male deaths from cirrhosis of the liver/100,000 males

Table 4A Canada (ten provinces), 1955, 1960, and 1964
Product-moment correlations

1)

	D	E	F	G	G¹	H	H¹	I	J	K	L	M	N
		$p < ·05$	$p < ·05$		$p < ·05$								
A	−0·127	−0·748	−0·719	−0·426	−0·753	−0·486	−0·500	−0·141	−0·170	−0·536	−0·361	−0·347	−0·616
B	−0·117	−0·533	−0·081	−0·287	−0·040	−0·024	+0·172	−0·430	+0·165	+0·229	+0·010	−0·113	+0·204
		$p < ·01$											
C	−0·261	−0·789	−0·310	−0·521	−0·432	−0·274	−0·131	+0·209	−0·027	−0·074	−0·232	−0·237	+0·001

2)

	D	E	F	G	G¹	H	H¹	I	J	K	L	M	N
		$p < ·01$	$p < ·001$		$p < ·001$	$p < ·01$	$p < ·001$			$p < ·01$	$p < ·05$		
A¹	+0·127	+0·771	+0·916	+0·436	+0·872	+0·799	+0·809	+0·513	+0·275	+0·790	+0·700	+0·426	+0·517

A   Road deaths/100 million vehicle-miles
A¹ Amended road deaths/100 million vehicle-miles (see *Table 4B*)
B   Road deaths/100,000 persons
C   Ratio of observed to expected road deaths
D   Accidental deaths/100,000 persons
E   Suicide deaths/100,000 persons
F   Homicide deaths/100,000 persons
G   Total sum of accident, suicide, and homicide deaths
G¹ Total sum of accident, suicide, and homicide deaths (weighted)
H   Offences of violence known to the police/100,000 persons

H¹ Offences of violence known to the police/100,000 persons (weighted)
I   Convictions for drunkenness per 10,000 persons
J   Convictions for drunken driving/100,000 persons
K   Divorce rates/10,000 persons
L   Extra-nuptial births as a percentage of live births
M   Juvenile delinquency: prosecutions/100,000 persons aged less than 20 years
N   Male deaths from cirrhosis of the liver/100,000 males

FIGURE 4 Canada (ten provinces) 1955, 1960, and 1964
Road deaths, violent death, violent crime, convictions for
drunkenness, convictions for drunken driving

A' = Corrected values for road deaths/10⁸ vehicle miles
G' = Weighted sum of other violent death (÷10)
H' = Weighted sum of violent crime   (÷100)
I = Convictions for drunkenness   (÷100)
J = Convictions for drunken driving   (÷10)

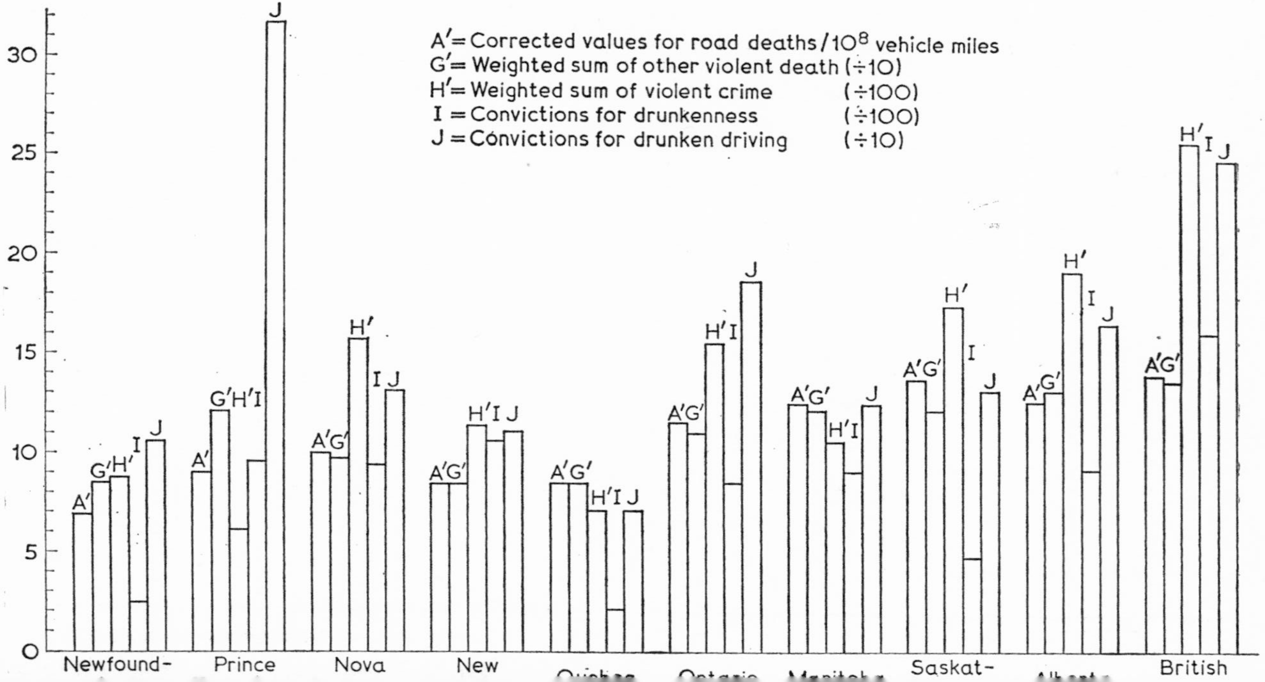

FIGURE 4A Canada, 1930–1966
Road deaths and suicides

Road deaths/100,000 population
Suicides/100,000 population

Table 4B Canada (ten provinces), 1955, 1960, and 1964
Snowfall, motor-vehicle numbers, and amended road-death
rates

		X	Y	Z
1	Newfoundland	113·8	0·14	6·91
2	Prince Edward Island	105·7	0·28	8·99
3	Nova Scotia	81·0	0·26	10·05
4	New Brunswick	107·1	0·23	8·33
5	Quebec	104·5	0·21	8·22
6	Ontario	72·6	0·34	11·43
7	Manitoba	51·3	0·31	12·19
8	Saskatchewan	43·1	0·37	13·33
9	Alberta	57·3	0·37	12·55
10	British Columbia	29·2	0·36	13·90

X Annual average snowfall in inches
Y Number of motor vehicles per head of population
Z Corrected values of road deaths/100 million vehicle-miles

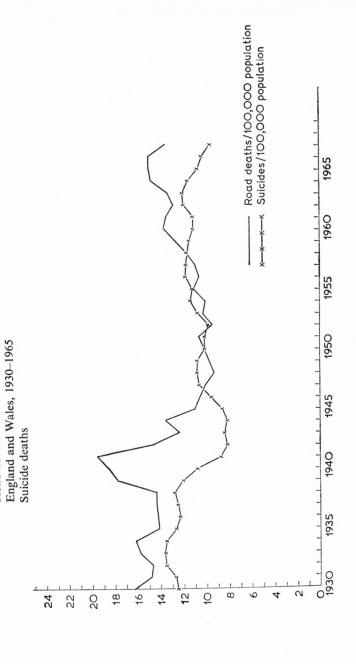

FIGURE 5 Great Britain, 1930–1965
Road deaths
England and Wales, 1930–1965
Suicide deaths

——————— Road deaths/100,000 population
×——×——× Suicides/100,000 population

Table 5 England and Wales, 1954–1964
Road-death rates and offences of drunkenness

	A	B		A	B
Barnsley	26·2	9·6	Manchester	53·9	14·1
Barrow in Furness	15·4	9·1	Merthyr Tydfil	18·7	7·4
Bath	13·2	6·3	Middlesboro'	60·3	12·0
Birkenhead	22·0	9·9	Newcastle/Tyne	66·7	12·5
Birmingham	45·4	11·5	Newport	29·6	10·0
Blackburn	26·0	10·0	Northampton	8·4	5·9
Blackpool	17·3	11·8	Norwich	3·8	8·0
Bolton	13·2	12·3	Nottingham	24·9	10·8
Bootle	17·0	8·4	Oldham	23·1	12·2
Bournemouth	12·1	9·7	Oxford	8·1	11·3
Bradford	37·0	13·6	Plymouth	17·2	7·2
Brighton	23·0	11·3	Portsmouth	25·9	10·3
Bristol	4·0	9·8	Preston	25·8	11·8
Burnley	9·4	10·5	Reading	22·5	7·9
Cardiff	21·4	9·7	Rochdale	16·5	13·9
Carlisle	12·8	10·7	Rotherham	15·7	13·8
Coventry	27·0	10·7	St Helens	8·5	10·8
Derby	27·3	13·5	Salford	65·0	11·5
Dewsbury	11·8	10·7	Sheffield	21·6	9·4
Doncaster	29·0	13·1	S. Shields	25·2	8·0
Eastbourne	6·7	7·7	Southampton	32·4	9·5
Exeter	8·6	7·3	Southend/Sea	7·2	7·6
Gateshead	46·1	10·5	Southport	4·5	7·1
Gt Yarmouth	11·9	9·8	Stockport	10·7	11·5
Grimsby	37·7	6·3	Stoke/Trent	8·9	9·4
Halifax	14·3	12·8	Sunderland	12·4	8·6
Hastings	7·7	8·5	Swansea	22·2	8·5
Huddersfield	6·2	12·4	Tynemouth	39·1	7·5
Ipswich	8·1	9·6	Wakefield	16·9	15·7
Kingston/Hull	28·4	8·6	Wallasey	9·8	6·0
Leeds	36·9	10·9	Warrington	16·3	10·9
Leicester	10·7	12·5	Wigan	10·9	9·2
Lincoln	8·7	10·6	Worcester	16·6	10·4
Liverpool	96·9	11·4	York	8·1	8·9
London MPD	42·7	9·8			

A Offences of drunkenness/10,000 population
B Road deaths/100,000 population

Table 5A England and Wales, 1954–1964
  Cities with high conviction rates for drunkenness compared
  with cities with low rates

High			Low		
	A	B		A	B
Liverpool	96·9	11·4	Halifax	14·3	12·8
Newcastle/Tyne	66·7	12·5	Bolton	13·2	12·3
Salford	65·0	11·5	Bath	13·2	6·3
Middlesboro'	60·3	12·0	Carlisle	12·8	10·7
Manchester	53·9	14·1	Sunderland	12·4	8·6
Gateshead	46·1	10·5	Bournemouth	12·1	9·7
Birmingham	45·4	11·5	Gt Yarmouth	11·9	9·8
London MPD	42·7	9·8	Dewsbury	11·8	10·7
Tynemouth	39·1	7·5	Wigan	10·9	9·2
Grimsby	37·1	6·3	Stockport	10·7	11·5
Bradford	37·0	13·6	Leicester	10·7	12·5
Leeds	36·9	10·9	Wallasey	9·8	6·0
Southampton	32·4	9·5	Burnley	9·4	10·5
Newport	29·6	10·0	Stoke/Trent	8·9	9·4
Doncaster	29·0	13·1	Lincoln	8·7	10·6
Kingston/Hull	28·4	8·6	Exeter	8·6	7·3
Derby	27·3	13·5	St Helens	8·5	10·8
Coventry	27·0	10·7	Northampton	8·4	5·9
Blackburn	26·6	10·0	Oxford	8·1	11·3
Barnsley	26·2	9·6	York	8·1	8·9
Portsmouth	25·9	10·3	Ipswich	8·1	9·6
Preston	25·8	11·8	Hastings	7·7	8·5
South Shields	25·2	8·0	Southend/Sea	7·2	7·6
			Eastbourne	6·7	7·7
			Huddersfield	6·2	12·4
			Southport	4·5	7·1
			Bristol	4·0	9·8
			Norwich	3·8	8·0

A Conviction rates for drunkenness
B Road-death rates

Table 5B England and Wales, 1961–1965
Prosecutions for drunken driving, etc. in seventy-two towns and cities

	A	B		A	B
Barnsley	29·7	9·9	Manchester	76·6	14·6
Barrow in Furness	13·5	11·4	Merthyr Tydfil	16·8	9·7
Bath	8·4	5·3	Middlesboro'	33·1	12·4
Birkenhead	22·4	10·7	Newcastle/Tyne	32·1	11·7
Birmingham	24·6	12·4	Newport	17·1	10·1
Blackburn	24·8	12·6	Norwich	10·5	8·7
Blackpool	22·4	12·6	Nottingham	9·2	11·4
Bolton	18·3	14·2	Oldham	21·8	13·8
Bootle	12·5	7·5	Oxford	24·2	11·6
Bournemouth	9·4	11·0	Plymouth	38·2	6·9
Bradford	18·7	15·4	Portsmouth	31·8	10·9
Brighton	24·9	12·4	Preston	35·4	12·3
Bristol	8·7	14·5	Reading	20·1	8·4
Burnley	28·6	14·5	Rochdale	14·1	15·3
Cardiff	18·0	10·4	Rotherham	22·0	14·0
Carlisle	42·5	10·4	St Helens	11·1	9·9
Coventry	16·6	13·0	Salford	95·2	13·1
Derby	28·3	14·1	Sheffield	15·2	11·1
Dewsbury	34·3	10·8	South Shields	27·5	10·6
Doncaster	18·6	15·2	Southampton	26·6	11·0
Dudley	10·3	13·7	Southend/Sea	13·0	8·4
Eastbourne	13·8	8·1	Southport	10·7	9·7
Exeter	27·3	7·5	Stockport	19·5	12·7
Gateshead	52·5	13·2	Stoke/Trent	15·9	11·0
Gt Yarmouth	4·9	9·0	Sunderland	8·6	9·3
Grimsby	24·6	7·9	Swansea	15·5	7·3
Halifax	13·6	16·2	Tynemouth	29·4	8·3
Hastings	19·1	11·0	Wakefield	18·0	17·7
Huddersfield	16·8	13·8	Wallasey	11·2	5·6
Ipswich	26·7	12·1	Walsall	11·5	13·5
Kingston/Hull	28·0	10·3	Warrington	15·4	12·1
Leeds	27·3	12·1	Wigan	14·8	10·7
Leicester	13·7	13·1	Wolverhampton	7·6	13·9
Lincoln	10·1	11·9	Worcester	23·8	10·4
Liverpool	23·5	12·2	York	25·4	10·8
London MPD	24·3	10·1			

A Prosecutions for drunken driving, etc/10,000 population
B Road deaths/100,000 population

Table 5C England and Wales, 1961–1965
    Towns and cities with high and low rates of prosecution for drunken driving

| High prosecution rates | | | Low prosecution rates | | |
	A	B		A	B
Salford	95·2	13·1	Wigan	14·8	10·7
Manchester	76·6	14·6	Rochdale	14·1	15·3
Gateshead	52·5	13·2	Eastbourne	13·8	8·1
Plymouth	38·2	6·9	Leicester	13·7	13·1
Preston	35·4	12·3	Halifax	13·6	16·2
Dewsbury	34·3	10·8	Barrow/Furness	13·5	11·4
Middlesboro'	33·1	12·4	Southend/Sea	13·0	8·4
Newcastle/Tyne	32·1	11·7	Bootle	12·5	7·5
Portsmouth	31·8	10·9	Walsall	11·5	13·5
Barnsley	29·7	9·9	Wallasey	11·2	5·6
Tynemouth	29·4	8·3	St Helens	11·1	9·9
Burnley	28·6	14·5	Southport	10·7	9·7
Derby	28·3	14·1	Norwich	10·5	8·7
Kingston/Hull	28·0	10·3	Dudley	10·3	13·7
S. Shields	27·5	10·6	Lincoln	10·1	11·9
Exeter	27·3	7·5	Bournemouth	9·4	11·0
Leeds	27·3	12·1	Nottingham	9·2	11·4
Ipswich	26·7	12·1	Bristol	8·7	14·5
Southampton	26·6	11·0	Sunderland	8·6	9·3
York	25·4	10·8	Bath	8·4	5·3
			Wolverhampton	7·6	13·9
			Gt Yarmouth	4·9	9·0

N 20
Mean prosecution rate 36·7
Mean road-death rate 11·35

N 22
Mean prosecution rate 10·5
Mean road-death rate 10·82

Author Index

Subject Index